We live in a time of alarming ignorance of the bedrock and transformational doctrines of the Christian faith. *Foundations* was crafted in response to the growing need for believers to learn, love, and live the timeless truths of Scripture.

—DR. KENNETH BOA, PRESIDENT, REFLECTIONS MINISTRIES

In an age when Bible doctrine is devalued, Tom Holladay and Kay Warren have coauthored a seminal work that has come to the kingdom for such a time as ours. *Foundations*, a well-devised tool with realistic learning levels in mind, will equip a new generation of informed believers. A biblical theology linked with practical relevance.

—HOWARD G. HENDRICKS, DISTINGUISHED PROFESSOR AND CHAIRMAN, DALLAS THEOLOGICAL SEMINARY

At last! A curriculum that will root hearts and heads in the solid ground of God's Word in a way that makes sense in this complex and challenging world. These studies are targeted to empower teachers and leaders to mentor others toward purpose, potential, and fruitfulness! I am thrilled to recommend it!

—DR. JOSEPH M. STOWELL, PRESIDENT, MOODY BIBLE INSTITUTE

This excellent curriculum shouts its message from the housetops that if the truth is broken down into small pieces so that all may read, mark, and inwardly digest it, it will be sweeter than honey, like fire in the bones of those who commit themselves to learn it. Never has our crazy world so needed such help.

—JILL BRISCOE, AUTHOR

Tom Holladay and Kay Warren have designed a winsome and accessible introduction to the basic beliefs of the Christian faith. It will be a gift both to those who teach and those who learn.

—JOHN ORTBERG, TEACHING PASTOR, MENLO PARK PRESBYTERIAN CHURCH

How refreshing to find a book on doctrine (often a dusty subject) that's down-to-earth, easy to grasp, with great illustrations and humor to boot! This is one book that makes the study of doctrine come alive.

—JUNE HUNT, AUTHOR

I can't affirm the value of this type of resource too strongly. Growth without depth and building without a foundation are two surefire approaches to delusion, disappointment, and eventual defeat, if not destruction. Thank God for the foresight as well as the insight that Tom Holladay and Kay Warren have shown in serving us with *Foundations*.

—JACK HAYFORD, INTERNATIONALLY KNOWN AUTHOR AND SPEAKER

Tom Holladay and Kay Warren have done for us and our churches what we all know we need to do—get people grounded in the core doctrines of the faith. As important as touching people's felt needs are to evangelism, so equally important is the grasping of biblical truth in a refreshing and applicational manner to discipleship. *Foundations* is the systematic, doctrinally sound, and applicationally relevant resource we've all been waiting for. Great work, Tom and Kay! I highly recommend it.

—CHIP INGRAM, PRESIDENT/CEO WALK THRU THE BIBLE

Thank God for Tom Holladay and Kay Warren! Their new curriculum, *Foundations*, is a powerful resource for anyone wanting to strengthen their understanding of basic Christian doctrine and build their lives on the foundation of truth. This twenty-four-session study in systematic theology for lay people has been completed by more than 3,000 members of Saddleback Church, as well as a number of other churches, and it is bound to change people's lives forever!

—JOSH D. MCDOWELL, AUTHOR AND SPEAKER

Tom Holladay and Kay Warren have given us a proven tool for one of the most vital needs in today's world—*Foundations*. This study answers the need of Christians who need a skeleton of biblical truth to support them. God will bless you and your church through this very practical and personal study of God's Word.

—AVERY WILLIS, SENIOR VICE PRESIDENT, OVERSEAS OPERATIONS, INTERNATIONAL MISSION BOARD

At last! This curriculum supplies the missing link in the study of theology by demonstrating on every page that theology is about life. Kay Warren and Tom Holladay have done us all a favor by removing the password protection from theology and making it accessible, inviting, and understandable for every Christian and by showing us how down-to-earth and practical knowing God can be. I highly recommend it!

—CAROLYN CUSTIS JAMES, INTERNATIONAL CONFERENCE SPEAKER AND AUTHOR OF *WHEN LIFE AND BELIEFS COLLIDE*

Tom and Kay are not content in producing converts. They are committed to turning converts into reproducing disciple-makers through time-tested truths presented in an accessible format.

—HANK HANEGRAAFF, HOST OF THE *BIBLE ANSWER MAN*

Foundations provides a thorough study of the core truths of the Christian faith. In a day when there is much confusion over what Christians really believe, this curriculum anchors the believer solidly in truth.

—STEPHEN ARTERBURN, FOUNDER AND CHAIRMAN, NEW LIFE MINISTRIES

Tom Holladay is a teaching pastor at Saddleback Church in Lake Forest, California. With Kay Warren, he developed the *Foundations* curriculum to teach in-depth doctrine to the largely unchurched congregation. In addition to his pastoral leadership and weekend teaching duties at Saddleback, Tom assists Rick Warren in teaching Purpose-Driven® Church conferences to Christian leaders all over the world. He and his wife, Chaundel, have three children.

Kay Warren is a teacher at Purpose-Driven events and other conferences around the world. She and her husband, Rick, began Saddleback Church in their home in 1980 with seven people. The church has since grown to become one of the largest in America and one of the most influential in the world. A mother of three children, Kay is also a Bible teacher and an advocate for women and children affected by HIV/AIDS.

11 CORE TRUTHS TO BUILD YOUR LIFE ON

foundations

A PURPOSE-DRIVEN® DISCIPLESHIP RESOURCE

Teacher's Guide
VOLUME ONE

tom HOLLaday & kay warren

ZONDERVAN™

GRAND RAPIDS, MICHIGAN 49530 USA

We want to hear from you. Please send your comments about this book to us in care of zreview@zondervan.com. Thank you.

ZONDERVAN™

Foundations Teacher's Guide, Volume 1
Copyright © 2003 by Tom Holladay and Kay Warren

Requests for information should be addressed to:
Zondervan, *Grand Rapids, Michigan 49530*

ISBN 0-310-24074-3

All Scripture quotations, unless otherwise indicated, are taken from the *Holy Bible: New International Version*®. NIV®. Copyright © 1973, 1978, 1984 by International Bible Society. Used by permission of Zondervan. All rights reserved.

Scripture quotations marked GNT (also known as the TEV) are taken from *Today's English Version*. Copyright American Bible Society 1966, 1971, 1976, 1992. Used by permission.

Scripture quotations marked LB are taken from *The Living Bible* © 1971. Used by permission of Tyndale House Publishers, Inc., Wheaton, IL 60189. All rights reserved.

Scripture quotations marked MESSAGE are taken from THE MESSAGE. Copyright © by Eugene H. Peterson 1993, 1994, 1995. Used by permission of NavPress Publishing Group.

Scripture quotations marked NASB are taken from the NEW AMERICAN STANDARD BIBLE ®, Copyright © The Lockman Foundation 1960, 1962, 1963, 1968, 1971, 1972, 1973, 1975, 1977, 1995. Used by permission.

Scripture quotations marked NCV are taken from *The Everyday Bible, New Century Version*, copyright © 1987 by Worthy Publishing, Fort Worth, TX 76137. Used by permission.

Scripture quotations marked NJB are taken from *The New Jerusalem Bible,* copyright © 1985 by Darton, Longman & Todd, Ltd. and Doubleday, a division of Bantam Doubleday Dell Publishing Group, Inc. Reprinted by permission.

Scripture quotations marked NKJV are taken from the *New King James Version*. Copyright © 1979, 1980, 1982 by Thomas Nelson, Inc. Used by permission. All rights reserved.

Scripture quotations marked NLT are taken from the *Holy Bible,* New Living Translation, copyright © 1996. Used by permission of Tyndale House Publishers, Inc., Wheaton, IL 60189. All rights reserved.

Scripture quotations marked RSV are taken from the *Revised Standard Version of the Bible,* copyright 1946, 1952, 1971 by the Division of Christian Education of the National Council of the Churches of Christ in the USA. Used by permission.

The website addresses recommended throughout this book are offered as a resource to you. These websites are not intended in any way to be or imply an endorsement on the part of Zondervan, nor do we vouch for their content for the life of this book.

All rights reserved. No part of this publication may be reproduced, stored in a retrieval system, or transmitted in any form or by any means—electronic, mechanical, photocopy, recording, or any other—except for brief quotations in printed reviews, without the prior permission of the publisher.

Interior design by Beth Shagene

Printed in the United States of America

03 04 05 06 07 08 09 /❖ ML/ 10 9 8 7 6 5 4 3 2 1

Contents

Volume 1

Volume 2

Foreword
What *Foundations* Will Do for You

I once built a log cabin in the Sierra mountains of northern California. After ten backbreaking weeks of clearing forest land, all I had to show for my effort was a leveled and squared concrete foundation. I was discouraged, but my father, who built over a hundred church buildings in his lifetime, said, "Cheer up, son! Once you've laid the foundation, the most important work is behind you." I've since learned that this is a principle for all of life: you can never build *anything* larger than the foundation can handle.

The foundation of any building determines both its size and strength, and the same is true of our lives. A life built on a false or faulty foundation will never reach the height that God intends for it to reach. If you skimp on your foundation, you limit your life.

That's why this material is so vitally important. *Foundations* is the biblical basis of the Purpose-Driven Life. You *must* understand these life-changing truths to enjoy God's purposes for you. This curriculum has been taught, tested, and refined over ten years with thousands of people at Saddleback Church. I've often said that Foundations is the most important class in our church.

Why You Need a Biblical Foundation for Life

- *It's the source of personal growth and stability.* So many of the problems in our lives are caused by faulty thinking. That's why Jesus said the truth will set us free and why Colossians 2:7 says, "Plant your roots in Christ and let him be the foundation for your life" (CEV).

- *It's the underpinning of a healthy family.* Proverbs 24:3 says, "Homes are built on the foundation of wisdom and understanding" (TEV). In a world that is constantly changing, strong families are based on God's unchanging truth.

- *It's the starting point of leadership.* You can never lead people farther than you've gone yourself. Proverbs 16:12 says, "Sound leadership has a moral foundation" (MESSAGE).

- *It's the basis for your eternal reward in heaven.* Paul said, "Whatever we build on that foundation will be tested by fire on the day of judgment. . . . We will be rewarded if our building is left standing" (1 Cor. 3:12–14 CEV).

- *God's truth is the only foundation that will last.* The Bible tells us that "the sound, wholesome teachings of the Lord Jesus Christ . . . are the foundation for a godly life" (1 Tim. 6:3 NLT) and that "God's truth stands firm like a foundation stone" (2 Tim. 2:19 NLT).

Jesus concluded his Sermon on the Mount with a story illustrating this important truth. Two houses were built on different foundations. The house built on sand was destroyed when rain, floods, and wind swept it away. But the house built on the foundation of solid rock remained firm. He concluded, "Therefore everyone who hears these words of mine and puts them into practice is like the wise man who built his house on the rock" (Matt. 7:24). The MESSAGE paraphrase of this verse shows how important this is: "These words I speak to you are not incidental additions to your life. . . . They are foundational words, words to build a life on."

I cannot recommend this curriculum more highly to you. It has changed our church, our staff, and thousands of lives. For too long, too many have thought of theology as something that doesn't relate to our everyday lives, but *Foundations* explodes that mold. This study makes it clear that the foundation of what we do and say in each day of our lives is what we believe. I am thrilled that this in-depth, life-changing curriculum is now being made available for everyone to use.

—RICK WARREN, AUTHOR OF *THE PURPOSE-DRIVEN LIFE*

Acknowledgments

Foundations is the result of ten years of faithful ministry by hundreds of people at Saddleback Church in Lake Forest, California. We are deeply grateful for those who have both participated in these studies and led in the teaching of the truth. While it would be impossible to thank them all by name, we do want to mention the wonderful contributions made to this material and program by Linda Johnson, Kerri Johnson, Tom Ulrich, Ron Rhodes, Elizabeth Styffe, Todd Wendorff, Rob DeKlotz, and Chaundel Holladay. Their ministry has made an imprint on the material you hold in your hand and, even more, on the lives of those whom they have taught and ministered to.

We also wish to acknowledge a group of God's servants who often go unnoticed. We thank God for the theologians of the church. For thousands of years, their ministry has helped God's people to keep their feet on the bedrock of God's truth. We did not quote many long theological excerpts in this material, choosing instead to use quotes from pastors and writers that would help to illustrate the truth. But make no mistake, every one of these quotes and every page of this material rests upon the faithful work of theologians.

—Tom Holladay and Kay Warren

Bring It to Life!

Get ready for a radical statement, a pronouncement sure to make you wonder if we've lost our grip on reality. *There is nothing more exciting than doctrine!*

Track with us for a second on this. Doctrine is the study of what God has to say. What God has to say is always the truth. The truth gives me the right perspective on myself and on the world around me. The right perspective results in decisions of faith and experiences of joy. *That* is exciting!

The objective of *Foundations* is to present the basic truths of the Christian faith in a simple, systematic, and life-changing way. In other words, to teach doctrine. The question is, Why? In a world in which people's lives are filled with crying needs, why teach doctrine? Because biblical doctrine has the answer to many of those crying needs! Please don't see this as a clash between needs-oriented and doctrine-oriented teaching. The truth is we need both. We all need to learn how to deal with worry in our lives. One of the keys to dealing with worry is an understanding of the biblical doctrine of the hope of heaven. Couples need to know what the Bible says about how to have a better marriage. They also need a deeper understanding of the doctrine of the Fatherhood of God, giving the assurance of God's love upon which all healthy relationships are built. Parents need to understand the Bible's practical insights for raising kids. They also need an understanding of the sovereignty of God, a certainty of the fact that God is in control that will carry them through the inevitable ups and downs of being a parent. Doctrinal truth meets our deepest needs.

Suggestions for Bringing Doctrine to Life

Teaching the deep truths of the faith can become a matter of complicated formulas and outlines. But it doesn't have to be that way. We have put together suggestions for teaching doctrine in a way that brings the truth to life. If you're already an experienced teacher, we hope you'll find one or two new ideas. If you're just starting to teach, consider what is described on these pages as your lifeline as you begin sharing the most exciting message in the world: the truth about God.

1. Make it personal.

- Talk about your doubts.
- Be vulnerable.
- Tell stories about your life.
- Think about the difference these teachings will make tomorrow.

2. Don't try to make the mysterious simple or the simple mysterious. Some truths are beyond our ability to grasp (the eternity and Trinity of God, for instance). Don't try to simplify a truth that has been grappled with for the last two thousand years; if you do, you'll inevitably leave out part of the truth as you try to make it "clearer." Feel comfortable with the fact that the Bible has some big truths in it. Doctrine sometimes is like a math equation, easily solved. But more often it's like a beautiful symphony; the longer you listen, the more you are awed by both its complexity and its simplicity.

Watch out for the opposite as well, the temptation to make everything too complex. A common mistake in teaching doctrine is using a complex picture to illustrate a simple truth. Look at Jesus. He knew how to use the simple things of everyday life to picture the deep truths of God. Jesus used birds to picture God's love (Matt. 6:26), flowers to picture God's blessings (Matt. 6:28–32), and seeds to picture God's Word (Matt. 13:4–9). You get the picture! Keep it as simple as possible.

3. Teach knowing that the truth will set people free. As you prepare for each session, and then right before that session begins, tell yourself, "Someone is going to be set free in a way that I may never know, but in a way that will have eternal impact!" Jesus promised that this will happen when he said, "The truth will set you free" (John 8:32). The truth of Christ has the power to break through the lies that keep us locked up.

4. Teach with passion in your voice. Having led a number of people as they taught this material, we can tell you that a common struggle is to teach with passion. What you are teaching is so important that Satan will tempt you to doubt the effectiveness of what you are saying even as you say it. You'll have the sinking feeling that no one is getting anything worthwhile out of it. Believe God's promise that the truths you are teaching change lives and your listeners will hear passion in your voice.

5. Connect with those you are teaching. Every time you talk on the phone, you're "connected" to the person at the other end of the line. But if suddenly the connection is lost, communication ends. The same is true when you're teaching. Throughout this teacher's guide you will find a number of teaching tips to help you stay "connected" with those you are teaching. Two of the best—keep the study personal and teach with passion in your voice—have already been mentioned.

As we close this section of personal encouragement to you as a teacher, it is our prayer that the words of Ecclesiastes 12:10 (NLT) will be true of each of us. "Indeed, the Teacher taught the plain truth, and he did so in an interesting way." We pray that God will use you to teach the truth in such a way that it becomes clear to people's minds and captures their hearts. We pray that your relationship with God will be refreshed as you share with others these truths that will never fail us.

— Tom Holladay and Kay Warren

How to Use This Guide

Features of the Guide

Throughout this teacher's guide you'll find resources designed to help you as a communicator. Our hope is that these will be invaluable for those new to teaching and a refresher for those who have been teaching for some time.

The following is a summary of the features and resources in this guide.

1. Teaching material. We've laid out this material to make life as easy as possible for you as a teacher. For each study you will find extensive teaching notes to guide you through what you will say. You'll want to add your own ideas and reflect your own personality, of course, but these materials are designed to be ready to teach. We've prepared the doctrinal outline for you, found good illustrations of that doctrine, and even helped you think through the application of this doctrine to everyday life. These materials will give you a significant head start as you teach these doctrinal truths.

A few things you should know about the format:

- The teaching material follows the outline given at the beginning of each study.
- To help you keep track of what is in the participant's guide without having to keep both guides open as you teach, all of the material that is common to the participant's and teacher's guides has been set in the teacher's guide in a bold font. Material that appears only in the teacher's guide has been set in a regular font.

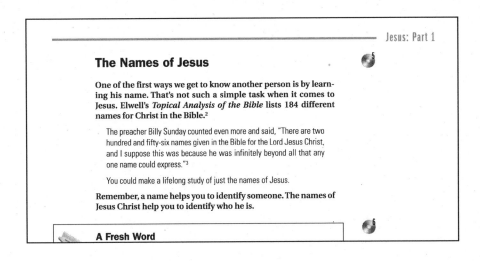

Jesus: Part 1

The Names of Jesus

One of the first ways we get to know another person is by learning his name. That's not such a simple task when it comes to Jesus. Elwell's *Topical Analysis of the Bible* lists 184 different names for Christ in the Bible.[2]

The preacher Billy Sunday counted even more and said, "There are two hundred and fifty-six names given in the Bible for the Lord Jesus Christ, and I suppose this was because he was infinitely beyond all that any one name could express."[3]

You could make a lifelong study of just the names of Jesus.

Remember, a name helps you to identify someone. The names of Jesus Christ help you to identify who he is.

A Fresh Word

- To help you to not miss any of the fill-in-the-blank answers where participants have blank lines in their guide, those answers are underlined and in bold capital letters in this teacher's guide. We use fill-in outlines for two reasons. First, because we want people to remember what is being taught. Studies show that we forget 95 percent of what we hear after seventy-two hours. That's a depressing statistic for any teacher! However, we forget only 30 percent of what we hear and write down after the same time period. The second reason we use fill-in outlines is so that the participant will have a reference to go back to. This reference is made more personal when it is partially written in their own handwriting. (We suggest you use the PowerPoint slides contained on the CD, which give not only the outline for each study but also the answers for the fill-ins.)

- Our goal in the teacher's guide is to help you make the truth clear. With that in mind, we've used material from a variety of sources: classic illustrations, quotes from church leaders, simple pictures, and personal applications. Our hope is that even if some of these sources don't fit your style, others will be of significant help. We encourage you to take a risk; try something new as a teacher. It's the only way to grow.

2. Highlight sections. Throughout this study you'll see four types of sidebar sections designed to help participants connect with the truths that God tells us about himself, ourselves, and this world.

- *A Fresh Word:* One aspect of doctrine that makes people "nervous" is the "big words." Throughout this study we'll take a fresh look at these words, words such as *omnipotent* and *sovereign.*
- *A Closer Look:* We'll take time to expand on a truth or to look at it from a different perspective.
- *Key Personal Perspective:* The truth of doctrine always has a profound impact on our lives. In these sections we'll focus in on that personal impact.
- *Acting on the Truth:* James 1:22 says, "Do what God's teaching says; when you only listen and do nothing, you are fooling yourselves" (NCV).

3. Teaching tips. We've interspersed more than sixty tips throughout this guide to strengthen your skills as a communicator. These Teaching Tips will help you to keep people's attention on the truth you are teaching as well as help *you* to keep your attention on God while you are teaching.

4. Discussion questions. You'll find Discussion Questions at the end of each study. We've discovered that teachers have two very distinct opinions on how to use them. Some like to use the questions throughout the study, interspersing discussion during their teaching. Others like to complete the teaching, then give people an opportunity to discuss. There is no right or wrong way; it's a matter of individual preference, taking into account the needs of the group. For those who prefer to intersperse discussion with teaching, you'll find sprinkled throughout each study suggestions for places where you can interrupt the teaching to discuss specific questions.

5. *Split session plan.* In each of the numbered studies, we've indicated a place where you can split the study into two sessions, if needed. Each full study is designed to take about 45 minutes for the teaching segment, with adequate time for discussion questions after that. The split session plan allows you to teach each half of the study in 20 to 25 minutes, with time for discussion questions at the end. You'll find a closing story or challenge before the split point and, to help you get the next session going, an interesting (we hope) introduction.

6. *Added material in an appendix.* A few studies have additional material in an appendix at the end of that study. In some cases this material is referred to in the study. In most cases, however, the appendix answers questions that may grow out of the study. It is meant not to be taught but to be referred to as a resource for those who want to know more.

7. *Memory cards.* There is a memory card for each of the eleven core truths in this study. Each card states the essence of the doctrine on one side, with a key verse concerning that doctrine on the other side.

8. *Additional material included on the CD:*

- *PowerPoint presentations:* The CD contains PowerPoint presentations for each session. These slides list the outline points and give the answers for the fill-ins to guide participants as you teach. Each slide is numbered and an icon with the corresponding number (such as the one shown here) is placed in the right margin of the Teaching Guides at the place where the slide should be shown.

- *Additional handouts:* As a bonus, we've included a few resources we didn't have space for in the printed guides. You'll find one- or two-page handouts on subjects such as the names of God, how to spend time getting to know Jesus, and the sending of the Holy Spirit. You may print them and copy them for use as additional handouts for the appropriate studies.

- *Programming resources:* To help you promote and set up the *Foundations* study, we've provided ideas for recruiting teachers, ideas for building groups, and sample letters for recruiting, organizing, and promoting *Foundations*. There's even a "final test" if you wish to use it. These materials are designed to give you a good head start in your planning.

Suggested Formats

This material is best taught in a large group, then discussed in small groups. Below are three formats in which the material has been used.

Midweek or Sunday night services

Start with fifteen minutes of singing, followed by forty minutes of teaching, which is capped off with fifteen minutes of discussion in small groups. Or allow sixty minutes for teaching and intersperse discussion questions as you go.

Foundations *Bible study program*

Foundations can provide a year's curriculum for any Bible study group. (Several thousand members of our church, Saddleback Church in southern California, have gone through *Foundations* in this format.)

Instead of seating people in rows, have everyone sit around tables in groups of eight to twelve. Round tables work best. When the program begins, assign each person to a group in which they will stay throughout the whole series of studies. This adds an important relational element to the study of doctrine since participants will be listening to the teaching and discussing the questions with the same people the entire year. Recruit and assign a leader and an apprentice leader for each group to guide the discussion time and to care for group members.

Below is a suggested schedule for a weekly two-hour Bible study program. On the CD we've included a number of other programming resources for this program.

1. 10–15 minutes of music
2. 5–10 minutes for announcements/memory review
3. 45–50 minutes for teaching
4. 20–30 minutes for discussion in groups
5. 10–15 minutes for prayer in groups

Sunday school or small group

Given the limited time available for most Sunday school classes and small group meetings, we advise you to use the split session plan, taking two weeks for each study.

Introductory Study

Life Change Objectives

- To trust in the power of God's truth to change your life.

- To anticipate in faith the changes that learning doctrine will make in you.

Summary Teaching Outline

Developing a Christian Worldview

Why Learn Doctrine?

    Because knowing the truth about God helps me know God better

    Because knowledge is an essential foundation

    Because doctrine feeds my soul

    Because knowing the truth enables me to serve others

    Because knowing the truth protects against error

    Because how I think determines how I act

    Because I am commanded to:

        1. Study the truth
        2. Live the truth
        3. Defend the truth

Warning: Knowledge all by itself can be very dangerous!

Developing a Christian Worldview

Teaching Tip

One quality of great teachers is their ability to connect with their students. As you teach, one of your primary jobs is to keep your listeners tuned in to what you are saying. Give them a sense of relationship with you. Refuse to allow them to slip into an "I'm watching and listening as if this were a TV show" mode! Keep them connected to and relating to you as the teacher.

In order to connect, you must focus on the people you are teaching rather than on yourself as a teacher. Be less aware of yourself and more aware of those you are talking to. It's amazing what a difference praying a simple prayer can make: "Lord, help me to not think about how my words sound as I teach but to focus instead on the needs of those I'm teaching."

Note: This introductory study and the wrap-up study are the only ones without a split session option. We suggest that you do this study in one sitting and give those present an opportunity, as you close, to commit to studying this material. If you're teaching this material in a shorter time frame, we suggest you shorten the last part of the section titled "Because knowledge is an essential foundation" as well as the next section titled "Because doctrine feeds my soul."

Welcome to *Foundations.* In this series of studies, we're going to talk about one of the most important aspects of everyone's life. It is at the center of how we live. It determines the decisions we make, how we treat the people we love, the emotions we experience throughout the day, and the eternal impact we make. I'm talking about our "worldview," the set of beliefs that form the "glasses" through which we see the world.

There are four classic worldview questions that we must grapple with:

1. Who am I?
2. Where am I?
3. What's wrong?
4. What's the remedy?

We'll find clear answers to those questions in this study series. To get us started, let's start with a simple example—the color red—and have some fun. I'm going to divide you into four groups, each holding a dif-

1.
2.
3.
4.

ferent worldview related to the color red. Those on my left and at the front, your worldview is that you *hate* the color red. On my right and at the front, the driving force in your view of the world is that you *love* red. On my left and at the back, your most cherished belief is that there is no such thing as the color red. And on the right at the back, your worldview is that we should all get along with each other regardless of what we think of the color red.

Now, with these worldviews in mind, let me ask you a question. How would you like to have a red apple? Quick! Shout out your answer!

Can you feel the energy that a worldview creates? If I'd asked that question before I outlined your different views, you would have answered it based on whether you were hungry or whether you liked apples. But now we're all focused on the color of the apple. Whether you recognize it or not, whatever is at the center of your worldview becomes the basis for the way you feel about issues and the basis for the decisions you make.

Teaching Tip

Obviously this illustration will be even more effective if you have a red apple to hold up.

That's why one of the most important things about you is your worldview. And yet most of us have haphazardly put together that worldview. Things we were taught as we grew up, the opinions we hear, truths we've been taught from the Bible—they all get thrown together into a worldview stew. Often the result is a view of the world that is more ours than God's. The good news is God doesn't want it to stay that way; he doesn't want to leave us in the dark. God wants to give us his knowledge, his insight. We can see this clearly in the fact that he sent his Son and gave us his Word. God wants us to know him.

Look at Philippians 1:9–10:

And this is my prayer: that your love may abound more and more in knowledge and depth of insight, so that you may be able to discern what is best.

—Philippians 1:9–10

Circle the words "knowledge and depth of insight." Our love and our ability to choose what is best are not ultimately a matter of feelings or even experiences. They grow out of the knowledge and insight we have about life: our worldview.

Charles Colson says:

> The term *worldview* may sound abstract or philosophical, a topic discussed by pipe-smoking, tweed-jacketed professors in academic settings. But actually a person's worldview is intensely practical. It is simply the sum total of our beliefs about the world, the "big picture" that directs our daily decisions and actions.[1]

Look at Jude 1:20:

> **But you, dear friends, must continue to build your lives on the foundation of your holy faith.**
>
> —Jude 1:20 (NLT)

This is the theme verse for this study. Circle the words "foundation" and "faith." Your view of this world is determined by the foundation that you choose to build your life on. Build your life on making money and you'll have one view of the world. Build on being popular and you'll have an entirely different view of what's happening around you. The foundation God wants us to build our lives on is faith in him.

Another word for worldview is *doctrine*. Stay with me. Don't let your mind go down the wrong path when you hear the word *doctrine*. Many of us can't think of anything more dry or boring. We envision a pastor lecturing on and on in a monotone while most of the students sleep.

A Fresh Word

What Is Christian Doctrine?

- **Christian doctrine is an <u>ORGANIZED</u> <u>SUMMARY</u> of what the <u>BIBLE TEACHES</u> about the most important issues of life.**

Or, to put it another way, doctrine is the study of what God has to say about questions such as:

How do I determine right from wrong?

What happens to me when I die?

Why do bad things happen to good people?

Why do people act the way they do?

Where do I find the life that I long for?

There's certainly not anything dry or boring about that!

Charles Swindoll says this about doctrine:

> What roots are to a tree, the doctrines are to the Christian. From them we draw our emotional stability, our mental food for growth, as well as our spiritual energy

---

and perspective on life itself. By returning to our roots, we determine precisely where we stand. We equip ourselves for living the life God designed for us to live.[2]

Another word you're going to hear a lot in this study series is *theology*.

- **A working definition of theology is: <u>FAITH</u> <u>SEEKING</u> <u>UNDER-STANDING</u>.**

The word *theology* literally means "the study of God." Study is an important part of theology; you can have no theology without study, without seeking understanding.

Christianity is a thinking faith! If you are *not* asking questions, you're not growing in faith. In fact, it's my hope that this study will stir up some questions! However, questions by themselves are not enough; we have to also seek the answers. This is a study that will often make you think, and that's not always easy. Someone has said, "Anyone who gives people the illusion that they are thinking will be loved by them, whereas anyone who actually prompts them to think will be hated."[3] Thinking about the truth is like exercising; we tend to resist it at first, but enjoy its benefits afterward.

> Discussion question 1 (on page 38 at the end of this study section) can be used here.

You may have come to this study series for many different reasons.

You may have questions. Not just questions about where verses are found in the Bible but deep questions about life. You want to reconcile your faith with the questions that arise from the mess of everyday life.

You may have doubts. You may even be unsure whether you believe in God.

I'm glad you're all here and invite you to dig into the truths of God. You may have heard someone say in regard to the Bible, "Don't think about it; just accept it." I want you to know that we're not going to do that here. God's truths can stand the closest scrutiny. You don't have to check your brain at the door when you come to church. After all, God made our brains!

You may just want to know more about the Bible; you're interested in what it has to say. As we study the Word of God together, you're going to find that the Bible is filled with answers. It often might not say what you expected to hear, but it will always have the ring of truth.

Whatever the reason for your coming here, you won't be the same person you are now when you complete this study series. I say that not because I think I'm a great teacher. The truth is I'm a person struggling to learn and to fit God's truth into my life, just like you. The promise of change isn't in the teacher but in the subject we'll be talking about. God's truth has the power to change everything—sometimes in an instant, more often slowly but certainly.

Now I want to whet your appetite for what God is going to do in your life by sharing with you seven reasons why we need to learn doctrine.

Why Learn Doctrine?

Because knowing the truth about God helps me KNOW GOD BETTER

J. I. Packer said,

We are cruel to ourselves if we try to live in this world without knowing the God whose world it is and who runs it. The world becomes a strange, mad, painful place . . . for those who do not know about God.[4]

—J. I. Packer

Living in this world without knowing God is like driving a car with the windows blacked out. It doesn't matter how hard you step on the accelerator or what direction you steer, you keep running into things and you never get anywhere.

We all have a deep desire to know God. You even hear it in phrases like "Oh God" or "My God" that people utter when they are shocked. The good news is God *wants* us to get to know him! That's why he sent Jesus, his Son, and has given us his Word.

Let's put this in perspective. Knowing truths about God is not enough to give you a relationship with him. We all know people who know truths about the Bible and about God but don't really know him in a personal way. Still, to get to know God better and better, you and I must learn more and more of the truth about him. The desire to read God's Word to learn about him is a sign of your love for God. Imagine a college student saying to his girlfriend back home, "I received the twenty-three love letters you wrote to me this semester and intend to read them as soon as things settle down a bit. But I really do love you!"

If you're going to get to know God, you have to know the truth about him. You cannot develop a relationship with God based on your guesses or wishes about what he is like. Relationships are built on the truth. You can't know someone if you believe a lie about them.

Proverbs 2:2–5 says:

Listen carefully to wisdom; set your mind on understanding. Cry out for wisdom, and beg for understanding. Search for it like silver, and hunt for it like hidden treasure. Then you will understand respect for the LORD, and you will find that you know God.

—**Proverbs 2:2–5** (NCV)

God has made us all for a purpose, yet sometimes we miss the most important purpose we were made for. You weren't made primarily to

have a successful career.

produce wonderful children.

write great books.

stop injustice in the world.

have your roses featured in *Better Homes and Gardens.*

make a lot of money.

You were made primarily to know God.

Knowing God will make you wise;
Knowing God will open your eyes;
Knowing God will give you hope;
Knowing God will help you cope.
—**Kay Warren**

There is a second reason why it's worth your time to learn God's truth.

Because knowledge is an ESSENTIAL FOUNDATION

Look at Hebrews 6:1–2:

Therefore leaving the elementary teaching about the Christ, let us press on to maturity, not laying again a foundation of repentance from dead works and of faith toward God, of instruction [doctrine] about washings [baptism] and laying on of hands, and the resurrection of the dead, and eternal judgment.

—**Hebrews 6:1–2** (NASB)

We all build our lives on a foundation that guides the decisions we make and the direction we take.

Sometimes we try to build our foundation on the opinions of others. But we get a lot of differing opinions.

Sometimes we attempt to make our feelings our foundation: "Do I feel like doing it?" This is a very popular one! Sometimes I feel like doing the wrong thing! Sometimes I just don't feel like doing the right thing. Is anyone else like that?

Sometimes we try to build our foundation on traditions. It has worked for others; it has to work for me.

But the only foundation that is strong enough to build on is knowledge of God. Just as you have to know your ABCs before you can read and write, you have to know the truth about G-O-D before you can live right.

You know that old phrase "Ignorance is bliss." It's not true! If I drive through a town going 55 and get pulled over by a police officer who tells me I didn't see the 35 mph sign, my ignorance is not bliss! If I see a bottle marked "strychnine" in my cabinet and decide it would be good flavoring for a chocolate cake, my ignorance would take my life.

Ignorance can put us at risk. And ignorance of God's truth is incredibly dangerous. Our joy is at stake. Our families are at risk. Our place in eternity is at risk.

Building a good foundation for life takes a great deal of time. And, to be honest with you, it's tough work. To build a foundation you have to get down and dig. I honor you for being here. By taking part in this study series you're saying, "I'm willing to dig in. I'm willing to do the tough work. I want God to build a lasting foundation for my life."

We all need to know answers to questions like:

> How do I grow as a Christian?
>
> How can I be sure that I'm saved?
>
> How do I handle the fact that there is evil in the world?

Only the Bible has the answers.

Look at the next two verses. One is in Ephesians; the other is in Matthew. One talks about life without a foundation; the other talks about the value of a foundation.

Life without a foundation

> . . . until we all reach unity in the faith and in the knowledge of the Son of God and become mature, attaining to the whole measure of the fullness of Christ. Then we will no longer be infants, tossed back and forth by the waves, and blown here and there by every wind of teaching and by the cunning and craftiness of men in their deceitful scheming.
> —Ephesians 4:13–14

Teaching Tip

One of the most important skills to develop in teaching doctrine is the skill of reading a Bible verse out loud. Remember, you're never telling the truth in purer form than when you read from the Bible. Yet it's easy to fall into the trap of reading a passage quickly to get to what *you* want to say. Equally distracting is reading so dramatically it sounds like you're an actor in a Shakespearean play. Don't just read Ephesians 4:13–14; communicate it! Remember to:

- Read slowly. (But not too slowly.)
- Read naturally. (Let your personality shine through.)
- Read clearly.
- Emphasize key words.
- Read passionately. (When you know you mean it, your listeners will know too.)
- Make the reading of this passage an expression of your love for the Lord.

This passage in Ephesians presents two clear pictures of what life is like without the foundation of God's truth:

1. **"Tossed back and forth by the waves . . ."**

Without truth I am vulnerable to <u>CIRCUMSTANCES</u>.

Have you seen the movie *Perfect Storm*? It's the story of a small fishing boat helpless in a raging sea. That's what life in this world is like without the anchor of God's truth.

2. **"Blown here and there by every wind of teaching . . ."**

Without truth I am victimized by <u>FALSE</u> <u>TEACHINGS</u>.

Have you seen the movie *Twister*? How about *Gone with the Wind*? That's you and me without God's truth.

Life with a foundation

Therefore everyone who hears these words of mine and puts them into practice is like a wise man who built his house on the rock. The rain came down, the streams rose, and the winds blew and beat against that house; yet it did not fall, because it had its foundation on the rock.
—Matthew 7:24–25

Circle the words "on the rock."

Did you notice the two things Jesus said our foundation is built on? It's built on *hearing* "these words of mine." But it's also built on what? Yes, on *putting* those words "into practice." It takes both! So in this study series, we're not going to just hear the truth, we're going to challenge each other to put the words into practice.

It's all too easy to have a "three little pigs" faith. We build our lives with the straw or the sticks of our own ideas and emotions. It's just easier and quicker to do it that way. But then the troubles of life inevitably come along to "huff and puff and blow our faith down." Not that I think we should get our theology from fairy tales, but in this case I'd encourage you to be like the pig that built with brick!

There's a third reason to know doctrine.

Because doctrine feeds my soul

Have you ever gone on one of those liquid diets? What happens? In just a few days you would sell your firstborn child for a carrot, anything with some crunch in it! You hunger for solid food. That's a sign of maturity; you need solid food to sustain you.

Doctrine is solid food for our soul. I was going to call it "soul food" but knew you all would groan! Look at Paul's encouragement to Timothy:

In pointing out these things to the brethren, you will be a good servant of Christ Jesus, constantly nourished on the words of the faith and of the sound doctrine which you have been following.

—1 Timothy 4:6 (NASB)

This nourishment of our soul is *not* automatic! We have to choose to eat this solid food. We have to chew for a while on some of the truths in the Bible in order to understand them. In Hebrews we are warned very clearly that if we don't decide to dig into God's Word, we'll remain baby Christians. Baby Christians are believers who always seem to have so many needs that they can never meet the needs of others.

For though by this time you ought to be teachers, you have need again for someone to teach you the elementary principles of the oracles of God, and you have come to need milk and not solid food. For everyone who partakes *only* of milk is not accustomed to the word of righteousness, for he is a babe. But solid food is for the mature.

—Hebrews 5:12–14 (NASB)

In that passage, circle the words "need again" and "have come to need." The new Christians, to whom this letter was written, had taken a step backward! You need solid food not only to keep growing in faith but also to sustain the spiritual life you already have. If you stop feeding on God's Word, don't think you'll stay where you are. Without God's Word, your spiritual life will weaken.

It's through continued feeding on God's Word that we are built up.

And now I commend you to God and to the word of His grace, which is able to build you up.

—Acts 20:32 (NASB)

Discussion questions 2 and 3 can be used here.

Because knowing the truth enables me to serve others

Notice the order in 1 Timothy 4:6:

If you give these instructions to the believers, you will be a good servant of Christ Jesus, as you feed yourself spiritually on the words of faith and of the true teaching which you have followed.

—1 Timothy 4:6 (GNT)

First you feed yourself, then you serve others by sharing with them what you have learned.

Would you like to encourage others? Look at Titus 1:9:

He must hold firmly to the trustworthy message as it has been taught, so that he can encourage others by sound doctrine and refute those who oppose it.

—Titus 1:9

One of the keys to real encouragement is knowing the truth of God. Without God's truth, your encouragement is just your words—and that's pretty weak encouragement.

Suppose a friend shows up on your doorstep one evening filled with discouragement over a tough situation at work—or maybe your friend is out of work. How are you going to provide comfort and encouragement? Invite your friend in to watch a video of *Rocky*? Make a banana split? Pat your friend on the back and say, "It'll be okay"? To which your friend probably would say, "How do *you* know it'll be okay?" And that question pinpoints the difference between our saying that things will be okay and what God promises. It's entirely different to remind a friend that God says he will never fail us or forsake us—that's encouragement your friend can bank on. *Then* you can make the banana split!

Because knowing the truth protects against error

So then, just as you received Christ Jesus as Lord, continue to live in him, rooted and built up in him, strengthened in the faith as you were taught, and overflowing with thankfulness. See to it that no one takes you captive through hollow and deceptive philosophy, which depends on human tradition and the basic principles of this world rather than on Christ.

—Colossians 2:6–8

Once you get rooted in God's Word, it will be difficult for anyone to throw you off with a false doctrine.

For example, in order to drive a car, you don't have to know anything about an internal combustion engine. You just push the gas pedal and the car goes. Likewise, you don't have to know all of the truths we're going to study to become a Christian. All you have to know and believe is that Jesus loves you, that he died for your sins, and that he was resurrected to give you new life.

But let's get back in your car. Let's say you're driving down the street and the car starts to make a horrible sound. You think the sound is coming from the engine but you're not sure. Spotting an auto repair shop, you pull in and ask a mechanic what might be wrong. The mechanic tells you, "You need to fill your gas tank with water. That will fix everything." At that point, even a little bit of knowledge about cars would be of great help to you.

The best way to protect yourself against errors of any kind is to know the truth. Agents at the United States Bureau of Engraving and Printing are taught to recognize a counterfeit bill not by looking at counterfeits but by staring at new money eight hours a day, looking for flaws. Once you know the truth, you can spot a counterfeit every time.

Look at Hebrews 5:14:

But solid food is for the mature, who by constant use have trained themselves to distinguish good from evil.

—**Hebrews 5:14**

Circle the words "trained themselves." Once you train yourself, then you are ready to train others!

How can we equip ourselves and our kids for survival in a disintegrating culture? With <u>TRUTH</u> firmly believed, clearly taught, and consistently lived out.

Because how I think determines <u>HOW I ACT</u>

For as he thinks within himself, so he is.

—**Proverbs 23:7** (NASB)

Beliefs determine behavior. Thoughts result in actions.

If I were to tell you that I had taped a hundred-dollar bill under one of the chairs in this room, you would all check the bottom of your chair. At least, if you believed me you would.

Let me stretch this illustration a little. We live in a world that tells us, "Here's where to find the hundred-dollar bills." So we spend our lives struggling to find fulfillment in our job or satisfaction in our vacations, and all we come up with is old bubble gum! The amazing thing is we often keep going back to the bottom of that chair again and again. You'd think we'd have learned the first time, but our beliefs keep determining our actions.

You cannot change the way you act without changing the way you believe.

God's truth changes the way we act. It will change the way you parent. It will change the way you work, the way you handle your business. It will change the way you think about the future and the past. It will change *you*.

Because I am commanded to:

1. <u>STUDY</u> <u>THE</u> <u>TRUTH</u>

Be diligent to present yourself approved to God as a workman who does not need to be ashamed, handling accurately the word of truth.
—2 Timothy 2:15 (NASB)

Knowing the truth enables you to better *use* the truth.

Second Timothy 2:15 isn't just for pastors; everyone is to learn how to accurately handle God's Word. The Bible doesn't tell us that all of us are to be teachers; that's a gift some have and others do not. But the Bible does tell us that we are all responsible to know the truth for ourselves. We're not to rely on just what others tell us. We are to study the truth for ourselves.

2. <u>LIVE</u> <u>THE</u> <u>TRUTH</u>

The prayer in Psalm 25 is a prayer you could pray every day of your life:

Teach me to live according to your truth, for you are my God, who saves me.

I always trust in you.
—Psalm 25:5 (GNT)

Listen to what Titus 1:1 says:

I have been sent to bring faith to those God has chosen and to teach them to know the truth that shows them how to live godly lives.
—Titus 1:1 (NLT)

There are two important facts in this verse. First, to live the truth, you have to know the truth. Second, to know the truth, you must first learn the truth. You wouldn't expect to pick up a trumpet and know how to play; you'd have to learn. It's the same with God's truth. You and I can't keep God's command to live the truth unless we take the time to learn the truth.

If we don't give our hearts to learning the truth, we become like Sheila. Interviewed about her faith, she revealed the self-centered attitude that many struggle with. She said, "I believe in God, but I can't remember the last time I went to church. My faith has carried me a long way. It's Sheila-ism. Just my own little voice."[5] That so-called faith might carry her a long way, but she has no idea what direction it will carry her! Depending on your spiritual instincts is not enough, not if you've never taken the time to learn the truth.

3. <u>DEFEND</u> <u>THE</u> <u>TRUTH</u>

The Bible demands that every one of us be ready and able to defend the truth of God's Word:

Sanctify Christ as Lord in your hearts, always *being* ready to make a defense to everyone who asks you to give an account for the hope that is in you, yet with gentleness and reverence.

—1 Peter 3:15 (NASB)

Notice that the Bible even tells us what attitude to have as we defend the truth. A lot of people "DEFEND THE TRUTH!" in loud capital letters, with an overbearing and even angry attitude. The Bible tells us to be reverent toward God and to be gentle toward others as we defend the truth. You'll discover that people who are confident about the truth, who have built a good foundation, are able to defend the truth with gentleness and a quiet reverence. It's those who are unsure who have to yell the loudest.

Before we leave this talk about the value of God's truth, I want to give you one warning.

Warning: Knowledge all by itself can be very dangerous!

Knowledge is the foundation, but it is just the beginning. Many believers fall into a subtle trap. Satan, knowing the magnificent things that God can build in our lives on the foundation of knowledge, sets a snare for us. He tempts us to think, "You really know a lot. In fact, you know *much* more than the guy sitting next to you in church. You may even know more than the pastor! You ought to be proud of how much you know." Satan is trying to get you stuck on your knowledge. But what's the use of a foundation if you never build anything on it?

How do you make sure you don't fall into this trap?

- **Knowledge must be balanced with <u>DISCERNMENT</u>.**

  And this is my prayer: that your love may abound more and more in knowledge and depth of insight, so that you may be able to discern what is best.

  —Philippians 1:9–10

  Discernment is the ability to see how the knowledge you've gained is to be used in living. We've all known people with great knowledge who can't seem to make it work in their own lives: the physician who is a chain smoker or the college psychology teacher who has had five divorces.

  Warning signs of knowledge without discernment: Knowledge remains theoretical; one person or group becomes a person's exclusive source of knowledge.

  Those without discernment easily fall prey to the personality of a false teacher.

- **Knowledge must be balanced with <u>GRACE</u>.**

  But grow in the grace and knowledge of our Lord and Savior Jesus Christ.

  —2 Peter 3:18

  You have to grow in both grace and knowledge. The knowledge of some people seems to have pushed all of the grace right out of them.

  Warning signs of knowledge without grace: Learning more about God without growing closer to God; legalism.

  Legalism, as many of you know, is the result of thinking you can grow closer to God just by keeping rules—or by forcing rules on others. Rules never produce growth. Never! Christianity is not a religion of rules; it's a relationship with God.

- **Knowledge must be balanced with <u>LOVE</u>.**

  Read 1 Corinthians 13:2 with me:

  If I . . . can fathom all mysteries and all knowledge . . . but have not love, I am nothing.

  —1 Corinthians 13:2

  17

  Nothing, nada, zilch, zero, goose egg—that's pretty clear, isn't it! You don't have to be a math expert to add that up.

  First Corinthians 8:1 tells us why knowledge without love is so dangerous:

  Knowledge puffs up, but love builds up.

  —1 Corinthians 8:1

Knowledge is not the problem; the problem is the lack of love.

Let me tell you a story. It was required in Jesus' day that you take care of your aging parents, even if it was a financial burden. A group of religious men called the Pharisees found a way around that. They would call a portion of their income or wealth "dedicated to God." Since God was more important than their parents, they would not have to spend that portion on their family. Of course, since these Pharisees were serving God, they could then justify spending the money on themselves in a variety of ways.

How does this true story make you feel? Maybe you're thinking, "I would never act like that!" Remember, knowledge puffs up. If instead you and I are able to think, "Lord, show me how I let what I know become an excuse not to love," we're on our way to the attitude Jesus wants us to have. Why do you think the New Testament is filled with stories of the judgmental Pharisees? Not so that you and I can feel morally superior to them! God put those stories there because all of us tend to act like the Pharisees.

Warning signs of knowledge without love: Knowledge leads to intolerance of others; growth in knowledge leads to a growth in pride.

Discussion question 4 can be used here.

We've looked at seven convictions and one warning regarding investing our hearts and time in knowing God's truth. It's an investment that pays eternal dividends!

Now look with me at the chart titled "Building a Foundation That Lasts," which outlines what we're going to study together in this series. These areas of doctrine are the foundation of a Christian worldview. We live in a time when many people—even many Christians—build their worldview on a poor foundation. But doing so is frustrating because your worldview keeps letting you down. You don't have to live with that frustration; God wants you to learn and love and live his truth, building on the only foundation that lasts—God's truth.

Look at the three headings across the top of the chart: learn it, love it, live it. The hard fact is that if you're not willing to live the truth that you'll be learning, all of your studying will be a waste of time. We learn the truth to be able to live it!

Let me read through the topics we'll be looking at, and I'll leave the rest of the chart for you to look at more closely when you go home.

Teaching Tip

This first study ends with a call for commitment. There are three important things to keep in mind when asking people to make a commitment:

1. *Be confident.* You're not trying to sell people a bad insurance policy; you are inviting them to make a commitment that will forever change their lives for the better. Your confidence is strengthened when you see yourself as God's representative.

2. *Be clear.* People need to know what they are committing to. Be careful not to ask for two or three different kinds of commitments at once; that always causes confusion.

3. *Be compassionate.* Love the people you are talking to with all your heart as you ask them to make a commitment to obey God.

As I read each topic, I invite you to affirm in your heart your desire to learn that doctrine so that you can love it and live it.

It will take some work. It won't be easy. But the work will be worth it. You'll never regret it.

You cannot leave a knowledge and conviction of these truths to chance; it starts with a commitment. That commitment is not to me as a teacher or even to this study series; that commitment is to God, the author of truth.

Will you make that commitment with me now?

The Bible: The Bible is God's perfect guidebook for living.

God: God is bigger and better and closer than I can imagine.

Jesus: Jesus is God showing himself to us.

The Holy Spirit: God lives in me and through me now.

Creation: Nothing "just happened." God created it all.

Salvation: Grace is the only way to have a relationship with God.

Sanctification: Faith is the only way to grow as a believer.

Good and Evil: God has allowed evil to provide us with a choice. God can bring good even out of evil events. God promises victory over evil to those who choose him.

The Afterlife: Heaven and hell are real places. Death is a beginning, not the end.

The Church: The only true "world superpower" is the church.

The Second Coming: Jesus is coming again to judge this world and to gather God's children.

Pray with me.

Father, thank you for sending your Son and giving me your Word so that I can know the truth about you and your world. I want to love your truth. I desire to be a person who knows how to live your truth. And so I commit myself to give my heart and my time to learn your truth. In Jesus' name, amen.

Teaching Tip

You may want to provide a commitment card for participants to sign at this point. It would say something like this: "I want to learn and to love and to live God's truth. By God's grace I commit to be at each of the *Foundations* studies, to memorize the eleven core truths and verses, and to discuss these truths in a group with others."

I encourage you to bring a friend with you next week because we all need God's truth in our lives.

Building a Foundation That Lasts

Three Levels of Truth

Here's a brief look at what we'll be studying together. This chart helps you to see the different levels of learning that go along with grasping a truth. Being able to quote a truth does not mean I've fully grasped that truth.

To grasp a doctrine I must . . .	Learn It (understand the truth)	Love It (change my perspective)	Live It (apply it to life)
The Bible	The Bible is God's perfect guidebook for living.	I can make the right decision.	I will consult the Bible for guidance in my decision about _____.
God	God is bigger and better and closer than I can imagine.	The most important thing about me is what I believe about God.	When I see how great God is, it makes _____ look small.
Jesus	Jesus is God showing himself to us.	God wants me to know him better.	I will get to know Jesus through a daily quiet time.
The Holy Spirit	God lives in me and through me now.	I am a temple of God's Holy Spirit.	I will treat my body like the temple it is by _____.
Creation	Nothing "just happened." God created it all.	I have a purpose in this world.	The reason I exist is to _____.
Salvation	Grace is the only way to have a relationship with God.	I am an object of God's grace.	I'll stop seeing _____ as a way to earn my salvation. I'll begin doing it simply in appreciation for God's grace.
Sanctification	Faith is the only way to grow as a believer.	I grow when I see myself in a new way.	I'll spend more time listening to what God's Word says about me and less time listening to what the world says about me.
Good and Evil	God has allowed evil to provide us with a choice. God can bring good even out of evil events. God promises victory over evil to those who choose him.	All things work together for good.	I am battling evil as I face _____ I will overcome evil with good by _____.
The Afterlife	Heaven and hell are real places. Death is a beginning, not the end.	I can face death with confidence.	I will have a more hopeful attitude toward _____.
The Church	The only true "world superpower" is the church.	The best place to invest my life is in God's church.	I need to make a deeper commitment to the church by _____.
The Second Coming	Jesus is coming again to judge this world and to gather God's children.	I want to be living alertly for him when he comes.	Someone I can encourage with the hope of the Second Coming is _____.

Discussion Questions

1. Since this is your first time together as a group, take a few minutes to get to know each other. Share your name, where you were born, and one reason you decided to participate in this study.

2. When did understanding the truth about the Bible first become important to you? Tell about a time when knowing a truth was a real lifesaver. How has a truth about God and faith
   - helped you deepen your relationship with God?
   - kept you from making a terrible mistake?
   - made you better able to serve God and others?
   - encouraged you in a time of trouble or temptation?
   - given you a new sense of freedom in your life?

3. If doctrine is so important, why do you think so many people seem to have a negative attitude toward the teaching of doctrine? Why do people so often see doctrine as something dry and boring, or loud and dogmatic?

4. Discuss things you can do to make sure your knowledge does not get out of balance. Don't just talk about what others should do; talk about what *you can* do. List two or three specific things that will help you and your group keep your knowledge balanced with love and grace and discernment.

The Bible
Part 1

Life Change Objective

To deepen (or to form) your conviction that the Bible, as God's Word, can be trusted more than your feelings, values, opinions, and culture.

Summary Teaching Outline

Three Important Words, Their Definitions, and Their Implications
  Revelation
  Inspiration
  Illumination

How Do We Know the Bible Came from God?
  First: The external evidence says the Bible is a historical book.
  Second: The internal evidence says the Bible is a unique book.
  Third: The personal evidence says the Bible is a powerful book.
  Fourth: Jesus said the Bible came from God.

How Do We Know We Have the Right Books?
  The testimony of the Bible
  The history of the church
  The power of God

What Does It Mean When We Say the Bible Is Inspired?
  Inspiration means God wrote the Bible through people.
  Inspiration means the Holy Spirit is the author.
  Inspiration means God's Word is to be our final authority.

Discussion questions 1 and 2 can be used here.

Take a look at the book I hold in my hand—the Bible. We also call it Scripture, the Word of God, God's love letter. Sometimes you'll hear people call the Bible "the Good Book." While the Bible certainly is a good book, I'd describe it more as a guidebook. Sometimes we'll refer to a book like *War and Peace* as a good book, a classic that looks great on your shelf. You can impress your friends with the fact that you have a copy sitting there!

The Bible isn't meant to stay on your shelf; it has no "shelf life." It's more like the *Thomas Guide* map book that you keep in your car. It's dog-eared with use. You refer to it frequently. It tells you how to get from where you are to where you want to be. The Bible, filled completely with God's truth, is our guidebook for life.

Teaching Tip

Bring a copy of *War and Peace*, a *Thomas Guide* (or other book of maps for your car), and a Bible to hold up during this introduction. Even in the age of video and PowerPoint presentations, the impact of holding up something in your hand is amazing.

Suppose that sitting next to you now is a friend who's never been to church. The two of you stop for coffee on the way home and start to talk about the Bible as a unique book containing God's truth.

Your friend says, "I'm sure the Bible is a great book, and I'm glad it helps you. But how is it different from any other great book?

"It bothers me that sometimes Christians act as if the Bible is the only holy book, like they have a corner on the truth. I'd like to have your trust in the Bible, but it's hard to get past the fact that people just like you and me wrote it and that it has been changed so much over the years.

"Anyway, it's so hard to understand."

Your friend has just raised three important points. These can be addressed by examining three words. To see the Bible for what it really is, we must first understand these three words.

The question, How is the Bible different from all other religious books? is answered by the truth behind the word *revelation*.

The question, Wasn't it written by people just like you and me? is answered by the truth behind the word *inspiration*.

The comment, It's so hard to understand, is addressed by the truth behind the word *illumination.*

We'll look closely at these three theological words in the next few weeks. Understanding them will not only help you answer your friend but will build your confidence in looking to the Bible to guide your life.

Let me give you a quick definition of these three words.

Teaching Tip

We'll focus on these three words in this study and in the next. As you introduce these truths, give people something to look forward to. A key skill for any teacher to develop is building anticipation. You can say something as simple as, "In a few minutes we're going to talk about . . ." or "At the end of today's study we'll look at . . ."

Three Important Words, Their Definitions, and Their Implications

Revelation

Revelation means that God has chosen to reveal his nature and his will to us through the Bible. The Bible was written so that God could show us what he is like and what he wants us to be like. An understanding of God comes solely through his decision to reveal himself to us.

> **And so I will show my greatness and my holiness, and I will make myself known in the sight of many nations. Then they will know that I am the LORD.**
>
> **—Ezekiel 38:23**

What do you say to someone who tells you the Bible is no different from any other book? In this study we'll look at four classic ways that we know the Bible is from God and three reasons why we know we have the right books.

Inspiration

Inspiration is the process through which God gave us the Bible. God worked in the hearts of human writers to inspire them to write down his words. God's words written through these people are perfect, infallible, and trustworthy.

All Scripture is inspired by God and is useful to teach us what is true and to make us realize what is wrong in our lives. It straightens us out and teaches us to do what is right.
— 2 Timothy 3:16 (NLT)

If what I read in the Bible are only the ideas of men, I can take it or leave it. Once I'm convinced that God said these words, what I read takes on the ring of authority. Toward the end of this study, we'll look at how understanding the word *inspiration* multiplies our confidence in the Bible.

Illumination

Illumination is the Holy Spirit's work of bringing light to the words of the Bible as we read them. Illumination is the means by which we understand the Bible.

Then he opened their minds so they could understand the Scriptures.
— Luke 24:45

In the next study we'll look at four ways that each of us can "turn the light on" when it comes to our personal study of the Bible. In Luke 24:45 we're told that when the disciples met with the resurrected Jesus, "He opened their minds so they could understand the Scriptures."

Listen to this wish expressed by Chuck Swindoll:

> If I could have only one wish for God's people, it would be that all of us would return to the Word of God, that we would realize that His Book has the answers. The Bible is the authority, the final resting place of our cares, worries, griefs, tragedies, sorrows, and our surprises. It is the final answer to our questions, our search.[1]

That's the goal of this study and the next: not only that each of us would have a new love for and commitment to the Bible's answers for our lives but also that we would be able to share that love for God's Word with others.

In the next study we'll focus on illumination. Now we'll look at three important questions related to the revelation and inspiration of God's Word:

1. How do we know the Bible came from God?
2. How do we know we have the right books?
3. What does it mean when we say the Bible is inspired?

How Do We Know the Bible Came from God?

You may be asking yourself, If the Bible shows us who God really is, how do I know I can trust it? What makes it more trustworthy than any other book? Is there any objective evidence that the Bible is a unique book?

YES! Every Christian needs to understand four classic proofs of the reliability of the Bible. These proofs answer the questions we hear from others and that you may be asking yourself: Why should I trust the Bible more than any other book? What is so special about the Bible?

First: The external evidence says the Bible is a historical book.

External evidence simply means the proofs for the reliability of the Bible that are outside the pages of the Bible itself. For instance:

- **The number of manuscript copies and the short length of time between the original manuscripts and our first copies of the New Testament**

Norman Geisler writes,

For the New Testament the evidence is overwhelming. There are 5,366 manuscripts to compare and draw information from, and some of these date from the second or third centuries. To put that in perspective, there are only 643 copies of Homer's *Iliad*, and that is the most famous book of ancient Greece! No one doubts the existence of Julius Caesar's *Gallic Wars*, but we only have 10 copies of it and the earliest of those was made 1,000 years after it was written. To have such an abundance of copies of the New Testament from dates within 70 years after their writing is amazing.[2]

—Norman Geisler

Why didn't God allow us to have the original rather than relying on a number of copies? One possibility: we would have worshiped an old document rather than reading and following his living Word.

By the way, it's important to understand that Bibles are translated from these original copies, which were written in Hebrew, Aramaic, and Greek. Many people have the idea that the Bible has been passed down from language to language over the centuries, and thus may have been changed many times. That's not true. When a Bible translation is done, the translator goes back to these early manuscripts in the original languages.

- **The extreme care with which the Scriptures were copied**

The earliest Jewish scribes (Old Testament copyists) followed a strict code to insure accuracy in their copies. Here are a few of the rules they followed meticulously:

1. Each scroll must contain a specified number of columns, all equal throughout the entire book.
2. The length of each column must not be less than forty-eight lines or more than sixty lines.
3. Each column's breadth must be exactly thirty letters.
4. The copyist must use a specially prepared black ink.
5. The copyist must not copy from memory.
6. The space between every consonant must be the size of a thread.
7. The copyist must sit in full Jewish dress.
8. The copyist must use a fresh quill to pen the sacred name of God. (The copyists held the Scriptures and the name of God in such reverence that they would even refuse to acknowledge the presence of a king while writing the name they held so holy.)

Later scribes added these requirements:

1. They could copy only letter by letter, not word by word.
2. They counted the number of times each letter of the alphabet occurred in each book, and if it came out wrong, they threw the scroll away.
3. They knew the middle letter of the Pentateuch (the first five books of the Old Testament) and the middle letter of the entire Old Testament. After copying a scroll, they counted forward and backward from this middle letter. If the number of letters did not match what they knew to be correct, they destroyed the scroll and started over.

- **Confirmation of places and dates by archaeology**

The confirmation through archaeological findings of places and dates helps many to see the reliability of the Bible.

The Dead Sea Scrolls are one of the most famous archaeological discoveries. What's so significant about them? Every one of the Old Testament books is found in these scrolls. Before their discovery, the earliest manuscripts we had of some of the Old Testament books were from 900 A.D.—almost a thousand years later than when these scrolls were made. Amazingly, when the Dead Sea Scrolls were compared with the later manuscripts, practically no differences were found. (The differences, about 5 percent, are mostly in word spellings.) That's almost no changes in 1,000 years!

The Bible's historical accuracy has been questioned repeatedly through the years, yet again and again, archaeology has proven the Bible to be right and the critics wrong. Erwin Lutzer writes in *Seven Reasons Why You Can Trust the Bible:*

> Here are some examples of where critics have had to change their mind about the Bible's reliability.
>
> - For years critics insisted that the story of Abram's rescue of Lot in Genesis 14 was not historically accurate. They said (1) that the names of the kings listed were fictitious, since they were not confirmed in secular histories; (2) that the idea that the king of Babylon was serving the king of Elam was historically impossible. . . . But archaeology had debunked these critics. The names of some of the kings have now been identified. And there is evidence that the king of Babylon did serve the king of Elam at this time.
> - For decades it was said that the Old Testament writers invented the Hittite tribe, since their existence could not be independently confirmed. However, in 1911–12 Professor Hugo Winchkler of Berlin discovered some ten thousand clay tablets at Bogazkoy, the site of the Hittite capital. The existence of the Hittite empire is now extensively proven and documented.
> - The existence of Solomon's reign and his thousands of horses was at one time questioned. But in Meggido, which was one of five chariot cities, excavations have revealed the ruins of thousands of stalls for his horses and chariots.[3]

Archaeology confirms that the places and people the Bible speaks about were historically accurate. This is true not only of the Old Testament but also of the relatively more recent history of the New Testament. Archaeologists have uncovered many of the places where New Testament events occurred. A few examples: portions of Herod's temple, the Areopagus in which Paul spoke in Athens, the theater in Ephesus where Acts 19 tells us a riot occurred, the pool of Siloam where a man was healed of blindness in John 9. The book of Acts is a model of historical accuracy. "In all, Luke names thirty-two countries, fifty-four cities, and nine islands without error."[4]

William Albright reminds us:

Discovery after discovery has established the accuracy of innumerable details, and has brought increased recognition to the value of the Bible as a source of history.[5]

—**William F. Albright**

Discussion question 3 can be used here.

Second: The internal evidence says the Bible is a unique book.

Internal evidence is the evidence that you see in the Bible itself. If you never studied archaeology or history, you could still see the reliability of the Bible just by reading it. Look with me at just two of the ways we can see from the pages of the Bible that it is trustworthy and unique.

- **The majority of the Bible is from eyewitness accounts.**

We all know the value of an eyewitness. When a prosecutor can call upon someone who saw what happened, the prosecution has a much greater chance of winning a conviction.

One piece of evidence that historians look for in assessing the reliability of any document is the number of generations that passed on a story before that story was written down. In other words, is the information firsthand or secondhand? The events of the Bible were primarily recorded in the generation in which they were experienced—by those who experienced them!

The Bible is filled with eyewitness accounts. Moses was there when the Red Sea split. Joshua saw with his own eyes the wall of Jericho falling. The disciples stood together in the Upper Room and saw and heard the resurrected Lord Jesus.

- **The amazing agreement and consistency throughout the Bible**

Josh McDowell writes,

The Bible was written over a period of about 1,500 years in various places stretching all the way from Babylon to Rome. The human authors included over 40 persons from various stations of life: kings, peasants, poets, herdsmen, fishermen, scientists, farmers, priests, pastors, tentmakers and governors. It was written in a wilderness, a dungeon, inside palaces and prisons, on lonely islands and in military battles. Yet it speaks with agreement and reliability on hundreds of controversial subjects. Yet it tells one story from beginning to end, God's salvation of man through Jesus Christ. NO PERSON could have possibly conceived of or written such a work![6]

—Josh McDowell

A Closer Look

What's the Difference?

The Bible is translated from 24,000 copies of the New Testament alone, with millions of people having seen some of these copies. Those copies have been translated by thousands of scholars.	**The Book of Mormon** is translated from a supposed single original that is claimed to have been seen and translated by one man: Joseph Smith (who was not an expert in languages). That original was "taken back." There are no copies of that original.
The Bible was written by more than forty different authors spanning over fifty generations and three continents. It speaks with agreement on all matters of faith and doctrine.	**The Qu'ran** is the writings and record of one man, Muhammad, in one place at one point in history. It differs at many points with the Old and New Testament accounts of history.
The Bible provides God's distinctive solution to man's problem with sin and focuses on God's work in actual, verifiable history.	**Hindu** scriptures claim all roads lead to the same place and focus on stories of things that happened in the "celestial realms."

Teaching Tip

You may not have time to cover all of the material in these studies. With sections such as "A Closer Look," you may want to say to participants, "You may have wondered what the difference is between the Bible and other so-called holy books. Although we don't have time to cover this thoroughly, here is some information to get you started."

Third: The personal evidence says the Bible is a powerful book.

The Bible is the world's best-selling book. Most people know that it was the first major book to be printed on a press (the Gutenberg Bible). The Bible, in whole or in part, has been translated into more than 1,300 languages.

Millions of lives have been changed through the truth in the Bible!

The truth of the Bible has changed my life. I can't tell you how many times just the right word at just the right time gave me God's direction at a crossroad.

Teaching Tip

You'll find that from time to time throughout this study series we'll include personal stories about how a doctrine has impacted our lives. We believe that to bring the truth to life, we must share how it has changed us. When you come across these stories, you have two choices:

1. Read the story as an example of one person's experience. You could say something like, "Tom Holladay, one of the writers of this study series, tells this story about how the truth of God's Word impacted his life in a personal way."

2. The second choice is, of course, for you to tell a story from your own life. We hope that's what you'll do in most cases. Let the following story remind you of a personal experience you've had with the power of God's Word. The most *personal* way to say a truth is the most *powerful* way to say it. For doctrine to come alive, those you are teaching must see the power God's truth has in your life.

I (Tom Holladay) remember the struggle I faced when my mother was in the last stages of cancer. She lived about a two-hour drive from the town I was living in. Once a week or so, I would drive through the valley and over the curvy mountain roads to spend a few hours with her. Although her tenacious spirit never allowed her to admit it, we all knew she didn't have long to live. She was a believer in Jesus Christ, and I was filled with a strong faith that she was heading for an eternity of joy in heaven. However, I was unprepared for the waves of emotion that would hit me as I watched her slipping away, the wave of her body growing weaker, the wave of her mind becoming confused. I felt drenched by the realities of her illness. Oh, I wanted her to be with the Lord, but not this soon and not like this. Everything in me wanted to do something to stop this. So I got on the activity merry-go-round. Frantically, I chased after ways to stop what was happening to my mother. Even if it had nothing to do with my mom, I found myself constantly doing to try to ease my hurting. (Please know that I'm not saying we shouldn't do all we possibly can for someone we love. My activities, however, were often nothing more than pointless exertion of energy.)

One night as I was driving home after seeing her, weariness overwhelmed me. As I rounded one dark curve after another, I was struck again and again with the thought: how could I possibly help my mother when I didn't even have the strength to face the fact that she was dying?

At that moment, Jesus' words from Matthew 11:28 pierced my soul: "Come to me, all you who are weary and burdened, and I will give you rest."

"I will give you rest!" The experience of these words coming into my mind was so powerful and personal; I could almost sense that Jesus was riding with me in that car. In the perfect timing of God, at that moment I rounded the last curve through the mountains and saw the expanse and the lights of the valley spread out in front of me. The thought hit me: God wants to broaden my perspective, to help me to be aware of the fact that he is working even when I can't. "I will give you rest." I must have repeated those words to myself hundreds of times during the weeks leading up to my mother's death. The hurt was real, but God's promise made his presence and strength just as real. His promise gave me the perspective I needed to face the death of my mother.

Remember, personal testimony is just one of the four proofs that the Bible is God's book.

People talk about how the book of Mormon has changed their life, or how the Qu'ran has made a difference, or even describe the impact of a line from the latest Star Wars movie! This, too, is personal testimony. It's subjective, meaning it is the account of one person's experience that has no objective proof.

The good news is, the Bible is shown to be reliable by both objective proof and subjective experience. You can see in the facts of archaeology and history that the Bible is a trustworthy book. And you can see in the personal experience of billions that the Bible is a book that changes lives.

> Discussion questions 4 and 5 can be used here.

Fourth: <u>JESUS</u> said the Bible came from God.

Have you ever heard someone say, "I trust what Jesus said, but not the rest of the Bible"? Jesus himself spoke with confidence about the Bible. If we trust what Jesus said, we have no choice but to trust all of the Bible.

1. **Jesus recognized the Spirit as the <u>AUTHOR</u>.**

   "Why, then," Jesus asked, "did the Spirit inspire David to call him 'Lord'? David said, 'The Lord said to my Lord: "Sit here at my right side until I put your enemies under your feet."'"
   —Matthew 22:43–44 (GNT)

Jesus, quoting from what David wrote in the Psalms, recognizes that the Spirit inspired David's words.

2. **Jesus quoted the Bible as <u>AUTHORITATIVE</u>.**

In Matthew 22:29 Jesus told the Sadducees that not knowing the Scriptures was the reason they lived in error and without God's power.

Jesus replied, "You are in error because you do not know the Scriptures or the power of God."

—Matthew 22:29

In Luke 11 Jesus clearly tells us that God's Word is not just history or poetry; it is to be obeyed.

He replied, "Blessed rather are those who hear the word of God and obey it."

—Luke 11:28

3. **Jesus proclaimed its uniqueness.**

Jesus reminded us that the Bible stands above all other books and all other writings. In fact, he told us that this book stands above all that we see in this physical universe.

Read with me what Jesus said in Matthew 5:18 and in John 10:35:

I tell you the truth, until heaven and earth disappear, not the smallest letter, not the least stroke of a pen, will by any means disappear from the Law until everything is accomplished.

—Matthew 5:18

Scripture is always true.

—John 10:35 (NCV)

4. **Jesus called it the "<u>WORD</u> <u>OF</u> <u>GOD</u>."**

Thus you nullify the word of God by your tradition that you have handed down. And you do many things like that.

—Mark 7:13

Even though Jesus did not possess the original writings of the Bible by Moses, David, and so forth, he nevertheless considered the manuscript copies used in his day to be "the word of God." This is a powerful and personal expression to us of the truth that God works to preserve the integrity and accuracy of the Bible through generation after generation.

5. **Jesus believed that people and places in the Bible were real.**
   - **He believed in the <u>PROPHETS</u> (Matt. 22:40; 24:15).**
   - **He believed in <u>NOAH</u> (Luke 17:26).**
   - **He believed in <u>ADAM</u> and <u>EVE</u> (Matt. 19:4).**
   - **He believed in <u>SODOM</u> and <u>GOMORRAH</u> (Matt. 10:15).**
   - **He believed in <u>JONAH</u> (Matt. 12:40).**

It's interesting that these last four (Noah, Adam and Eve, Sodom and Gomorrah, and Jonah) are found in the portions of the Bible most often attacked as fables or just good stories by those who distrust its historical reliability. The very parts of the Bible that are doubted today are affirmed by the words of Jesus himself.

John MacArthur writes:

> The Bible is the only completely trustworthy source of knowledge about God. Man can't learn all he needs to know about God from human reason, philosophy, or even experience. God alone is the source of the knowledge about Himself, and He has chosen to reveal Himself in the Bible and in no other book.[7]
>
> —John MacArthur Jr.

I want to make sure that as we discuss the historical reliability of the Bible, we keep in mind its impact on our lives.

Though the Bible is the record of how God revealed himself to men and women down through history, he gave us this book to personally reveal to us what he is like. He gave us this book to change *our* lives.

Before we go on, I'd like you to answer in your minds two intensely personal and incredibly important questions about this book:

First, what changes has God's Word worked in your life, or what changes would you like to see the truth of God's Word bring about in your life?

Take a moment to think about that.

Second, how has this book, the Bible, shown you who God really is, or how do you need God to reveal himself to you through this book?

Again, take a moment.

Split Session Plan: If you're teaching this study over two sessions, end the first session here. With a few small modifications, you can use the material directly above this note to close the first session, and the material directly following this note as your introduction to the next session.

Now, let's continue our look at the reliability of God's book.

The latest and most publicized attack on the Bible is from a group of seventy-four scholars who call their meetings "The Jesus Seminar." These self-proclaimed authorities meet twice a year to determine which sayings of Jesus are really authentic and which are not. They present papers, discuss biblical texts, and then, in a theatrical way, vote on how we should view the sayings of Jesus.

They vote not by raising their hands or by writing on little slips of paper but rather with colored beads.

- A red bead means "Jesus undoubtedly said this or something very like it."
- A pink bead means "Jesus probably said something like this."
- A gray bead means "Jesus did not say this, but the ideas are close to his own."
- A black bead means "Jesus did not say this; these words come from a later time."

After dropping their beads in a bucket for six years, the Jesus Seminar published what they consider to be the ultimate red-letter Bible, which they call *The Five Gospels,* with the subtitle *What Did Jesus Really Say?*[8] What have they concluded? That Jesus never said 82 percent of what the Gospels claim he said, and that it is doubtful whether he said most of the remaining 18 percent.

Because this group is very media savvy, you've likely read their ideas in a newspaper or in a magazine such as *Time* or *Newsweek.* The truth is, much of their so-called scholarship is based on subjective standards. Most of us don't know how to combat ideas such as this. In fact, you may have wondered yourself whether what you read in the Bible is really *all* God's Word.

As we continue in this study, I believe you'll have a greater confidence that the Bible you hold in your hand is God's Word—not just in part but in whole. You'll also be better able to explain to someone else—a friend or your children—the foundation upon which that belief is built.

We've looked at four tests, or proofs, of the Bible's reliability. By every one of these four tests—external, internal, personal, and scriptural—the words of the Bible are clearly shown to be God's revelation to the people of every generation. There is, however, one nagging question that continues to bother some people regarding the reliability of the Bible.

How Do We Know We Have the Right Books?

16

A common misconception is that although God may have written the Bible, the books that are included in it were chosen by a committee of men who could have easily left out some books. Let's clear that up and look at the truth. The bottom line is that if God wrote the books, he is certainly powerful enough to make sure those books are included in his Word. Here are three reasons we know that we have the right books.

The testimony of the _BIBLE_

- **Jesus recognized the Old Testament canon. The word** _canon_ **refers to the list of books that are accepted as Scripture.**

  Jesus said:

  This is what I told you while I was still with you: Everything must be fulfilled that is written about me in the Law of Moses, the Prophets and the Psalms.
  —**Luke 24:44**

  When Jesus mentions the Law, the Prophets, and the Psalms in Luke 24, he is affirming all three major divisions of the Old Testament.

- **Peter recognized part of the New Testament canon.**

  Peter wrote:

  Some things in Paul's letters are hard to understand, and people who are ignorant and weak in faith explain these things falsely. They also falsely explain the other Scriptures, but they are destroying themselves by doing this.
  —**2 Peter 3:16** (NCV)

  Circle the words "the other Scriptures." These letters of Paul had just been written, and they were already being recognized as Scripture by the church.

- **Paul recognized the _EQUAL_ inspiration of the Old and New Testaments in a single verse.**

  For the Scripture says, "Do not muzzle the ox while it is treading out the grain," and "The worker deserves his wages."
  —**1 Timothy 5:18**

  This is an amazing verse. In it Paul quotes from Deuteronomy 25:4 in the Old Testament and from Luke 10:7 in the New Testament, and calls them both Scripture!

  Students of Bible history believe that Luke's gospel was written in 60 A.D. and that the book of First Timothy was written in 63 A.D. This means that the gospel of Luke was being recognized as Holy Scripture within only three years of its writing.

The history of the church

When you look at how books actually came to be included in the Bible, you realize that it was not the result of one vote taken at a single meeting.

Books were included in the New Testament on the basis of three things:

1. **The authority of an _APOSTLE_**

The New Testament stands on the foundation of the apostles, men who intimately knew Jesus. God decided to use those who were closest to Jesus to tell the story of his life and to show us how to live as Jesus lived.

The New Testament has eyewitness authority. Take the writers of the Gospels, for instance. Matthew was an apostle, Mark wrote down Peter's remembrances, Luke was a friend of Paul, and John was an apostle.

2. The teaching of the <u>TRUTH</u>

The first people to read the New Testament books saw the light of God's truth in them. The clear ring of truth in the words caused them to see these books as something entirely different from other religious writings of that day.

As more and more people read these books, a third affirmation resulted:

3. The confirmation of the <u>CHURCH</u>

Many people think that the New Testament books were chosen by a council of a few people. That is not true. A council did recognize the books of the New Testament (around 400 A.D.), but that was after the church had been using these books for 300 years. The council formally recognized the books in response to false teachers who were trying to add books to the Bible.

The misconception is that what gives these books authority is the fact that they were "voted in." The opposite is true. What caused these books to be recognized as God's Word is the fact that these books had the authority of God behind them.

The power of God

The grass withers and the flowers fall, but the word of our God stands forever.

—Isaiah 40:8

Our assurance that we have the right books is a matter of <u>FAITH</u>. God would not have allowed any part of what he had chosen to stand forever to be left out.

You can erase from your mind the thought that someday they'll discover in some cave a book of the Bible that should have gotten in—a "lost" book of the Bible. Do you think God would let that happen? Of course not!

What Does It Mean When We Say the Bible Is Inspired?

We are bombarded with words every day, words with varying degrees of authority behind them. Suppose you're driving down the road and see a billboard that says, "Pull off at the next off-ramp." You may or may not pull off. But if you see a flashing light in your rearview mirror and hear a voice from the police car behind you saying, "Pull off at the next off-ramp," you would react quite differently! Of all the voices we hear calling to us each day, none speaks with more authority than the Bible. Because God said it, and because he knows and controls everything, each word in the Bible has immeasurable authority behind it. This authority of God's Word is what the doctrine of inspiration is about. Look at this definition.

A Fresh Word

Inspiration

Inspiration does not mean simply that the writer felt enthusiastic, like Handel composing "The Messiah." Nor does it mean that the writings are necessarily inspiring, like an uplifting poem. As a process, it refers to the writers and the writings being controlled by God. As a product, it refers to the writings only, as documents that are God's message.[9]

—Norman Geisler

What do we mean when we say that the Bible is "inspired?"

Inspiration means God wrote the Bible through PEOPLE.

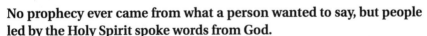

No prophecy ever came from what a person wanted to say, but people led by the Holy Spirit spoke words from God.

—2 Peter 1:21 (NCV)

The details of how God inspired the Bible are a matter of great debate and conjecture. One thing is obvious as you read the Bible: he didn't use people as robots. You can clearly see people's personalities and passions in what they wrote. God created a perfect Bible through real people. He moved them internally to create a Word that will last eternally.

For those of you who doubt whether God could create something perfect through a fallible human being, I'd remind you that Jesus was born into this world through a faith-filled but imperfect woman named Mary. And Jesus was perfect.

Inspiration means the Holy Spirit is the __AUTHOR__.

Look at these verses:

The Scripture had to be fulfilled which the Holy Spirit spoke long ago through the mouth of David . . .

—Acts 1:16

The Holy Spirit spoke the truth to your forefathers when he said through Isaiah the prophet . . .

—Acts 28:25

Then the Spirit of the LORD came upon me, and he told me to say . . .

—Ezekiel 11:5

Who wrote the Bible? God did! He worked through people, but ultimately he is the author. The fact that God created a perfect book through so many imperfect people is one of his greatest miracles. Splitting the Red Sea is nothing compared with that!

We have to be careful, of course, to see that the authority is in God's words and not in our opinions about his Word. God always has a way of humbling us when we try to speak for him rather than allowing him to speak for himself. A church bishop of a century ago pronounced from his pulpit and in the periodical he edited that heavier-than-air flight was both impossible and contrary to the will of God. His name was Bishop Wright. . . . You've already guessed that his two sons were named Orville and Wilber!

Two important words to understand:

Verbal: God inspired the __WORDS__, not just the ideas (Matt. 5:18; 22:43–44—Jesus based his argument on the single word "Lord").

Plenary: God inspired __ALL__, not just part (2 Tim. 3:16).

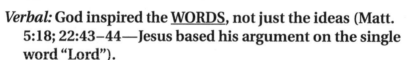

As for God, his way is perfect; the word of the LORD is flawless. He is a shield for all who take refuge in him.

—Psalm 18:30

So when you hear someone say we believe in the "verbal, plenary inspiration of God's Word," now you know what they mean.

Some books and portions of the Bible will be more inspiring to you than others, but that doesn't change the fact that all of the Bible is inspired. Augustine gave us a clear warning of the danger of our deciding which parts of the Bible are inspired:

If you believe what you like in the Gospel, and reject what you don't like, it is not the Gospel you believe, but yourself.

—Augustine

Inspiration means God's Word is to be our __FINAL AUTHORITY__.

How can a young person stay pure? By obeying your word and following its rules.

—Psalm 119:9 (NLT)

For the word of the LORD holds true, and everything he does is worthy of our trust.

—Psalm 33:4 (NLT)

- Understanding inspiration increases my __CONFIDENCE__ in the Bible.

- The truth behind inspiration is that I can trust his Word above my __FEELINGS__, __VALUES__, __OPINIONS__, and __CULTURE__.

J. I. Packer defines authority as when you "treat his words as having decisive force" for your life.[10] This means that:

Whenever there is a conflict between what the Bible says and the way I feel or what I've been taught or the opinions of others or what seems reasonable to me—whenever I have a difference of opinion with the Bible for any reason—the Bible is always right!

Discussion questions 6 and 7 can be used here.

Sometimes you'll hear a person say that it is closed-minded to accept the Bible as authoritative truth. Belief in the authority of the Bible is not being closed-minded; it is being right-minded. It is not closed-minded to say that on a compass there is only one true north, or that on a map there is only one geographical location for your destination. Since God inspired the Bible, it is not closed-minded to say that it has the final say in our lives.

Teaching Tip

This would be a good moment to talk about how you are learning to trust the Bible more and more every day. It's good for people to see that learning to trust is a process that takes time. It is also good for them to see that it is a process that works, that when we trust the Bible, it is not always easy, but we are always glad we did in the end.

Listen to what C. H. Spurgeon once said:

I would recommend you either believe God up to the hilt, or else not to believe at all. Believe this book of God, every letter of it, or else reject it. There is no logical standing place between the two. Be satisfied with nothing less than a faith that swims in the deeps of divine revelation; a faith that paddles about the edge of the water is poor faith at best. It is little better than a dry-land faith, and is not good for much.[11]

—C. H. Spurgeon

Pray with me:

Father, we reaffirm our faith in your Word. We want a faith that swims in the depths of your truth. Our prayer is that you would enable us not only to talk about the authority of your Word but also to live that truth in our lives. Help us to see, right now, where it is that your Word is calling us to act and to change. We pray that you would give us the faith to take you at your word. Help us to step out in faith to make the decision your Word is telling us to make. In Jesus' name, amen.

Acting on the Truth

How Should We Respond?

The Bible shows us God. How should we respond to this book?
- **With awe (Ps. 119:120)**
- **With delight (Ps. 1:2)**
- **With appreciation (Ps. 119:72)**
- **With praise (Ps. 119:62)**
- **With joy (Ps. 119:111)**
- **With love (Ps. 119:47, 97)**
- **With obedience (Deut. 5:32; James 1:22; John 14:15)**

Use the verses above in your quiet time before the next session. Take a few moments not only to read the verse but also to do what it says. It's amazing how our faith in God's Word is increased through this simple step of telling God how we value his Word.

Begin working on *Foundations* memory card 1, "The Truth about the Bible."

Teaching Tip

As a study in doctrine, this series contains a great deal of content. Using these memory cards will help that content stick in participants' minds. But only if you emphasize them by going over them from time to time. A good time to do this is at the beginning or at the end of each study. Start with the next session!

Discussion Questions

1. Take a moment to get to know each other better by filling in some of the following details of your personal histories.

   My Life Story
   > Place I was born:
   > Favorite subject in high school:
   > One of my favorite TV shows growing up:
   > The model and year of the first car I owned:
   > My first job:
   > My favorite candy bar as a kid:

2. Do you have a favorite verse or passage or book in the Bible? What is it and why?

3. Tell about a time when the Bible had an impact on your life.

4. What difference does it make whether the Gospels—or the other books of the Bible—are historically reliable?

5. In your reading of the Bible, what evidence have you seen that the Bible is both amazing and unique?

6. Give some examples of the struggle to

   trust God's Word above your feelings.

   trust God's Word above the values you've grown up with.

   trust God's Word above your opinions.

   trust God's Word above your culture.

7. How has this study helped you to see that trusting in the Bible as God's Word is more than just a feeling we have? What truths that we have looked at are the most convincing to you of the wonder and reliability of the Bible?

The Bible
Part 2

Life Change Objective

To give you deep and lasting confidence in your God-given ability to understand the Bible.

Summary Teaching Outline

Four Things Necessary for Illumination

Love God's Word Deeply

How does the Bible picture its potential for changing our lives?

1. Seed
2. Sword
3. Food
4. Fire and Hammer
5. Mirror

Understand God's Word Spiritually

Two truths about every believer in Christ

1. The Holy Spirit makes me able to understand the Bible.
2. The Holy Spirit makes me responsible for understanding the Bible.

Handle God's Word Accurately

Seven rules of Bible study

Study God's Word Diligently

When you walk into a dark room, what's the first thing you do? You run your hand along the wall until you find the light switch. You want to illuminate the room so you won't stub your precious little toe.

When characters in cartoons get an idea, what picture pops above their heads? Right, Road Runner gets a great idea for eluding Wile E. Coyote, and with a "ding," you see a little lightbulb appear. He has had an illuminating thought, a thought that brings light to his circumstances.

We are meant to have this kind of experience with God's Word. God wants to illuminate his Word for us so we'll know what the Bible means and how its truth fits into our lives. He wants to show us the light switch. He wants us to experience that "ding" of the light coming on as we see a verse in a way we've never seen it before.

In fact, I hope that some illumination from God's Word happens during this study!

Remember the three words: revelation, inspiration, illumination?

- **Revelation has been completed (Heb. 1:1–2).**

- **Inspiration has been completed (1 Peter 1:10–12).**

- **Illumination is going on right now.**

  In this study, we're going to talk about how illumination happens. I don't know about you, but I've noticed that it doesn't happen every time I read the Bible or listen to it being read. Sometimes I get a lot of illumination; other times I feel like I'm in a dark room.

  Why the difference? Why do some seem to be able to understand the Bible better than others? Is it that some Christians are smarter? Absolutely not. Is it that some have been to Bible school? Of course not. Illumination has to do with inner qualities. It is not automatic, but it is the result of choices we all can make. In this study we're going to talk about four choices every one of us can make that lead to life-changing illumination from the Bible. God is light, and he promises to bring us light.

  Look at Psalms 18:28 and 119:105:

  LORD, you have brought light to my life; my God, you light up my darkness.

  —Psalm 18:28 (NLT)

  Your word is a lamp to my feet and a light for my path.

  —Psalm 119:105

A Fresh Word

Illumination

Illumination is the supernatural influence or ministry of the Holy Spirit, which enables all who believe in Christ to understand the Scriptures.

Picture it this way: with his revelation and by his inspiration, God sent the light of his Word into our world. Through illumination, the blinders are taken off our eyes so we can see the light that is already there.

Four things are necessary for illumination in a believer's life:

Love God's Word <u>DEEPLY</u>

Circle with me some words in these three verses in your outline. In Psalm 119:97, circle "all day long."

How I love your teachings! I think about them all day long.
—**Psalm 119:97** (NCV)

Circle "finest gold" in Psalm 119:127.

Truly, I love your commands more than gold, even the finest gold.
—**Psalm 119:127** (NLT)

In Proverbs 2:3–6 circle "silver" and "hidden treasure."

And if you call out for insight and cry aloud for understanding, and if you look for it as for silver and search for it as for hidden treasure, then you will understand the fear of the LORD and find the knowledge of God. For the LORD gives wisdom, and from his mouth come knowledge and understanding.
—**Proverbs 2:3–6**

Notice the value placed on God's Word here. Illumination starts with God; he's the one who turns the light on. But I'm never going to see that light if I don't value the Bible enough to pick it up and read it, to search out its truth.

I love the pictures of gold and silver and hidden treasure; these pictures tell me how the valuable truths of God get into my life. You don't find gold or silver just lying around on the ground; you have to dig for it. You can't find hidden treasure without a map—"X marks the spot." You have to search it out and dig it up. God gives us his Word and says, "X marks the spot." Here is the place where you can find the hope you need, the power to love, and a deeper faith than you ever imagined. But you have to open the Bible and read it. And many times you have to dig a little. Understanding doesn't come immediately; it takes thought and prayer. If you don't love what God's Word can do in your life, you won't open this book—and you certainly won't take the time to dig into it.

Discussion question 1 can be used here.

I want to help you deepen that love right now. Look with me at some pictures of what the Bible tells us happens when we read God's truth.

How does the Bible picture its potential for changing our lives?

1. SEED

Read with me 1 Peter 1:23:

For you have been born again, not of perishable seed, but of imperishable, through the living and enduring word of God.

—1 Peter 1:23

Help me with this very simple quiz. If a farmer plants corn seed in his field, what's going to grow? Corn! If he plants wheat seed, what will he get? Wheat. Watermelon seed? Watermelon.

This verse talks about two kinds of seed: perishable and imperishable. If you plant perishable seed, what will you get? Things that perish. If you plant imperishable seed, you'll get things that never fade away.

Look at me for a moment.

Teaching Tip

Believe it or not, not everyone is listening to you every moment that you speak. Some may be distracted by their thoughts, by writing their notes, or by someone else in the room. It's important to draw people's attention when you are about to say something you want to make sure no one misses. (Jesus did this using the phrase "Truly, truly....") You could say "Listen," or "I don't want you to miss this," or "The one truth I want to make sure you take away from this study is ..." Often it's most effective to say, "Look at me for a moment." You say this not in a demanding way but with quiet passion in your voice. This draws everyone's attention away from distractions and gets them to focus on the truth you are about to teach.

One of the reasons you and I face so many struggles is that we expect perishable seeds to give us imperishable crops.

We want more joy in life, so we plant a lot of happy circumstances and experiences. So we get a crop of happiness. But happiness fades very quickly; it's perishable. You can't grow imperishable joy out of seeds of perishable happiness.

We want more fulfillment in life, so we throw ourselves into our careers. We get success in our careers, but we're still not fulfilled. The fulfillment our heart longs for is an imperishable quality; you can't grow it out of a job.

God's Word is the seed for the imperishable things we all want. If you want a crop of hope, plant God's Word. A harvest of inner fulfillment comes only from God's truth. You cannot get genuine security out of any seed this world offers; it comes only through God's Word.

2. Sword

Look at these two verses:

Take the helmet of salvation and the sword of the Spirit, which is the word of God.

—**Ephesians 6:17**

For the word of God is living and active. Sharper than any double-edged sword, it penetrates even to dividing soul and spirit, joints and marrow; it judges the thoughts and attitudes of the heart.

—**Hebrews 4:12**

The dividing of soul and spirit, where what I want and what God wants clash. That can be a real battleground!

I want you to notice:

In Ephesians the sword is in our hand, defending against the enemy. In Hebrews, the sword is in God's hands, penetrating and deeply impacting our lives.

God's Word is our defense against our spiritual enemies.

When Jesus was tempted by Satan in the desert, he did not turn to a self-help book or advice from a talk show. He used the Bible as a sword of defense against Satan. Jesus knew that the Word of God had the power to defend him from temptation.

God's Word is also a sword that is used on us!

Have you ever felt God's Word cut into your heart? You've gone to the Bible and it has sliced you in a way that opens your heart. You may have had everyone else fooled, even yourself, but God's Word showed the truth of your motives and your sin. It hurts, doesn't it?

When God uses his sword on us, he uses it not as an enemy trying to destroy us but as a surgeon who wants to heal us. He knows how to cut in just the right place at just the right time to bring healing to our lives, to cut out the spiritual cancer that could destroy our lives.

3. <u>FOOD</u>

Read with me the following verses:

When your words came, I ate them; they were my joy and my heart's delight, for I bear your name, O Lord God Almighty.

—Jeremiah 15:16

Jesus answered, "It is written: 'Man does not live on bread alone, but on every word that comes from the mouth of God.'"

—Matthew 4:4

Like newborn babies, crave pure spiritual milk, so that by it you may grow up in your salvation.

—1 Peter 2:2

Jeremiah actually ate the scrolls upon which God had told him to write his words. That's a high-fiber breakfast! Obviously God wanted to make a point by commanding the prophet to consume these scrolls. "[Your words] were my joy and my heart's delight," says Jeremiah.

Matthew compares God's Word to the daily bread we need. The spiritual nutrition we need is God's Word. Anytime God's Word is taught, preached, read, or studied, we are fed. If you're in a church in which the Bible is taught, you are being faithfully fed. Sometimes you hear people say, "That preaching is not feeding me." That's inevitable if the Bible isn't part of what is being taught. But when the Word is taught, you are fed. If the Word is shared faithfully, you are getting food.

Be careful of falling into the trap of thinking, "That doesn't feed me," when the real issue is simply that the Word is being taught in a different style than you are used to. Sometimes believers get a taste of God's Word being presented or taught in one style, and when they hear it taught with a different style they think, "I can't learn from that." Maybe you're used to a "paper plate" teaching of the Word and you find yourself in a church that serves it on fine china. The question isn't style; the question is, Is the Bible being taught?

You may be thinking, "I'd like to be fed from God's Word, but I just can't seem to understand it." Look again at 1 Peter 2:2. The Bible also calls itself milk, the kind of food that even new believers can benefit from. If you're having a hard time understanding the Bible as you begin reading it (and who doesn't!), here's what you do. Find the simple and clear truths that you *do* understand, and live on them. Don't get caught up in what you don't understand as yet; just live out what you do understand. God says, "Stop lying," and "Love your neighbor," and "Think about good and pure things"; these are truths that anyone can understand. As you drink them in and live them, you'll find yourself growing stronger and understanding more.

Don't fall into the trap of thinking, "I'm not going to live the clear truths until I understand it all." That would be like a baby saying, "I'm not going to drink this milk unless you let me have that steak!" Frankly, I still have a difficult time understanding some of the truths in the Bible. But I'm not going to let that keep me from the blessing of living out what I do know.

4. Fire and Hammer

 12

"Is not my word like fire," declares the LORD, "and like a hammer that breaks a rock in pieces?"

—Jeremiah 23:29

The joy that comes from what God's Word does in our lives is not always an easy joy. Sometimes God's Word is like a fire. It refines us, and that process of burning out the impurities is painful.

Sometimes God's Word is like a hammer.

Teaching Tip

The following is a personal story from Kay Warren's experience. As we noted in the previous study, we hope this will cause you to think of a story in your own life of when God's Word acted as a hammer.

Have you ever felt God's Word acting like a hammer? I (Kay Warren) have. I will never forget teaching a women's Bible study at Saddleback Church about forgiveness and our need to love one another. I blithely read out of 1 John how if anyone does not love his brother, the truth is not in him. It was a verse I'd picked out and studied during the week, but as I read it that day, all of a sudden God's hammer hit me on the head and I was absolutely broken. All I could do was put my head down on the lectern and sob.

At that time, my younger brother was a drug addict, and his addiction was tearing the heart of my parents and myself. I was watching my parents die by inches. I honestly didn't love my brother at that time; I was filled with anger at him for the pain he was causing and for the waste of his life. When I read that verse, so confident of how God was going to use it in someone else's life, I heard the words, "If anyone loves God but hates his *brother,* the truth is not in him," in a way I never had before. God used that experience to give me a tender heart toward my brother.

Why would God need to use a hammer on us? Because sometimes we have hard hearts.

5. Mirror

Anyone who listens to the word but does not do what it says is like a man who looks at his face in a mirror and, after looking at himself, goes away and immediately forgets what he looks like. But the man who looks intently into the perfect law that gives freedom, and continues to do this, not forgetting what he has heard, but doing it—he will be blessed in what he does.

—James 1:23–25

How many of you looked in a mirror at least once today? Of course you have. If you hadn't, you'd run the risk of walking around all day with a piece of breakfast in your teeth!

God's Word shows us the spiritual truth about ourselves. But it cannot show us if we don't look. It's amazing how even a quick look at God's Word will show you the truth about an attitude you're struggling with.

Sometimes we look in other mirrors to try to figure out who we really are. For some it's the mirror of others' opinions. It may be the mirror of our family's expectations, or the mirror of our culture. All of these mirrors are like fun house mirrors—they give a distorted reflection. God's Word is a perfect mirror; it lets you see yourself for who you really are and this world for what it really is, both the good and the bad. Both! If you think when you look into the mirror of God's Word that all you'll see are bad things about yourself, you're dead wrong. You'll see the promise and potential God has built into your life; you'll see joy and significance that you never dreamed could be a part of your life.

> Discussion question 2 can be used here.

What emotion do you feel when you see the Bible? For many of us, it's become just a familiar part of our lives; we don't feel much. Sometimes we need to take a few minutes to be reminded, as we've done in this study. Do you realize how valuable this book truly is? The value is not in the leather binding or the wafer-thin pages; its value is in the personal sacrifice that has been paid.

Do you realize the sacrifice that it took to get this book into your hands today? For the first 1,500 years of church history, the Bible was available only to an elite group of church leaders and teachers—and then mostly in Latin. William Tyndale, the man who first translated the Bible into the English language, paid for that translation with his life. He was burned at the stake for the crime of translating the Bible into English. The leaders of the church felt that the Bible should not be translated into the language of common people because it would be misinterpreted and abused. He paid with his life for your freedom to read the Bible. This book is a treasure!

Understand God's Word SPIRITUALLY

Once you've begun to highly value and read and study God's Word, you'll need to understand God's Word spiritually, not just intellectually.

Two truths about every believer in Christ:

1. The Holy Spirit makes me ABLE to understand the Bible.

That's true for every believer. Open your Bible with me to 1 Corinthians 2:12–15.

Teaching Tip

We strongly encourage you to ask people to open their Bibles during these studies. Although most of the verses are printed in the learner's guide, it's important for people to open the Bible and see the context in which the verses were written. We want them to open their Bibles because of the very point being made here: people are personally able and responsible to understand God's Word. Anytime you're reading from a longer passage, that's a great opportunity to say, "Open your Bible with me."

And God has actually given us his Spirit (not the world's spirit) so we can know the wonderful things God has freely given us. When we tell you this, we do not use words of human wisdom. We speak words given to us by the Spirit, using the Spirit's words to explain spiritual truths. But people who aren't Christians can't understand these truths from God's Spirit. It all sounds foolish to them because only those who have the Spirit can understand what the Spirit means. We who have the Spirit understand these things, but others can't understand us at all.
—1 Corinthians 2:12–15 (NLT)

Have you ever read a book and wished the author was there to explain what you just read? The author of the Bible is always available! His Spirit has been put into the lives of believers—into our lives. God didn't go to the trouble of sending his Spirit into your life only to have you leave your Bible on the shelf.

But when he, the Spirit of truth, comes, he will guide you into all truth.
—John 16:13

I like the word *guide*. Sometimes we think understanding just washes over us all at once. It doesn't work that way. If I have a guide to get me through a jungle, he's going to guide me step by step. If he tried to tell me all at once what I need to know, I'd forget much of what he said. I wouldn't understand because he would be talking about places I hadn't seen yet. God *guides* us into his truth by his Spirit. Step by step you understand more and more of God's Word. You take a step, and he shows you more truth.

The Holy Spirit makes me able to understand the Bible, and then:

2. The Holy Spirit makes me <u>RESPONSIBLE</u> for understanding the Bible.

Read with me from 1 John 2:20, 27:

But you have an anointing from the Holy One, and all of you know the truth. . . . As for you, the anointing you received from him remains in you, and you do not need anyone to teach you. But as his anointing teaches you about all things and as that anointing is real, not counterfeit—just as it has taught you, remain in him.

—1 John 2:20, 27

Not only are you able to understand the Bible, you are responsible to understand the Bible. God has given us great teachers and preachers and writers to help us to learn and apply God's Word, but you cannot depend on them alone.

> Discussion question 3 can be used here.

You are responsible to learn the truth of God's Word for yourself.

Most of us have three or four Bibles in our homes. That's a wonderful gift, but it is also an incredible responsibility. You and I have the opportunity to know more truth than most believers down through history, and God will hold us accountable for that. We need to take that responsibility very personally.

We're responsible to know the truth, and that means the whole truth. The question is, How much of the Bible have you taken the time to know and understand? Most of us have favorite parts of the Bible, and that's good. But if those are the only parts that you ever read you are going to miss out on some incredible blessings that God wants to give to you. Dr. Donald Grey Barnhouse used this story to emphasize the benefits of exploring the entire Bible.

> Dr. Donald Grey Barnhouse was an American preacher of the last generation, and nobody ever sparkled when he preached like Dr. Barnhouse.
> One time he was telling his audience why they needed to read the whole Bible. He reminded them how God said to Abraham, "I'm going to give you this

land [Palestine], so go walk around it. Every place you set your foot will be yours" (loose wording of Genesis 13:14, 17; Deuteronomy 11:24; and Joshua 1:3).

The way Dr. Barnhouse told it, that evening Abraham took a walk, walking around about an acre—and that night he owned an acre.

The next day he walked around a mile, and he owned the mile.

And when the sheep had grazed there, he took them over to the next valley, and he owned the valley. ("Every place where you set your foot will be yours.")

It wasn't too many years until he owned everything from Dan to Beersheba— just by setting his foot down.

And, said Dr. Barnhouse with his sparkle, lots of Christians possess a very small Bible. They have John 3:16 and the Twenty-third Psalm and a few other little passages, and they keep going back and forth from one to another, maybe grazing those little spots down to bare rock. And that's all they have. But God says, "Go walk through the length and breadth of the land. Every place where you set your foot will be yours—full of wonderful truths just for you."[1]

You are responsible to check out the truth that you're taught.

If you follow a false teacher and one day stand before the Lord and say, "It was their fault," the Lord will say, "It was your responsibility." There are two terrible tragedies with a false teacher such as Jim Jones (who you might remember called more than nine hundred of his followers to commit mass suicide in Guyana). The first is with the false teacher, that someone would so twist and pervert God's words for their selfish ends. But the other tragedy is with those who accept the words of the false teacher. They have all the resources they need to show his teaching to be a lie if only they will take the time to read the Bible for themselves.

Never accept what you're taught without checking it out in God's Word.

Being responsible means that you and I are also accountable for dealing with the doubts that can keep us from leaning on the truth in God's Word.

If you've ever found yourself struggling with doubts about the Bible, you're in some pretty good company. At the time that Billy Graham was about to see his ministry explode into national prominence, he found himself wrestling with questions about the reliability of the Bible. A respected peer in ministry had told him that it would be "intellectually dishonest" to accept all of the Bible as truth. Graham was troubled over whether the Bible was actually the Word of God or just the words of men about Jesus. While speaking at a youth conference in the San Bernardino Mountains, he decided to take a walk in the forest to settle this issue in his heart.

As he walked he said, "Lord, what shall I do? What shall be the direction of my life?" He saw that intellect alone couldn't resolve the question of the Bible's inspiration and authority. It ultimately became an issue of faith. He thought of the faith he had in many everyday things that he did not understand, such as airplanes and cars, and asked himself why it was only with the things of the Spirit that such faith was considered wrong.

> "So I went back and got my Bible," he recalled, "and I went out in the moonlight. And I got to a stump and put the Bible on the stump, and I knelt down, and I said, 'Oh God, I cannot prove certain things. I cannot answer some of the questions some are raising, but I accept this Book by faith as the Word of God.'"[2]

From that point on, his ministry did nothing but expand. And the most familiar phrase in his messages became "the Bible says."

Split Session Plan: If you're teaching this study over two sessions, end the first session here.

You and I have to come to grips with just how powerful the Bible is. That's why it has to be handled responsibly.

The story of Jesus' temptation in the wilderness teaches some sobering truths about the Bible. Jesus went into the desert to fast for forty days and nights before beginning his public ministry. At the end of that time, Satan tempted Jesus. Satan used the most powerful tool at his disposal. It wasn't money or fame; he tempted Jesus by trying to twist the truth of the Bible:

> The devil led him to Jerusalem and had him stand on the highest point of the temple. "If you are the Son of God," he said, "throw yourself down from here. For it is written: 'He will command his angels concerning you to guard you carefully.'"
> —Luke 4:9–10

Satan knows the power of God's Word, and he is not afraid to attempt to use it against us. Jesus resisted the temptation by quoting the real truth of the Bible back to him. Would you or I be able to do the same?

How do we keep from getting fooled? We need to learn to handle God's Word accurately.

Handle God's Word <u>ACCURATELY</u> 16

Be diligent to present yourself approved to God as a workman who does not need to be ashamed, handling accurately the word of truth.
—2 Timothy 2:15 (NASB)

It's amazing how people will try to twist the Bible to say anything they want, often even throwing out rules of common sense. You can't just ignore all the rules for understanding a language or a book when you pick up the Bible. As we get to know the Word, it's vital that we understand a few simple guidelines for Bible study. By knowing them, you'll be able to spot anyone who is twisting the truth of the Word.

Here are seven rules for understanding the Bible that will help you to follow God's command in Timothy to be a workman who is "handling accurately the word of truth."

Seven rules of Bible study

Rule 1:   Faith and the Holy Spirit are necessary for proper interpretation.

Do you ever wonder why those who are not yet believers scratch their heads in confusion over so much of what the Bible says? Is it that the Bible really doesn't make sense? No, it's that the Bible is understood by faith. To make sense of the whole of what the Bible says and means, you have to have a personal relationship with the author. And for someone who is not yet a believer, even the smallest step of faith will give them insight to understand God's Word.

Rule 2:   The Bible interprets itself.

When someone asks me, "What's the best commentary on the Bible?" my first answer is always, "The Bible." You have to look all the way through the Bible to see what the Bible teaches. Scripture best explains Scripture.

Application: **Learn to do cross-reference studies.**

To do cross-reference studies, you'll need a Bible with cross-references in the margin—a listing of other verses that relate to the verse you're reading. For instance, a verse about forgiveness will point you to several other verses about forgiveness. Or verses about Jesus' resurrection will point you to other verses and passages on the Resurrection.

Rule 3:   Understand the Old Testament in light of the <u>NEW TESTAMENT</u>.

The Old Testament can sometimes be a scary place without the light of the New Testament. Picture it like this: The Old Testament is a dimly lit room filled with treasures. The New Testament brings more light into the room. It allows you to see the real beauty of the treasures contained in the Old Testament.

Example: **The Old Testament Law**

The sacrificial laws in the Old Testament can be very confusing. Why did God want all of those sheep and cattle killed—why all that blood? But as soon as you read in the New Testament about Jesus' sacrifice for us—his blood being spilled for our forgiveness—the light goes on.

Rule 4: Understand unclear passages in the light of <u>CLEAR</u> passages.

People violate this rule all the time. They find one verse they don't understand, decide how to interpret it, and then try to make other verses fit with their unique interpretation.

Example: **"Now if there is no resurrection, what will those do who are baptized for the dead?" (1 Cor. 15:29).**

We don't know for certain what Paul meant by "baptized for the dead"; several possible interpretations center on the fact that Paul is referring to what some were doing at the time. He is not directing us to do the same. Cults and false teachers will often take a verse such as this and make it seem that the Bible agrees with what they teach. For instance, they might say, "What this verse means is that you should be baptized for your relatives in order to assure them a place in heaven." But to say that, you would have to set aside many clear verses about salvation being a decision everyone must make for themselves. Let the clear passages about baptism help you understand this unclear passage, and not vice versa.

Rule 5: Understand words and verses in the light of their <u>CONTEXT</u>.

Example: **"Take life easy; eat, drink and be merry" (Luke 12:19).**

Does Luke 12:19 mean we're to be party animals? The next phrase says, "For tomorrow you die." It's good to know that! It's not a commandment; it's a *warning*.

There are so many words on so many subjects in the Bible. It's easy to take a few of them out of context to prove just about anything you want.

Rule 6: Understand historical passages in the light of <u>DOCTRINAL</u> passages.

Examples:

> **"The king must not take many wives for himself, because they will lead him away from the LORD" (Deut. 17:17 NLT).**

"Very early in the morning, while it was still dark, Jesus got up, left the house and went off to a solitary place, where he prayed" (Mark 1:35).

I'm sometimes asked, "How about all of those guys who had more than one wife?" History records that David had a number of wives, and that his son Solomon had three hundred wives. Does that mean having more than one wife was okay with God? Not when you understand the doctrinal passage. Genesis 2 teaches that two shall become one, not that three hundred and one shall become one! Deuteronomy specifically warned the king, "The king must not take many wives." These doctrinal passages help us to see clearly that David and Solomon were sinning by having many wives and to see how that sin led them astray.

Jesus never left the country of his birth. Does that mean we can never leave our country? No, there is no command attached to this example.

Look at Mark 1:35. Jesus often prayed early in the morning. Does that mean we're commanded to get up at 4 A.M. and pray? No. (Some of you are saying, "Thank you, Lord," right now!) God may convince you that this is a good habit for your life, but he does not command every believer to pray early in the morning. You cannot turn the story of when Jesus prayed into a command.

Rule 7: Understand personal experience in the light of Scripture.

This probably is the rule that believers break most often. We tend to understand Scripture in the light of personal experience, and we make our personal application of Scripture into a command for others to follow.

Example: **"Owe nothing to anyone" (Rom. 13:8 NASB).**

As an example, let's say you read Romans 13:8 and think, "I owe thousands on my credit cards. I need to do something about that." The application for you is to pay off your debt and cut up your credit cards. That's a good, God-honoring application.

But then suppose that from your experience you say to others, "The Bible teaches here in Romans 13:8 that every Christian must cut up their credit cards." No, it does not! The words *credit card* are not in the original Greek. It might be that other believers can handle having a credit card without going into debt, paying their balance off each month. The Bible is the truth. Your application of the Bible is a way of living out that truth.

You can accurately say, "This verse helped me to make a tough decision and cut up my credit cards." But it's not handling God's Word accurately to say, "The Bible says in Romans 13:8 that you can't have credit cards."

This is where we often get legalistic. We take our personal application and force it on others.

> Discussion question 4 can be used here.

To allow the illumination of God's Word to shine clearly into our hearts, we must love God's Word deeply, understand God's Word spiritually, and handle God's Word accurately. But there is a fourth thing we must do for the Bible to impact our lives.

Study God's Word <u>DILIGENTLY</u>

It takes diligence to study God's Word because the payoff does not always come immediately. Howard Hendricks talks about the different stages we go through in Bible study:

> Psalm 19:10 says that Scripture is sweeter than honey, but you'd never know that judging by some believers. You see, there are three basic kinds of Bible students. There are the "castor oil" types. To them the Word is bitter—Yech!—but it's good for what ails them. Then there is the "shredded wheat" kind. To them Scripture is nourishing but dry. It's like eating a bale of hay.
> But the third kind is what I call the "strawberries-and-cream" folks. They just can't get enough of the stuff. How did they acquire that taste? By feasting on the Word. They have cultivated . . . an insatiable appetite for spiritual truth.[3]

Our commitment to reading God's Word is always rewarded, but diligence comes first.

I don't know about you, but I find it much easier to talk about diligence than to actually be diligent. How do we bridge the gap between our desire to study God's Word and our decision to dedicate the time and effort to dig out the truths in the Bible?

How do you decide to study God's Word as a lifetime commitment?

1. Vow before the Lord to trust in and commit to the truth of his Word.

Read with me 1 Timothy 4:15–16:

Be diligent in these matters; give yourself wholly to them, so that everyone may see your progress. Watch your life and doctrine closely. Persevere in them.

—1 Timothy 4:15–16

You may have some doubts about God's Word; can you really trust it? In these two studies about the Bible, you've seen proof in history and in changed lives, but ultimately this is a matter of faith. Will you decide, right here and right now, to trust the truth of God's Word?

2. Cultivate eagerness by examining God's Word for answers.

They [the Bereans] received the message with great eagerness and examined the Scriptures every day to see if what Paul said was true.
—**Acts 17:11**

Be like the Bereans in Acts 17:11, who as soon as they heard the Word from Paul went back and examined it for themselves.

When you have a question, go to the Bible. Search. When you find that answer for yourself, you'll have a spiritual high like you've never before experienced.

3. Tell others what you're learning from God's Word.

Listen to what Colossians 3:16 says:

Let the word of Christ dwell in you richly as you teach and admonish one another with all wisdom.
—**Colossians 3:16**

This will keep you from growing stagnant in your faith.

In Israel there are two seas. In the north is the Sea of Galilee, and in the south the Dead Sea. The Sea of Galilee is a beautiful body of water, still a vacation spot in Israel, filled with fish and teeming with life. The Dead Sea is called dead for a good reason. It is so filled with minerals that little can survive in or around this desolate site. What's the difference? Water flows into the Sea of Galilee from the northern mountains and then out through the Jordan River. The Dead Sea has no outlet, so it fills with sediment and minerals.

These two seas are a good parable for your life as a Christian. If you only take God's Word in, you'll soon find yourself growing stagnant in your faith. The most exciting truth in history will seem stale. It is as you share the truth with others that the living water continues to flow in fresh and inspiring ways through your heart.

4. *Act* on what you learn as you study the Bible.

Read with me from James 1:22:

Do not merely listen to the word, and so deceive yourselves. Do what it says.
—**James 1:22**

27

G. K. Chesterton was one of the great Christian minds of the early twentieth century. He had a way with words not unlike Mark Twain. Chesterton once said, "The Bible tells us to love our neighbors, and also to love our enemies; probably because they are generally the same people."

Chesterton was asked what one book he would want with him if he were stranded on a desert island. Everyone of course expected him to say "The Bible," with a wonderful explanation why. His surprising and exceedingly sensible answer was, *"Thomas' Guide to Practical Ship-building."*[4] Of course! If you were stranded on an island, a guide to ship-building would show you what to do to safely get home.

We are all stranded, in a way, on this island we call Planet Earth. We long for the day when we will be together in heaven, but we are not there yet. While we wait, God has given us an amazing gift: the Bible, the one book we need.

It is a book that gives us hope.

It is a book that gives us direction.

It is a book that will see us safely home.

Pray with me:

> *Lord, I need the truth of your Word. Forgive me for those times when I've relied on my thoughts rather than seeking out what you have to say. I make a fresh commitment to read and study and follow the truth of your Word. I know, Lord, that this will not be easy. I'm asking for your strength, and I pray for the wisdom to remember to look for answers in your Word, to share what you're teaching me with others, and to act on what I hear. Grow in me for the rest of my life a deepening love for your Word. In Jesus' name, amen.*

**Finish memorizing *Foundations* memory card 1,
"The Truth about the Bible."**

Discussion Questions

1. Tell about an experience that caused you to feel that you really love the Bible. What kinds of experiences cause you to feel this way? When do you most deeply feel the truth that the Bible is a treasure?

2. Discuss together your answers to the following:

   The Bible was like a seed to me when . . .

   The Bible was like a sword to me when . . .

   The Bible was like food to me when . . .

   The Bible was like a hammer to me when . . .

   The Bible was like a fire to me when . . .

   The Bible was like a mirror to me when . . .

3. The Holy Spirit gives us understanding of God's Word individually. John says we don't "need anyone to teach us." Yet the New Testament talks about, and even tells us to honor, the gifts of teaching and preaching. Why do we need teachers? How do these two truths fit together?

4. Which of the seven rules of Bible study do you think Christians most often stretch or break? How can we remind ourselves to handle the Bible accurately?

For Further Study

Anders, Max. *The Bible.* Nashville: Nelson, 1995.

Elwell, Walter, ed. *Topical Analysis of the Bible.* Grand Rapids, Mich.: Baker, 1991.

Little, Paul. *Know What You Believe.* Wheaton, Ill.: Victor, 1987.

McDowell, Josh. *The New Evidence That Demands a Verdict.* Nashville: Nelson Reference, 1999.

Mears, Henrietta. *What the Bible Is All About.* Ventura, Calif.: Regal, 1997.

Rhodes, Ron. *The Heart of Christianity.* Eugene, Ore.: Harvest House, 1996.

Warren, Rick. *Personal Bible Study Methods.* Available at www.Pastors.com.

God
Part 1

Life Change Objectives

- To gain a deeper sense of God's love for you as a Father.

- To act in some new way on the fact that God is your Father.

Summary Teaching Outline

God Is Real

    How do we know God exists?

God Is Revealed

God Is Relational

    The truth about God

    The number 1 way we see that God is relational

How does the truth of God's reality fit you in a personal way? Worship!

Look at this thimble. Imagine trying to fit the Pacific Ocean into this thimble. That's how I feel as we begin this study of the person of God. Someone as inadequate as I am is going to use something as small as words to try to describe the greatness of God.

Sounds impossible. Let's just give up and go home!

If we were left to our own intelligence and intuition to try to describe God, what we could say about him would amount to less than a thimbleful. One person's guess about God would be as good as another's. None of us would really have anything worthwhile to say.

Look at this Bible, God's book given to us. In it he tells us about himself—his character, his values, his love. In ways that we can understand, that our minds can grasp, God invites us to get to know him.

Through this book, he brings the ocean to us, an ocean of understanding about the one who loves us the most. As we talk about God today, it's my prayer that you won't feel as if we're looking at who he is from afar. My prayer is that you'll feel like you're diving into the ocean. My prayer is that you'll feel as if you're being hit by wave after invigorating wave of understanding God's person and appreciating God's power and enjoying God's presence.

Our goal is not just to learn more facts about God, as important as that might be. The goal of this study and the next is to get to know God in a more powerful and personal way. I can say with confidence that there is no subject more important for us to talk about. Life's major pursuit is not knowing self but knowing God.

As we launch into this look at the person of God, two attitudes are crucial: expectancy and humility.

Expect that God will do something great in your life today as we talk about who he is and how he shows himself to us. A. W. Tozer wrote,

What comes into our minds when we think about God is the most important thing about us.[1]

—A. W. Tozer

God is so great, and our belief in him is so important, that even the smallest change in our perspective on who he is and how he acts can transform our lives. Our beliefs about God set the course of our lives.

Think about the impact the truth about God can have on your everyday life. What you believe about God sets your moral compass and shapes your attitude toward fortune, fame, power, and pleasure. Trusting the truth about God strengthens us in hardship and pain; keeps us faithful and courageous when we are outnumbered; prompts our praise and enhances our worship; dictates our philosophy and determines our lifestyle; gives meaning and significance to our relationships; shows us when to say yes and when to say no. Knowing God gives us the hope to go on. It is the foundation upon which everything rests.

We must also have a humble heart as we study the person of God. Augustine, one of the early leaders of the church, said,

If you can understand it, it's not God.

—Augustine

For you to understand God on your own would be like an ant attempting to understand you. Only by God's grace and revelation of himself do we know anything of what he is like. Instead of approaching this study with a desire to "figure God out," begin with the humble intention to let God show you what you need to know about him.

Children have a way of asking the right questions about God. "What does God look like? Where does God live? How big is he?" At some point many of us stopped asking those questions—maybe because we never got any answers! Today, let's give ourselves the freedom to be kids again, to ask those "simple" questions again.

Some of you will remember this story. A little girl comes to her mother and says excitedly, "I'm going to draw you a picture of God!"

"Oh, honey," replies her mom, "no one knows what God looks like."

With the characteristic confidence of a five-year-old, the girl replies, "After I'm done with my picture they will."

Close your eyes and bring to mind your picture of God. Do you see an ancient man long in beard, robe, and tooth? Is it the picture of someone who doesn't understand modern things like nuclear physics, computers, and lasers, sort of a grandfatherly type who's there when you need him? Do you see pure light, or a king on a throne, or thunder and lightning? In order to see a better picture of God, it's good to start with thinking about how you picture him now.

> Discussion question 1 can be used here.

As we look at God's existence, we need to remember three key truths:

1. **God is real.**
2. **God is revealed.**
3. **God is relational.**

In this study we're going to look at these three truths about God. At first glance they may seem simple, but there's nothing simple about God. These truths form the basis for filling in a picture of who God is and how he works in our lives.

God Is Real

God is not a character in a story, in some fairy tale. He is as real as we are.

How do we know God exists?

Maybe in school you had to study the philosophical arguments for God's existence: ontological arguments, teleological arguments, cosmological arguments. While these arguments make it clear that logically some kind of higher being must exist, they also make belief in the existence of God sound complicated and confusing. Interestingly, the Bible does not present arguments for God's existence; it assumes it.

We all have moments when we think, "Is this stuff about God real, or am I just fooling myself?" But there are good reasons why 96 percent of Americans believe that there is a personal God.[2] To the vast majority, the fact that there is a God is intuitively obvious. Here are three reasons why.

1. **We see God's <u>CREATIVITY</u> in what he has made (Gen 1:1; Rom 1:19–20; Acts 14:16–17).**

Read with me from Psalm 19:

The heavens declare the glory of God; the skies proclaim the work of his hands. Day after day they pour forth speech; night after night they display knowledge.

—Psalm 19:1–2

Look up into the sky on a clear night in a field (away from city lights), or out on a lake, or in the mountains. Wow! Something in us is drawn at that moment to see the greatness of God in the greatness of what he has made. Do you realize how vast this universe is? Avery Willis gives us this picture:

> Step on a rocket with me and catch a glimpse of the greatness of God. We travel at the speed of light, 186,282 miles per second. As we blast off, our seats afford us a clear view of earth. One second later earth has dropped away until it appears no larger than a huge balloon. In two seconds we have shot past the moon and stolen a glance at the now-famous moon shot of earth. Eight and one-half minutes later we pass the sun. Earth appears to be a speck 93 million miles away in the darkness of space.
>
> Five hours later we leave our solar system and can no longer distinguish earth from myriads of other planets and stars. After four years of travel at the speed of light, we zip by the nearest star, Alpha Centauri. For almost 100,000 years we travel across the Milky Way, our own galaxy. After that, we travel another 1,500,000 years before we reach the Great Nebula, most distant of the six other galaxies in what astronomers call the Local Group. Up to this point we might compare our journey to a family traveling across country whose five-year-old asks before they get out of town, "How much farther is it?" In the great vastness of space, we must travel at least 12 *billion* years at the speed of light before we begin to reach the area of the universe that cannot be seen with telescopes from our planet. And who knows how much lies beyond?
>
> Yet Isaiah says God "hath measured the waters in the hollow of his hand, and meted out heaven with the span" (Isa. 40:12). He measures space by the width of his hand.[3]

Teaching Tip

When you are reading a clipping from a newspaper, book, or magazine, it's good to print or write the clipping out on a separate card and to pick up the card and read from it as you teach. This accomplishes two things: it allows you to move away from the podium as you read, and, more important, it lets those who are listening know that you have put some time into studying what you are talking about. Some people, especially those with more exacting personalities, love to see that you as a teacher have taken the time to do research.

2. **We see God's <u>THUMBPRINT</u> on human history.**

> **From one man he made every nation of men, that they should inhabit the whole earth; and he determined the times set for them and the exact places where they should live. God did this so that men would seek him and perhaps reach out for him and find him, though he is not far from each one of us.**
>
> **—Acts 17:26–27**

History really is "his story." Even while he waits to finish the story, it's very evident that God is the author and director and main character in the story we call life.

Sociologist Grace Davie "cites a recent survey that asked Britons whether they believed in God. Most respondents said they did. The next question: 'Do you believe in a God who can change the course of events on Earth?' A popular response: 'No, just the ordinary one.'"[4]

Acts 17:26–27 reminds us that there is nothing ordinary about God. He determines both the times and the places of world history. He sets the course of events on earth. He determined when this earth began, and it is on his timetable that it will come to an end. He alone decided when the world would start fresh with a flood, when Abraham would go to the Promised Land, when Moses would lead the Israelite slaves out of Egypt. Going through the Old and New Testaments, you would find hundreds of examples of God's being at the helm of history. It's still true today. He may allow an evil leader or an injustice to exist for a time, but never to prevail. God decides when and how a Hitler will fall. He puts an Abraham Lincoln at the right place at the right time. He decided when Communism would unravel in the Soviet states. And as Acts 17 tells us, he does it "so that men would seek him and perhaps reach out for him and find him."

3. **We see God's <u>ACTIONS</u> in our lives.**

Look at the story of Elijah and his battle with the false prophets on Mount Carmel in 1 Kings 18:24–39.

Teaching Tip

Never be afraid to take the time to tell a story from the Bible; Bible stories are among our best illustrations. You'll be surprised at how many people have never heard them, at how many have heard them but not understood their significance, and at how much those who know them well will be inspired by hearing them again.

When telling a story from the Bible remember three things:

1. Tell it as if your audience is hearing it for the first time.
2. Tell it with excitement in your voice, not as if it's a list of facts but as a living experience.
3. Tell it knowing that someone in your group will be able to see themselves in the story. (In the case of the story of Elijah, they may know what it is like to feel outnumbered by unbelievers in their workplace.)

For years Elijah has been battling the false prophets of a god called Baal. Passionate about defeating their influence on the nation of Israel, he finally challenges them to a test on Mount Carmel. Four hundred and fifty prophets of Baal show up to battle this one lone prophet of God. For Elijah, that's what I'd call a poor "prophet" margin. (Go ahead, groan.) The prophets build an altar, and Elijah's challenge is that the god who burns up the sacrifice of a bull placed on that altar will be shown to be the real God. The prophets of Baal pray and chant all day, but of course nothing happens. You can't squeeze blood out of a turnip, and you can't squeeze miracles out of a false god. Elijah then has water dumped on the altar until it fills a small moat around the place of sacrifice. He prays a simple prayer, and God sends a fire that consumes not only the sacrifice but the wood, the stone altar, and the ground under the altar, and dries up the water that had collected in a trench around the altar.

God works in clear and personal ways in our lives. Your experience likely has never been as dramatic as Elijah's, but it was just as real. You may have seen his power at work in a restored relationship or in a habit he enabled you to set aside. Maybe he has given you peace when you've been overwhelmed by worry or he's given you courage to take a step of faith. Every believer has experienced the action of God in his sending his Son to give his life for our forgiveness. His action on the cross was dramatic, and it was personal. It was not just a historical event; the cross was God's personal action in your life. Jesus died for you.

It's easy to forget what God has done. Elijah, two days after the victory over the prophets of Baal, got depressed and hid in a cave. We easily forget the power of what God has done and get caught up in the details of the day. Faith grows when we take the time to remind ourselves of God's actions in our lives.

 A Closer Look

What Does God Look Like?

The Bible tells us that no one has actually seen God (John 1:18). God is spirit (Ps. 139:7–12; John 4:24); God is invisible (John 1:18; Col. 1:15; Heb. 11:27). The natural assumption, when hearing the phrase that we are all "made in his image," is to think that God must look something like us: with two arms and two legs. What a scary thought! God, who fills this universe, obviously couldn't look like a man. When the Bible speaks of God having "strong arms" or "sheltering wings," these are not literal descriptions but pictures of how God relates to us.

Discussion question 2 can be used here.

God Is Revealed

God is not discovered by us, he <u>REVEALS HIMSELF</u> to us (Gen. 35:7; Ps. 98:2).

When seeking to understand who God is, we must not make the mistake of acting like some spiritual Christopher Columbus, thinking that we can discover God for ourselves as Columbus discovered America. We can't build a ship that can sail far enough to discover God for ourselves. God must reveal himself to us. Even more important, we must not fall into the trap of being a spiritual Thomas Edison, inventing our own God. Neither human energy nor human ingenuity are great enough to determine the truth about God. God is so much greater than we are. He *must* reveal himself to us. To understand how God reveals himself, we need to know about three theological ideas: God's general revelation, God's special revelation, and God's personal revelation.

1. God reveals himself to us through <u>HIS</u> <u>CREATION</u>.

Romans 1:20 says,

From the time the world was created, people have seen the earth and sky and all that God made. They can clearly see his invisible qualities— his eternal power and divine nature. So they have no excuse whatsoever for not knowing God.

—**Romans 1:20** (NLT)

Earlier in this study we saw that God reveals himself to us in three ways: through nature, through his actions in history, through our experiences. Theologians call these God's *general revelation* of himself.

While we can see God clearly through these things, he wanted to show himself to us even more clearly. So he revealed himself a second way.

2. God reveals himself to us through <u>HIS</u> <u>WORD</u>.

Look at 2 Peter 1:20–21:

Above all, you must understand that no prophecy in Scripture ever came from the prophets themselves or because they wanted to proph- esy. It was the Holy Spirit who moved the prophets to speak from God.

—**2 Peter 1:20–21** (NLT)

You might remember that these prophets weren't so much predictors of the future as they were spokesmen for God. God would audibly speak to them, and they would tell the people the exact words God had said. Whether it was Moses recording the words of the commandments on the mountain or Jeremiah dictating the words for his secretary, Baruch, to write on a scroll, they heard the voice of God and told the people. In New Testament days, men such as Paul and Luke wrote down the words the Spirit inspired in their hearts. These writings are God's *special rev- elation*. The Bible, from Genesis to Revelation, is the record of God's special revelation to us.

It may seem that this is the greatest extent to which a God we cannot see could go to reveal himself to us. But he wanted us to see him even more clearly, so he revealed himself a third way.

3. God reveals himself to us through <u>HIS</u> <u>SON</u>.

God became a man! Jesus' coming to earth was more than general rev- elation or special revelation; it was God's personal revelation of him- self. In the New American Standard version, John 1:18 tells us that Jesus came to "explain" God to us.

No one has seen God at any time; the only begotten God, who is in the bosom of the Father, He has explained Him.

—**John 1:18** (NASB)

Jesus came to give us understanding (1 John 5:20). Jesus chose to reveal the Father to us (Matt. 11:27). God has revealed himself in many ways, but his last word and clearest revelation is in Jesus (Heb. 1:1–2).

If you wanted to explain to your dog what it's like to be a human, how could you best do that? Become a dog!

To best explain humans to rabbits, you would have to become a rabbit. To best explain us to ants, you would have to become an ant.

To explain God to us, Jesus became a man. If you think it would take humility for you to take on the form of an ant, that's nothing compared to the step Jesus made when he took on human flesh. He said to us in the clearest way possible, "God wants to know you!"

Have you been trying to figure God out on your own? I have some good news for you. God's deepest desire for you is to reveal to you who he truly is. There is no prayer that he will answer more quickly than "God, show me who you really are!" In fact, he's already answered that prayer by sending his Son.

> **Split Session Plan:** If you're teaching this study over two sessions, end the first session here.

Understanding who Jesus shows God truly to be is more critical than a trip to the ER! If your belief about God is wrong, then the more devout you are, the more lost you become.

Gallup surveys consistently show 96 percent of Americans believe that God is real. For most people, whether God exists is not the issue. The real issue is, What kind of a God is he? What does Jesus reveal to us about God?

God Is Relational

I don't know of any story Jesus told that more clearly pictures what God is really like than the story of the prodigal son. Because it is familiar to some of us, we miss the shocking nature of Jesus' love. Listen to Philip Yancey's story of a prodigal daughter. I hope it will help us see anew the relational love at the core of Jesus' parable.

> A young girl grows up on a cherry orchard just north of Traverse City, Michigan. Her parents, a bit old-fashioned, overreact to her nose ring, the music she listens to, and the short length of her skirts. They ground her a few times, and she seethes

inside. "I hate you!" she screams at her father when he knocks on the door of her room after an argument, and that night she acts on a plan she has mentally rehearsed scores of times. She runs away.

Because newspapers in Traverse City report in lurid detail about the gangs, the drugs, and the violence in downtown Detroit, she concludes her parents will not look for her there. They might look in California or Florida, but not Detroit. On her second day in Detroit, she meets a man who drives the biggest car she's ever seen. He offers her a ride, buys her lunch, arranges a place for her to stay. He gives her some pills that make her feel better than she's ever felt before. She was right all along, she decides; her parents were keeping her from all the fun.

The good life continues for a year. The man with the big car—she calls him Boss—teaches her a few things that men like. Since she's underage, men pay a premium for her. She lives in a penthouse and orders room service whenever she wants. Occasionally she thinks about the folks at home, but their lives now seem so boring and provincial she can hardly believe she grew up there.

After a year the first sallow signs of illness appear, and it amazes her how fast the boss turns mean. "These days, we can't mess around," he growls, and before she knows it she's out on the street without a penny. When winter blows in she finds herself sleeping on metal grates outside the big department stores. "Sleeping" is the wrong word—a teenage girl in downtown Detroit at night can never relax her guard. Dark bands circle her eyes. Her cough worsens. One night as she lies awake listening for footsteps, everything about her life suddenly looks different to her. She no longer feels like a woman of the world. She feels like a little girl, lost in a cold and frightening city. Something jolts a memory and a single image fills her mind: of May in Traverse City, when a million cherry trees bloom at once, with her golden retriever dashing through the rows of blossoming trees chasing a tennis ball.

"God, why did I leave?" she says to herself, and pain stabs at her heart. "My dog back home eats better than I do now." She's sobbing, and she knows in a flash that more than anything else in the world, she wants to go home.

She calls home three times but only gets the answering machine. The first two times she hangs up without leaving a message, but the third time she says, "Dad, Mom, it's me. I was wondering about maybe coming home. I'm catching a bus up your way, and it'll get there about midnight tomorrow. If you're not there, well, I guess I'll just stay on the bus until it hits Canada."

It takes about seven hours for the bus to make all the stops between Detroit and Traverse City, and during that time, she realizes the flaws in her plan. What if her parents are out of town and miss the message?

Shouldn't she have waited another day or so until she could talk to them? And even if they are home, they probably wrote her off as dead long ago. She should have given them some time to overcome the shock. On the bus her thoughts bounce back and forth between those worries and the speech she is preparing for her father. "Dad, I'm sorry. I know I was wrong. It's not your fault; it's all mine. Dad, can you forgive me?" She says the words over and over, her throat tightening even as she rehearses them.

When the bus finally rolls into the station, its air brakes hissing, the driver announces in a crackly voice over the microphone, "Fifteen minutes, folks. That's all we have here." Fifteen minutes to decide the course of her life. She checks herself in a compact mirror, smoothes her hair, and licks the lipstick off her teeth. She looks at the tobacco stains on her fingertips and wonders if her parents will notice—if her parents are even there.

She walks into the terminal not knowing what to expect. Not one of the thousand scenes that have played out in her mind prepares her for what she sees. There in the bus terminal in Traverse City, Michigan, stands a group of forty brothers and sisters and great-aunts and uncles and cousins and a grandmother and a great-grandmother to boot. They're all wearing goofy party hats and blowing noisemakers, and taped across the wall of the terminal is a computer-generated banner that reads, "Welcome home!"

Out of the crowd of well-wishers steps her dad. She stares out through the tears in her eyes and begins the memorized speech: "Dad, I'm sorry, I know—"

He interrupts her. "Hush, child. We've got no time for that. You'll be late for the party. A banquet's waiting for you at home."[5]

That's the way God loves you! But the picture in this parable of a father running to his struggling child is very different from the image many of us have of God.

Let's look at some popular ideas about what kind of a God lives in heaven and see what the Bible has to say about the real God.

The truth about God

The popular idea is: God is distant.

 17

The truth is: God is <u>NEAR</u> (Ps. 139:7–12; James 4:8).

God is awesomely near to all of us. God's presence is not beyond the farthest star; he is as near as our next heartbeat. He does not just watch us; he is with us. We may feel that God is distant from us at times, even as believers. But that does not change the fact that he is near! David writes in Psalm 139, "Where can I go from your Spirit? Where can I flee from your presence?" (Ps. 139:7). God is near us, whether we're thinking of him or not, because his presence is everywhere. That is why James is able to give us the promise, "Come near to God and he will come near to you" (James 4:8). Though God in his greatness is above and beyond the created universe, he is at the same time right here with us, intimately involved in his creation. Our God is an awesome God!

The popular idea is: God watches our actions from afar.

 18

The truth is: God is intimately involved in <u>EVERY</u> <u>DETAIL</u> of our lives (Matt. 6:25–30; Luke 12:6–7).

Jesus tells us in Matthew 6:25–30 that God is interested in details like what we wear and what we eat and how we spend the hours of our day. In Luke 12 he amazes us with the statement that God even has the hairs on our head numbered. (For some aging pastors, God's job gets a little easier every day!) Just because the details of life don't always work out as we want them to does not mean that God doesn't care about those details. He does! Many people think that they should save their times of talking to God for the "big stuff." The problem with that is much of our lives is caught up in the details, and we're left not talking to God about a large part of how we spend our days. Just look at the intricate design in a tiny flower and you'll know: God cares about the details.

The popular idea is: God is anxiously waiting to judge those who do wrong.

The truth is: God is waiting to <u>FORGIVE</u> all who ask (John 3:17).

> For God did not send his Son into the world to condemn the world, but to save the world through him.
>
> —John 3:17

Many people picture God up in heaven with his finger on a button labeled, "Zap them now." Of course, God isn't like that. If he were, it wouldn't be safe to drive down the freeway because of all the people he'd be zapping for what they were saying about all of the other drivers—including you! The fact that God hasn't judged you for your sin is not because he hasn't noticed. He sees everything. It is because he is patiently waiting for you to ask him to forgive you.

The popular idea is: God is either powerless against or doesn't care about much of the evil in the world.

The truth is: God allows an evil world to continue to exist so that more people might be saved out of it (2 Peter 3:8–9).

When someone says, "I can't believe in a God who would callously allow children to suffer or rapes to occur," you can say to them, "I don't believe in that kind of a god either. I believe in a God who, more than you and I, cares about and hurts over the sinful things we do to each other. I believe in a God who will one day stop evil in its tracks by shutting down this world and taking us to live with him in a perfect place called heaven. The only reason he hasn't already done it is because he is waiting for more people to trust in him so they can spend eternity with him. In order to give more people the opportunity to come to know him, he is willing to endure more hurt and pain than we can imagine over the evil that we do to ourselves."

Discussion question 3 can be used here.

A Fresh Word

Four theological words provide the background for the statements we've covered about the real person of God:

1. **God's immanence:** God is awesomely near to all of us. God is not beyond the farthest star; he is as near as our next heartbeat. He does not just watch us; he is with us.

2. **God's omnipresence:** God is everywhere (omni = all + present). His presence fills the universe. He is everyplace all at once.

3. **God's omniscience:** God knows everything (omni = all + scient = knowing). He knows everything that has happened, is happening, and will happen. He knows what I will think before I think it.

4. **God's omnipotence:** God is all mighty (omni = all + potent). He has the power to do anything—*anything*—he wants. Immediately!

To sum it up: In a world in which people see God as UNAPPROACHABLE, the truth is that God is RELATIONAL.

The number 1 way we see that God is relational

Jesus taught us to call God our FATHER.

Teaching Tip

As you begin this section, realize that many people struggle with the idea of God as our Father. The struggles they had with or the pain that was caused by their earthly fathers makes it difficult to picture God as a heavenly Father. Pray that God will use you to help someone picture God as the Father they never had, the Father they truly need.

God relates to us as a perfect Father.

As our Father, God wants to meet our needs. As his children, we need God to be a Father to us every day of our lives. Listen to this list of ways God meets our needs as a Father. As you listen, think about which one of these you most need to hear . . . *today.* How can your needs as God's child be met—*right now*—by seeing his desire to relate to you as a loving Father?

1. **Our Father is willing to make <u>SACRIFICES</u>. He sent his Son into the world to die as our Savior (John 3:16; 1 John 4:14).**

   Maybe you need to see in a new or fresh way your need for the sacrifice God made for you. You need to be reminded that God loves you that much.

2. **Our Father has <u>COMPASSION</u> and love for his children (Ps. 103:13; 2 Cor. 1:3).**

   Do you need to sense that God deeply cares about everything you are facing right now?

3. **Our Father <u>GUIDES</u> his children (Prov. 3:12).**

   Are you trying to make it through life on your own? When was the last time you asked for God's guidance?

4. **Our Father knows our needs before we ask (Matt. 6:8; 7:9–11); that's why we pray "Our Father" (Matt. 6:9).**

   If he knows our need before we ask, why do we have to ask? Because when we pray, we are not informing God of our need; we are depending on God to meet our need. Have you been afraid to ask God to give you something you need?

5. **Our Father <u>REWARDS</u> us (Matt. 6:20; Heb. 11:6).**

   Do you see God as one looking to judge you, or as one who delights in the fact that one day he will reward your faith?

6. **Our Father makes us his heirs (Rom. 8:15–17).**

   Do you allow yourself to rejoice in the eternal riches God has promised you as his child?

7. **Our Father <u>ENCOURAGES</u> us (2 Thess. 2:16–17).**

   Have you ever sent up a quick prayer, "God, I'm feeling down today; please encourage me as only you can"?

8. **Our Father shows no <u>FAVORITISM</u> among his children.**
   - **He gives access to all equally (Eph. 2:18).**
   - **He blesses all richly (Rom. 10:12).**
   - **He judges each person impartially (1 Peter 1:17).**

   You are as privileged to enjoy these blessings of God your Father as any other believer who ever has walked or will walk the face of this planet.

   How do I know this is how God desires to act toward me? When something inside me starts to say, "I feel like God is out to get me," how do I see God for who he really is?

Jesus told us: "Anyone who has seen <u>ME</u> has seen the Father" (John 14:9).

Jesus came to this earth to help us to get to know the Father, our real Father. He came to say to us, "You have a Father who loves you more than you can imagine, who wants to get to know you in a deeper way than you've ever dreamed." He didn't teach us to pray, "Our impersonal force in heaven," or "Our higher power in heaven," or "Our benevolent ruler in heaven." He didn't even teach us to pray, "Our God in heaven." He taught us to pray, "Our Father, who art in heaven."

Discussion questions 4 and 5 can be used here.

Teaching Tip

Take the time to lead the group in the prayer below. Approach this with real compassion, knowing that people are hurting over this issue. But also approach it with real faith, knowing that lives can be changed in these few moments.

Key Personal Perspective

You may be having a hard time thinking of God as a Father because of the poor father you had growing up. One of the most refreshing breakthroughs in your life will happen when you begin to see God as the Father you never had, to see God as the Father who fulfills what your father never was.

Start or strengthen this new perspective in your life by praying the following prayer. (Pray those parts that are appropriate for your life and add to the prayer where you need to.)

God, I now accept you as the Father I never had. I was disappointed by my father, but you will never disappoint me. I never knew my earthly father, but you want to know me. I was hurt by my earthly father, but I am healed by you. I was ignored by my earthly father, but I have your full and constant attention. I could never meet the expectations of my earthly father, but I can find freedom from expectations in your grace. Amen.

Maybe you had an earthly father who, although he was not perfect, gave you the kind of love that put you on the road to finding a relationship with God through Jesus. You need to pray,

Thank you, God, for my earthly father. I know he wasn't perfect in the way he raised me, but he was good and he was kind and he was a man of character. He made decisions in his life that helped me to see a little bit of what you are like, decisions that made it easier for me to get to know you. Thank you for the gift he gave me. Amen.

Acting on the Truth

Truth can seem cold and distant until we see how it fits into our lives. How does the truth of God's reality fit you in a personal way? Worship!

Worship is acting like God is your Father. Make no mistake, he *is* your Father if you have put your faith in Christ. The problem is we often don't act like it. We act like God is a distant friend or a terrible tyrant or (heaven help us) a business partner. He is your Father in heaven! Here are some ideas for how you can act on that truth; try one this week.

Remember our picture of the thimble and the ocean as we began this study? You aren't going to be satisfied with the thimble, are you? Dive in! Get drenched! Immerse yourself in the greatness of God.

1. Before the next session, read the following passages of Scripture, in which God speaks about his reality. As you read, focus on listening to God. Hear him speaking directly and personally to you.

   "You are my witnesses," declares the Lord, "and my servant whom I have chosen, so that you may know and believe me and understand that I am he. Before me no god was formed, nor will there be one after me."
   —Isaiah 43:10

   See now that I myself am He! There is no god besides me. I put to death and I bring to life, I have wounded and I will heal.
   —Deuteronomy 32:39

   This is what the Lord says—Israel's King and Redeemer, the Lord Almighty: I am the first and I am the last; apart from me there is no God. . . . Do not tremble, do not be afraid. Did I not proclaim this and foretell it long ago? You are my witnesses. Is there any God besides me? No, there is no other Rock; I know not one.
   —Isaiah 44:6, 8

2. Concentrate on God's power and control as you remember some of the significant things he has done in your life.

   You don't have to be a history major to see God's work in human history. Think about the fact that all of history is divided by the life of Christ. Consider how history has shown us that the most powerful of human governments rise and fall. Get out a piece of paper and use it to finish the sentence, "God, I see your control over human history when I look at . . ."

   Now finish the sentence, "God, I see your control over my life when I look at . . ."

3. Consider God's beauty and creativity as you close your eyes and think about something he has made. Better yet, get out there and see it!

4. Jesus taught us to call God "Abba." The word *Abba* is the intimate name for a father that a little child would use, like our word *Daddy*. In your prayers this week, try addressing God as Abba or even Daddy. (Don't think of it as irreverent; it's a word that expresses your intimate connection with and your ultimate dependence on God.)

5. It helps some people to picture being in the presence of God. We don't worship the picture; it simply helps us to worship God. Picture God as your Father. Picture him walking up to you, taking your face tenderly in his hands, and asking you, "What do you want me to do for you today?"[6]

Begin working on memory card 2, "The Truth about God."

Discussion Questions

1. When you think of God, do you have a picture in your mind? What is that picture?

   Small Group Leaders: (We are including these small group tips for you to use as you ask these questions of the group. Or you can pass these tips along to those leading your small groups.) Stress to your group that we're not testing their theology. We're just taking a survey of the different pictures of God that they might have grown up with.

2. **What is the one thing that for you makes it seem as if God is in the room with you? What makes God seem the most real to you? Seeing what he has made? Being in church? Reading the Bible? Looking at human history?**

   Small Group Leaders: You might ask your group to share times when they have been especially aware of God's existence through his creation—a time when they looked at the stars and were awed by God's greatness, or saw great mountains or trees, or noticed God's creativity in a flower.

3. **Look at the list of popular ideas about God and the truths about God. In this list, which popular idea do you think is potentially the most damaging? Which truth is the most difficult for you to accept (perhaps because of the teaching or the culture you were brought up in)?**

   Small Group Leaders: Make it clear to your group that it's okay to admit we have a harder time accepting some truths in the Bible than others. We may *know* it's all true but have a more difficult time feeling some truths than others.

4. **Is there any part of this study that wasn't made as clear to you as you would like? What question that you had about what we discussed was not answered?**

   Small Group Leaders: These questions may help people in your group talk about what they didn't understand. We want them to feel it's okay not to know everything. In fact, we're all lifelong learners, and admitting that you don't know something is often the first step toward learning. Notice that we didn't say, "What didn't *you* understand?" We take the burden off of them and put it on us by asking, "What didn't *we* make clear?"

5. **What is it about God's love that most helps you to see him as a perfect Father? How has God shown his love as a Father to you? For ideas, review the list we covered of eight ways God meets our needs by relating to us as a Father.**

   Small Group Leaders: Be aware that many people struggle with the fact that their fathers did not love them the way they needed to be loved. Help them to see that only the love of God our Father can fill that gigantic hole.

God
Part 2

Life Change Objective

To develop a sense of amazement about God that results in a decision to spend time getting to know him.

Summary Teaching Outline

Three aspects of God's person that we all need to know and understand

God Exists as a Trinity

    Pictures and statements regarding the Trinity

    The truth of the Trinity is shown by the Bible's teaching

    Glimpses of the Trinity

God Is Absolutely Sovereign

God Is Perfectly Moral

We are fascinated by celebrities, people who are rich or powerful or popular. We want to know about what they do, how they live, and even what they wear. Just look at many of the most popular magazines; they focus on stories about these people.

What if *People* magazine did an article about God? He is, after all, the most powerful personality in the entire universe. No one is richer than God! It is from his person that everything began, and it is before him that we will all eventually stand. God is a personal God, and his story is the greatest story of all. If *People* did such an article, what would it cover? Obviously not details such as his clothes and house. But wouldn't you like to know what interests God most? Wouldn't a question like, "God, what has caused you the deepest hurt, the greatest joy?" spark your interest? Wouldn't you like to know what God is really like?

I give you this picture not to minimize God's power but to emphasize God's person. Of course God cannot be reduced to the pages of a magazine. But neither should we ignore the truth that he is a person, one who has passions and interests and plans. This is the second part of our study of the person of God: the characteristics that most help us to understand who he really is.

We read about a personal God in the most personal book ever written: the Bible. There is no more intriguing book about people than this one. Think of some of the people whose stories are told in the Bible:

A couple whose sin changed the fate of the human race

A father who waited twenty-five years for a son

A slave from Israel who rose to become the second highest ruler of Egypt

A woman who was the greatest military leader of her time

A prophet who was willing to risk his life as he confronted King David about his sin

Some shepherds who were surprised by angels

A mother who watched her son die on a cross

Some simple fishermen who turned the world upside down

And all of these intensely personal stories are just subplots to the most important story of all—God's story.

> Discussion questions 1 and 2 can be used here.

In this study, we're going to focus on three characteristics unique to the person of God.

God is a person. Let that sink in for just a moment. Anytime we think of God in impersonal terms, we've missed the very center of who he is. God is The Person—the one from whom and by whom all that we are as persons was created.

We looked in the last study at the clearest expression of the truth that God is personal: the fact that he is our Father. We are going to focus today on three additional aspects of God's person that we all need to know and understand. If God took a personality test, he would not be described with terms as limited as "sanguine," "dominant," or "introspective." The following three characteristics are unique to the person of God.

God Exists as a <u>TRINITY</u>

Suppose I hand you a mystery novel and tell you that it is by far the best story I've ever read, that I especially love the exciting surprise ending. You take the book home and read it, only to discover that the last two pages have been ripped out. It would drive you crazy! It's part of our nature that we hate unsolved mysteries. We want to know the solution; we want to figure it all out.

I have news for you.

You can't figure God out. To completely understand God, you would have to be as great as God, and we all know how ridiculous that idea is. One of the truths about God that most strongly demonstrates our inability to completely understand God is the truth that God is a trinity.

A Fresh Word

Trinity

God is three in one—Father, Son, and Holy Spirit. He is not three Gods, nor is he one God acting in three different ways. The Bible tells us that God is three different and distinct persons, and that these three different and distinct persons are one in the being of God.

Teaching Tip

One way to keep people's attention is to ask questions, but it is important to ask questions in a way that builds your relationship with those you are teaching. To build this relationship you must look for (and sometimes even insist on) some kind of response from the group. For instance, when you ask in the next paragraph, "Wouldn't you agree that the idea of the Trinity is a little beyond our grasp?" don't just slide past the question. Look at them for their response. If, as often happens, you get no response, ask the question again! Look at the group and say something like, "If you'd agree with me that this is tough to grasp, raise your hand," or, "Am I the only one who has to struggle with understanding this truth?"

Take a look at this definition of the Trinity. Would you agree that the idea of the Trinity is a little beyond our grasp? Like the concept of infinity, we know that it exists, but it's beyond our minds to comprehend. Our belief in the Trinity is not a matter of human understanding or philosophy; it grows instead out of God's revelation of himself to us. In a few moments we're going to focus on the evidence in the Bible for the Trinity. But before we do that, let's put this truth in perspective by looking at some pictures and statements regarding the Trinity.

Pictures and statements regarding the Trinity

You don't have to understand (or even have heard about) the truth of the Trinity to become saved. However, understanding the Trinity is invaluable in getting to know God for who he really is.

The doctrine of the Trinity is not found in any single verse of the Bible. It is to be found in a study of the whole of the Bible.

Although the word *trinity* isn't in the Bible, we'll see in a moment how the Trinity is taught throughout God's Word. By the way, the word *relationship* isn't in the Bible either, but obviously God's Word is all about how to have a relationship with him and with others.

St. Patrick's picture of the Trinity was the three-leafed shamrock.

Three leaves but tied together in one plant.

Some use the picture of the three forms of water: ice, liquid, and steam. Water under pressure and in a vacuum at a given temperature below freezing exists simultaneously as ice, liquid, and gas; yet it is identifiable always as water (H_2O), its basic nature. In physics this is called "the triple point of water."

Others use a much simpler picture: Neapolitan ice cream! The three flavors are distinct and separate, yet without any one of them it would not be Neapolitan.

When I first began to study the Bible years ago, the doctrine of the Trinity was one of the most complex problems I had to encounter. I have never fully resolved it, for it contains an aspect of mystery. Though I do not totally understand it to this day, I accept it as a revelation of God.[1]
—Billy Graham

Billy Graham reminds us that there is always a bit of mystery when *we* try to grasp the greatness of God. We use the eyes God made to read the words God gave us so we can think with the minds he fashioned and talk with the mouths he formed about the infinite person of God.

These pictures and statements are reminders of the truth that God is three persons in one God. God wants us to understand this truth because he wants us to know him for who he truly is.

When we say that God is a trinity, what does it mean? What does it *not* mean? Look at this picture of the Trinity that believers have turned to for centuries.

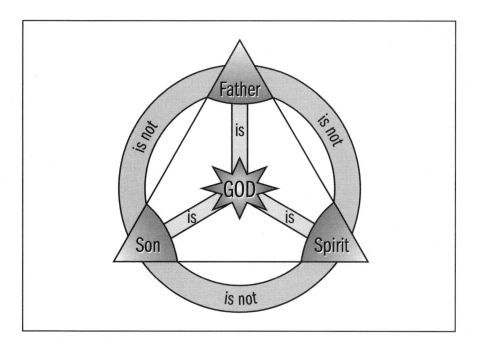

God is Father, Son, and Spirit, but that does not mean that somehow the Father takes on the role of the Son or sometimes shows himself as a Spirit. It's not a matter of one person showing himself in three different ways or taking on different roles at different times. God is three distinct persons in one unique personal being.

I know, I know, you may be feeling like I've ripped out the last pages of that mystery novel we talked about. Three persons but only one being; isn't that a contradiction? No, it's a mystery, a wonderful mystery that God wants us to understand because he is a God who truly wants us to know the depths of who he is.

I said a moment ago that the Trinity is not taught in any one verse of the Bible. How then do we know that the doctrine of the Trinity is true? Let's walk through the Bible's clear teaching of the triune nature of God.

Teaching Tip

At the beginning of this guide, in "Bring It to Life!" we discussed one of the keys to making doctrine come to life: "Don't try to make the mysterious simple or the simple mysterious." As you teach the truth of the Trinity, you have the perfect opportunity to apply this principle. On the one hand, it is good to let people see that the truth that God is a trinity is beyond our understanding. On the other, it's helpful to show how simply and clearly the Bible reveals this truth, as we'll see in the following material.

The truth of the Trinity is shown by the Bible's teaching that . . .

1. **God is <u>ONE</u>.**

   The LORD our God, the LORD is one.

   —Deuteronomy 6:4

   I am God, and there is no other; I am God, and there is none like me.

   —Isaiah 46:9

   There are not two gods or three gods or five gods; there is only one God. That teaching is at the core of what God reveals about himself in the Old Testament. In the New Testament, he shows us even more.

2. **Father, Son, and Spirit are all called God.**

   - **The Father is God.**

     Grace and peace to you from God our Father and from the Lord Jesus Christ.

     —Romans 1:7

   - **Jesus is God.**

     Thomas said to him, "My Lord and my God!"

     —John 20:28

     In John 20, Thomas calls Jesus God, and Jesus does not deny it. This is just one of the many places in the Bible that clearly tell us Jesus is God. We'll look more closely at this when we study the person of Jesus.

     In the beginning the Word already existed. He was with God, and he was God.

     —John 1:1 (NLT)

   - **The Spirit is God.**

     And I will ask the Father, and he will give you another Counselor to be with you forever—the Spirit of truth. The world cannot accept him, because it neither sees him nor knows him. But you know him, for he lives with you and will be in you.

     —John 14:16–17

     Ananias, how is it that Satan has so filled your heart that you have lied to the Holy Spirit. . . . You have not lied to men but to God.

     —Acts 5:3–4

     Sometimes we make the mistake of talking about the Holy Spirit as if he were an "it." God's Spirit is a person just as much as the Father and the Son are. This is clear from Jesus' words about the Holy Spirit in John 14:16–17.

The Holy Spirit as a person is equated with God throughout the Bible. In Acts 5:3–4 Peter says that Ananias lied to the Holy Spirit, and a few phrases later he says that this lie was to God. He speaks of God and the Holy Spirit as the same person.

Teaching Tip

This is just a quick look at the truths that Jesus is God and that the Spirit is God. In the upcoming studies of Jesus and the Spirit, we'll take a deeper look at these truths.

3. **Father, Son, and Spirit are <u>DISTINCT</u> from one another.**

Jesus is distinct from the Father. (He prayed to the Father in John 17.)

If Jesus had simply been God the Father appearing as a Son on the earth for a time, whenever he prayed he would have been praying to himself—quite a ridiculous picture when you think about it! It is obvious that while Jesus was on this earth, he was relying on a Father in heaven who was distinct from himself. The Father is referred to by Jesus as someone other than himself more than two hundred times in the New Testament. The Father sent the Son (John 3:17), the Father loves the Son (John 3:35), and the Father knows the Son just as the Son knows the Father (John 10:15). They are clearly distinct from one another.

The Spirit is distinct from the Father (John 14:26).

The Spirit is sent by the Father; they are spoken of as distinct from one another.

The Son is distinct from the Spirit (John 14:16–17).

Jesus would not have called the Spirit "another Counselor" if God's Spirit were simply Jesus coming to us in a different form. Again and again, the Bible uses language that shows the Father and the Son and the Spirit to be distinct from one another.

The conclusion is: God is one in being, but he exists in three persons.

Add these three truths up and you get the conclusion:

> God is one
> + Father, Son, and Spirit are all called God
> + Father, Son, and Spirit are distinct persons
> = the Trinity (one God in three persons)

Anyone who denies the truth of the Trinity is denying one of these three truths. False teachers use emotion and human reasoning to teach against the truth of the Trinity. You can count on the fact that they don't believe one or more of these three essentials about God. They don't believe that the Son and the Spirit are also God (this is most often the case). Or they don't believe God is distinct in three persons. And some don't believe there is only one God. To have a God who makes more sense to them, they choose not to believe what the Bible specifically tells us about God.

Let's look at a number of the places in the Bible where we can glimpse God at work as a trinity.

Glimpses of the Trinity

- **God speaks of himself as "<u>US</u>" in four places in the Old Testament (Gen. 1:26; 3:22; 11:7; Isa. 6:8).**

- **All three persons were involved in Creation (the Spirit—Gen. 1:2; the Father—Heb. 1:2; the Son—Col. 1:15–16).**

- **We are <u>BAPTIZED</u> in the name of the Father, the Son, and the Spirit (Matt. 28:19).**

- **All three persons were at Jesus' <u>BAPTISM</u> (Mark 1:10–11) and in Jesus' <u>BIRTH</u> <u>ANNOUNCEMENT</u> (Luke 1:35).**

- **The Bible tells us all three persons were the power behind Jesus' <u>RESURRECTION</u>. In John 2:19, Jesus said he would raise his body. In Romans 8:11 we're told that the Holy Spirit raised Jesus. In Acts 3:26, the Father raised the Son. This makes sense only when you understand the truth of the Trinity. Only God can raise someone from the dead.**

- **Paul's prayer in 2 Corinthians 13:14: "the grace of the Lord Jesus Christ, and the love of God, and the fellowship of the Holy Spirit."**

- **Jesus' promise to his disciples in John 14:16–17: Jesus says he will ask the Father for the Spirit.**

Discussion question 3 can be used here.

**Key Personal
Perspective**

Why Is This Important?

We've taken a good amount of time to focus on these pictures and proofs and glimpses of the Trinity. You might be wondering why. If we don't have to know the truth of the Trinity to be saved, why study this?

Theologically: **Understanding the truth of the Trinity prevents us from adopting inadequate views of God.**

It prevents us from seeing Jesus and the Spirit as less than God; from seeing Jesus and the Father as exactly the same; and from thinking that there are three gods rather than just one.

One of our inevitable temptations as human beings is to see God as less than who he is. The truth of the Trinity helps us to resist this temptation.

Personally: **The Trinity is a reminder of the majesty and mystery of the God who gave himself for us on the cross.**

You trust the truth of the Trinity:

- **When you ask for salvation (the Spirit convicts—John 16:8; the Son sacrifices—Heb. 10:10; the Father gives—John 3:16).**
- **Every time you pray (the Spirit communicates—Rom. 8:26; Jesus intercedes—Rom. 8:34; the Father answers—John 16:23–24).**

Relationally: **The Trinity shows us that God in his very essence is relational.**

Even before he created us, there was a perfect relationship between God the Father, God the Son, and God the Spirit. God did not need to create us in order to have someone to relate to, because he already had the perfect relationship in the Trinity. Our ability to relate to one another and to enjoy our relationship with God grows out of his relational nature.

This Person who exists as a trinity created you and me for the purpose of our getting to know him and enjoy him. This great God loves you more than you can possibly imagine.

I'm not going to let you leave today thinking that the truth of the Trinity is simply a matter of dry theological discussion or biblical argument. We're talking about getting to know the depths of the one who loves us more than anyone else! I want you to know—to really know—God; to deepen your relationship with him, you need to know that he exists as a trinity.

Split Session Plan: If you're teaching this study over two sessions, end the first session here.

As we try to come to grips with God's greatness, our constant temptation as human beings is to minimize what we cannot quite understand. We're like the fourth grader who was asked by his parents on the way home from church what he had learned in Sunday school. He said, "We learned that Moses was sent by God to be the general to deliver the Israelites out of Egypt. He went down there and organized them into an army and led them out to the edge of the Red Sea. There he ordered his corps of engineers to build a pontoon bridge across the Red Sea. When all the people of Israel had passed over on the pontoon bridge, the Egyptians tried to follow. When they got out into the middle, the Israelites blew up the bridge, the Egyptians were drowned, and the Israelites escaped."

His parents were a little suspicious of this story and said, "Is that what the Sunday school teacher taught you?"

And the boy said, "Well, no, not exactly. But if I gave it the way she told it, you'd never believe it!"

We are talking about some awesome, even overwhelming, ideas about God. Resist the temptation to minimize them. I encourage you to let them overwhelm you; take great comfort in the fact that God is so much greater than we are.

Since we're looking together at big ideas about a great God, let me throw a second mind-boggling truth about God at you.

God Is Absolutely <u>SOVEREIGN</u>

14

God does not have to consult with or depend on anyone to make a decision, and God does not have to answer to anyone for the decisions he makes. He is sovereign.

Sovereign is one of those words we don't use much these days. The idea of being the one who's absolutely in charge is difficult for us to grasp. It's not like being a manager; a manager has to answer to the CEO, and the CEO has to answer to the board, and the board has to answer to the stockholders. In England a few hundred years ago, people understood what sovereign meant; the king or queen was a sovereign ruler, answerable to no one. It's more difficult for us to understand sovereignty because the American government has a system of checks and balances.

Does God's sovereignty mean you and I are just pawns on his chessboard? No! In some amazing way God is able to be in absolute control and yet also give us genuine choice. One Bible handbook explains it like this, "What makes God's sovereignty effective is that his will is ultimately done—sometimes along with, sometimes in spite of, our free choices."[2] We'll talk about our free will more in a later study; let's keep the focus now on God's sovereignty. What does it mean when we say that God is sovereign?

Sovereignty refers not to God's attitude but to the reality of who he is. God is not someone with a dominating personality; he is a person who is absolutely dominant. God is not controlling; he is in ultimate control. God does not need to take charge because he always is in charge.

Let's get a little more specific about what sovereignty means:

1. **He is greater than and exists above his creation: he is <u>TRAN-SCENDENT</u>.**

   But will God really dwell on earth? The heavens, even the highest heaven, cannot contain you. How much less this temple I have built!
   —1 Kings 8:27

   One God and Father of all, who is over all and through all and in all.
   —Ephesians 4:6

   - **He is greater than time (Isa. 57:15; Deut. 33:27; Ps. 90:2).**
   - **He is greater than place (Ps. 139:7–10; Jer. 23:23; Acts 17:24–28).**
   - **He is greater than circumstance (James 1:17; 1 Sam. 15:29; Mal. 3:6).**

Psalm 90:2 tells us that "from everlasting to everlasting you are God." He not only will always exist; he always has existed. Take a blank piece of paper and put the smallest dot you can right in the middle of that page. Stare at that dot for a moment.

God can look at all of human history like you and I could look at that dot. He can see it all at once. He can take it all in with a glance—every moment, every life, every day. He is transcendent.

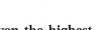

Discussion question 4 can be used here.

One thing this means is:

Nothing <u>SURPRISES</u> God (Ps. 139:2–4).

Psalm 139:2 in the NCV says, "You know when I sit down and when I get up. You know my thoughts before I think them." God isn't surprised by anything that happens, by anything you do. You will never hear God saying such things as, "I didn't see that one coming," or "You could have fooled me," or "Now that's a real shock!" He sees it all, and he knows it all.

2. **He never needs permission or help: he is <u>ALL-SUFFICIENT</u>.**

> And he is not served by human hands, as if he needed anything, because he himself gives all men life and breath and everything else.
> —Acts 17:25

> Who are you, a mere human being, to criticize God? Should the thing that was created say to the one who made it, "Why have you made me like this?"
> —Romans 9:20 (NLT)

It's important to remember that as much as God loves us, he does not need us. He never has, and he never will. He did not need to create us because he was lonely or lacking in some way; he created us as an act of love. He does not choose to use us because he couldn't get it done without us. Don't make the mistake of thinking that because God has chosen to work through people, he is somehow limited to what we can think or do. He is not limited in any way. He uses us as an act of his grace.

In Romans 9:20 (NLT), when Paul asks, "Who are you, a mere human being, to criticize God?" he reminds us that God does not need our help or advice. Sometimes we are tempted to play armchair quarterback with God. "If only he had done this, he could have avoided that natural disaster. If he'd have allowed a different government to rule, all would have been well." It is as if we are saying, "If I were God, things would be different." You've got to be kidding! As if we could do it better than God.

3. **God can do anything he wants: he is <u>ALMIGHTY</u>.**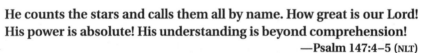

> He counts the stars and calls them all by name. How great is our Lord! His power is absolute! His understanding is beyond comprehension!
> —Psalm 147:4–5 (NLT)

Fifty-six times the Bible says that God is the Almighty One.

Let's talk for a moment about how this truth about God's power fits into our daily lives. In the current age of day planners and PDAs, you would think keeping things under control would be a cinch. Yet something still seems to be lacking. The marketers of these products would have us believe that with the right organizational tool (the one they're pushing, of course), our lives would be in perfect order. Have you noticed that God's plans don't always fit into your DayTimer? Sometimes he surprises us. Often he is doing something bigger than we can imagine.

Of course, planning is valuable; it can help us fulfill God's direction for our lives. However, there are four words we should never forget. These four words should be on the top of every page of our planners; they should jump out from our computer screens each time we open our calendars. The words? "God is in control."

When you recognize God's sovereignty as the most important aspect of your daily plans, you'll see amazing things begin to happen.

Annoying distractions will turn into anointed directions.

An impossible situation will turn into an opportunity for faith.

The feeling that your world is falling apart will turn into the assurance that God is at work in even the worst that life throws at you.

A Fresh Word

For just a moment, think again about the words we've been using to describe God. These words are often misunderstood. They have taken on meanings that make us feel that God is an impersonal God. This should be no surprise since one of Satan's schemes is to twist and degrade the name and person of God in order to lessen his impact in the world and in our lives. Satan is at the head of an evil PR campaign that seeks to defame the character of God. Here's the truth about some of the words we commonly use to describe God.

Holy does not mean God is picky or judgmental or "holier than thou." To be holy, literally, is to be separate and distinct. Holy means God has perfect integrity. In fact, he is the only being in the universe with perfect integrity.

Eternal does not mean that God is old or tired or out of date. God has always existed. He stands outside of time, able to see the entire history of the universe at a glance.

Transcendent does not mean that God cannot understand our needs and hurts. It does not mean, as in the Bette Midler song, that he's watching us "from a distance." The fact that God stands above and beyond his creation does not mean he stands outside his creation. He is both transcendent (above and beyond his creation) and immanent (within and throughout his creation).

Almighty does not mean that God does whatever he wants with no thought to the impact on us. He uses his power to create and to love his creation.

All-knowing does not mean that God is some kind of cosmic Big Brother, watching and judging us but never really caring about us. We know that as human beings we could not see all of the pain in the world without somehow becoming numb to it, but God is not like that. He can see all that happens and still deeply care about everything that happens.

As we prepare to look at a third truth about the person of God, let me give you a picture of how I feel as we look at these truths. To me, it's as if we were standing in the midst of the Himalayan Mountains, trying to take in the absolute grandeur of what's in front of us. It's simply breathtaking. It is so huge it feels as if I can't take it all in. These truths about God are like that for me. Breathtaking . . . awe-inspiring. We're talking about the very greatness of God, the God who is great enough to make those mountains.

Lord, take our breath away as we look at your greatness!

Look with me at a third truth about the person of God—a third mountain peak. We've touched on (and I do mean just touched on) the awe-inspiring truths of the Trinity and God's sovereignty; let's add a look at God's morality.

God Is <u>PERFECTLY</u> <u>MORAL</u>

Say this with me:

"God is good, all the time.

"All the time, God is good."

How do you get your arms around what it means for God to be good, truly good, more wonderfully good than we can imagine? My fear is that when I say, "God is moral," the picture that comes to many of our minds is of a heavenly Boy Scout helping old ladies across the street. Not that there's anything wrong with helping others, but God's goodness is so much more than that, and so much greater.

It is an old habit of mankind to allow our current thoughts about morality to determine our ideas of God's morality. There is no better example of this than the Greek gods who were worshiped during Jesus' day, gods who were seen as just as jealous and angry and selfish and lustful as the people were, only with a lot more power. It would be wonderful to say that this habit went out of fashion with the Greek toga, but it's still around today.

The tendency of human beings is to try to remake God in our image. The Greeks saw their gods as jealous and angry. A twenty-first century American thinks of God as having a nonjudgmental attitude toward sins that are tearing our lives and families apart. We have it backwards— God made us in his image. And the more we look at who God truly reveals himself to be in his Word, the more he transforms our hearts and character into his image.

Look at who he is and who he wants to grow us to be.

Teaching Tip

The difference between a good study and a great study is in the way you end it. You could read the following as a list of the attributes of God's morality and it would be true and even meaningful. But if you will take a few moments to prepare yourself and your heart to lead those you are teaching toward a time of personal and practical commitment, it will dramatically change how the study ends. This moves people toward the goal of teaching God's Word: making a genuine difference in the way lives are lived.

- **He acts in <u>HOLINESS</u> (Lev. 11:44; Isa. 6:1–3).**

Let me read for you Isaiah 6:1–3.

In the year that King Uzziah died, I saw the Lord seated on a throne, high and exalted, and the train of his robe filled the temple. Above him were seraphs, each with six wings: With two wings they covered their faces, with two they covered their feet, and with two they were flying. And they were calling to one another:

> **"Holy, holy, holy is the Lord Almighty;**
> **the whole earth is full of his glory."**

> —Isaiah 6:1–3

God is holy!

Just as we did at the end of the last study, let's take this opportunity to focus on the impact that the person of God is going to make on our daily lives. Your life may seem routine and ordinary at times. Not true. Absolutely not true! You and I live in the presence of the holy God that Isaiah wrote about here. The most exciting single experience of this prophet's life was this encounter with the presence of God in the temple of God. As a believer you are now a living temple; the holy God lives within you! That radically changes the way you look at the so-called routine of daily life.

Let me ask you, Are you willing to look at your life differently between now and the next session? Even the seemingly ordinary moments of life? I invite you to say to yourself in the midst of the routine, "I am living in the presence of a most holy God!" Just watch and see how that simple statement changes the way you wash dishes or drive carpool or mow the lawn.

- **He relates in <u>COMPASSION</u> (Ex. 34:6; Lam. 3:22; James 5:11).**

In James 5:11 we're reminded that the motivation for casting all of our cares on him is our recognition of the fact that he cares for us. Do you believe that God cares, really cares, about what you're going through right now? He does! Take a moment to sense his compassion for what you are facing and to trust your cares—the circumstances that are causing you worry or stress—into his hands.

- **His <u>FAITHFULNESS</u> can be trusted (Ps. 36:5; Heb. 10:23).**

  Psalm 36:5 tells us, "Your faithfulness [reaches] to the skies." Hebrews 10:23 reminds us, "He who promised is faithful."

  Other people have let you down. God never will! That may very well be the truth that gets you through the next week.

- **His <u>GOODNESS</u> is unequaled (Ps. 34:8; 2 Peter 1:3).**

  I love Psalm 34:8: "Taste and see that the LORD is good." He desires to do good things in your life, more than you could ever imagine. Even in and through the difficulties and trials that we'll all face in this world, God wants to do good things in your life. Look for the good things that he's doing this week; I guarantee that they are there!

- **His <u>JUSTICE</u> is impartial and fair (Isa. 30:18; Luke 18:7–8).**

  When it seems to you that others are getting away with things that you aren't, or that they are getting undeserved blessings, don't let yourself fall into the "poor me" syndrome. God is always impartial and he is always fair. In the end his perfect justice will prevail. One of the healthiest things you might do this week is remind yourself of that truth.

- **He reacts to sin in <u>WRATH</u> (Gen. 6:5–8; Rom. 2:5–9; 1 Thess. 2:16).**

  God hates sin. We sometimes ignore this side of God's character, and even more often, we misunderstand it. Some people see God's wrath against sin as a temper tantrum, as if God were in a bad mood. Genesis 6:5–8 shows us that God hurts and grieves as he sees sin. Romans 2:5–9 reminds us that he does not stand idly by and let this sin forever hurt and wound his creation; he judges sin in wrath. Of course he has wrath against sin: he sees clearly as none of us can what that sin does to those who are oppressed, to those who are hurting. He sees what sin does to our children, to our marriages, to our potential, to our relationship with him. He sees how sin separates us from him, both now and—for some—for eternity. God is not an angry God in the Old Testament and a loving God in the New. The same side of God's character that causes him to deal with sin in sweeping judgment caused him to send his Son to die on the cross to take the penalty for our sin.

- **He is <u>LOVE</u> (1 John 4:7–11; John 3:16).**

  The greatest expression of God's love for us is in the sacrifice he made for us: "He gave his one and only Son." Who do you need to make a sacrifice for, even a seemingly small sacrifice?

Key Personal Perspective

The Bible often talks about God's nature in terms of a personal challenge to us. We are created in his image (Gen. 1:27). What he is like in character is what we should become like. Some of God's attributes are his alone, such as omnipotence or eternalness, but we are to reflect others in our lives. How can that happen? A simple truth of human nature applies here: we become like those we spend the most time with. When I spend time with God, I inevitably become more like him.

His person empowers my character!

If I spend my time with critical people, I become critical. If I spend my time with people who are reaching for the top at any cost, I begin to reach for the top at any cost. Guess what? The more time I spend with God, the more I act and think like God! The problem is some of us spend more time watching our favorite television personalities than we do with God. That's scary!

The thought of being like God in any way seems beyond us. How can we be holy? How can we love like God loves? Let me remind you that it is not the strength of our will or the amount of our effort that makes the difference. It's our dependence on the God who has these qualities and wants to share them with us. Before you leave, take a moment to circle one of the qualities in the list we just looked at that you want to grow in this week. Maybe you want to be more holy, more patient, maybe you want to have more love—circle that in your notes. If you circled *wrath*, I'm a little worried about you! I joke about that, but the truth is, some of us really should desire a greater hatred for sin in our lives. If we could only see our sin as God sees it, we would change.

How will these things happen? How will the quality that you've circled begin to make its way into your life? By making the simple choice to spend time with him.

Discussion questions 5 and 6 can be used here.

**Finish memorizing memory card 2, "The Truth about God."
If you invest a little time each week memorizing these truths,
you'll increase your ability to apply them to your everyday life.
You'll also be able to share them more clearly with others.**

Appendix
Theology of the Trinity

Introduction	The word *Trinity* is never used, nor is the doctrine of Trinitarianism ever explicitly taught, in the Scriptures, but Trinitarianism is the best explication [detailed explanation] of the biblical evidence. It is a crucial doctrine for Christianity because it focuses on who God is, and particularly on the deity of Jesus Christ. Because Trinitarianism is not taught explicitly in the Scriptures, the study of the doctrine is an exercise in putting together biblical themes and data through a systematic theological study and through looking at the historical development of the present orthodox view of what the biblical presentation of the Trinity is.	
Essential Elements of the Trinity	God is One. Each of the persons within the Godhead is Deity. The oneness of God and threeness of God are not contradictory. The Trinity (Father, Son, and Holy Spirit) is eternal. Each of the persons of God is of the same essence and is not inferior or superior to the others in essence. The Trinity is a mystery which we will never be able to understand fully.	
Biblical Teaching	**Old Testament**	**New Testament**
God Is One	"Hear, O Israel: The Lᴏʀᴅ our God, the Lᴏʀᴅ is one" (Deut. 6:4; cf. 20:2–4; 3:13–15).	"Now to the King eternal, immortal, invisible, the only God, be honor and glory for ever and ever. Amen" (1 Tim. 1:17; cf. 1 Cor. 8:4–6; 1 Tim. 2:5–6; James 2:19).
Three Distinct Persons as Deity	The Father: "He said to me, 'You are my Son; today I have become your Father'" (Ps. 2:7).	". . . who have been chosen according to the foreknowledge of God the Father" (1 Peter 1:2; cf. John 1:17; 1 Cor. 8:6; Phil. 2:11).
	The Son: "He said to me, 'You are my Son; today I have become your Father'" (Ps. 2:7; cf. Heb. 1:1–13; Ps. 68:18; Isa. 6:1–3; 9:6).	"As soon as Jesus was baptized, he went up out of the water. At that moment heaven was opened, and he saw the Spirit of God descending like a dove and lighting on him. And a voice from heaven said, 'This is my Son, whom I love; with him I am well pleased'" (Matt. 3:16–17).
	The Holy Spirit: "In the beginning God created the heavens and the earth. . . . and the Spirit of God was hovering over the waters" (Gen. 1:1–2; cf. Ex. 31:3; Judg. 15:14; Isa. 11:2).	"Then Peter said, 'Ananias, how is it that Satan has so filled your heart that you have lied to the Holy Spirit . . . ? You have not lied to men but to God'" (Acts 5:3–4; cf. 2 Cor. 3:17).
Plurality of Persons in the Godhead	The use of plural pronouns points to, or at least suggests, the plurality of persons within the Godhead in the Old Testament. "Then God said, 'Let us make man in our image, in our likeness . . .'" (Gen. 1:26).	The use of the singular word "name" when referring to God the Father, Son, and Holy Spirit indicates a unity within the threeness of God. "Therefore go and make disciples of all nations, baptizing them in the name of the Father and of the Son and of the Holy Spirit" (Matt. 28:19).

Appendix *cont.*

	Attribute	Father	Son	Holy Spirit
Persons of the Same Essence: Attributes Applied to Each Person	Eternality	Ps. 90:2	John 1:2; Rev. 1:8, 17	Heb. 9:14
	Power	1 Peter 1:5	2 Cor. 12:9	Rom. 15:19
	Omniscience	Jer. 17:10	Rev. 2:23	1 Cor. 2:11
	Omnipresence	Jer. 23:24	Matt. 18:20	Ps. 139:7
	Holiness	Rev. 15:4	Acts 3:14	Acts 1:8
	Truth	John 7:28	Rev. 3:7	1 John 5:6
	Benevolence	Rom. 2:4	Eph. 5:25	Neh. 9:20
Equality with Different Roles: Activities Involving	Creation of the World	Ps. 102:25	Col. 1:16	Job 33:4
	Creation of Man	Gen. 2:7	Col. 1:16	Gen. 1:2; Job 26:13
	Baptism of Christ	Matt. 3:17	Matt. 3:16–17	Matt. 3:16
	Death of Christ	Heb. 9:14	Heb. 9:14	Heb. 9:14

Source: Taken from *Charts of Christian Theology and Doctrine* by H. Wayne House. Copyright © 1992 by H. Wayne House. Used by permission of Zondervan.

Discussion Questions

1. Did you find yourself thinking more about God as your Father this week? Share the place or circumstance in which you were reminded that he is your Father.   27

2. Share what you experienced in the four worship exercises from the last study mentioned in the bullets below.   28

   - After reading through the passages of Scripture in which God speaks about his own reality, what truths hit you?

   - As you took some time to concentrate on God's power and control by remembering some of the significant things he has done in your life, what did you remember?

   - What did you write about how you can see God's hand in human history?

   - Share with the group your experiences as you took some time to consider God's beauty and creativity by thinking about or taking a closer look at his creation.

3. It's easy to react to the teaching of the Trinity with a feeling of, "Who cares . . . just so I know Jesus loves me." How has this study helped you see why the truth of the Trinity is important?

   - What false teachings about God does the truth of the Trinity combat?
   - How does (or how could) this truth help you personally?

4. How does the truth that God is greater than time or place or circumstance help you to deal with a specific situation you're facing right now?

   Small Group Leaders: Pray for a real sense of "God is bigger than anything we can face" during this part of your discussion.

5. As we come to the end of our look at the person of God,

   - What new thing did you learn about God?
   - What did you learn that made God seem a little closer, a little less distant?
   - What did you learn about God that made you smile, made you able to enjoy him more?
   - What did you learn about God that made you feel more loved by him?
   - What did you learn about God that helped you understand his greatness in a clearer way?
   - What did you learn about God that increased your desire to devote your life to him?
   - What did you learn about God that increased your sense of security in everyday life?

   Small Group Leaders: Don't feel like you have to use every one of the questions above. Use them as ideas to help people to talk about what they learned and experienced in this study.

6. The ways that God acts toward us are an obvious guide for how he wants us to act toward others. While we cannot have many of the characteristics of God (none of us is all-powerful or perfect), all of us can develop more of the character of God (compassion, love, goodness, forgiveness) and display it to the world around us.

   God desires for his character to be shown in the world. One of the ways we express faith as believers is to pray that his character will be revealed through us in the world. Use the following questions to develop a prayer list that will be a part of your "group prayer list." One of the most exciting things that you will experience as a group is the way that God will answer many of the prayers you put on this list.

- Where in this world (or in your world) would you most like to see people recognize God's compassion?
- Who do you most hope could tie in to God's wisdom?
- Who or what are you counting on God to be patient with?
- What relationship would you like to see God make right?

(Be specific in your prayer requests. If your concern is for your sister, don't say "my family." Let the group in on the details of what you would like them to pray for.)

Small Group Leaders: Don't look at this as a wish list. Look at it as a prayer list. Help your group to see that when our prayer requests are based on what God has already told us he wants to do in our lives, those prayers are much more powerful.

For Further Study

Elwell, Walter, ed. *Topical Analysis of the Bible.* Grand Rapids, Mich.: Baker, 1991.

Little, Paul. *Know What You Believe.* Wheaton, Ill.: Victor, 1987.

Packer, J. I. *Knowing God.* Downers Grove, Ill.: InterVarsity Press, 1973.

Rhodes, Ron. *The Heart of Christianity.* Eugene, Ore.: Harvest House, 1996.

Sproul, R. C. *The Character of God.* Ann Arbor: Vine, 1982.

Tozer, A. W. *The Pursuit of God.* Camp Hill, Penn.: Christian Publications, 1982.

Zacharias, Ravi. *Can Man Live without God?* Nashville: Word, 1994.

Jesus
Part 1

Life Change Objectives

- To enable you to get to know your best friend, Jesus Christ, better than you ever have before.

- To encourage you to act on the truth that Jesus is your best friend in one specific way.

Summary Teaching Outline

Why Is This Important?

The Names of Jesus

The Details of Jesus' Life

    What did Jesus do before he was born?

    Jesus' life on earth

    The eternally existent Christ

This study is all about a relationship. As we talk together about Jesus, I don't want you to hear this in any way as a study of someone who lived two thousand years ago. Any doctrinal study of Jesus is, most importantly, a relationship-building study. As we look at what the Bible says about the person of Christ, we are doing so as ones who are developing a lifelong relationship with Jesus.

> Discussion question 1 can be used here.

Because this is a study about a relationship, let me tell you how my relationship with Jesus began. I (Tom Holladay) had grown up all of my life hearing about and even studying Jesus in Sunday school and church. Through the years, I developed an idea of what it means to be a Christian. To me, being a Christian meant that you went to church, tried to be a good person, and believed that Jesus lived and died and was resurrected two thousand years ago. However, as I grew older I began to suspect there was something wrong with my definition of Christianity. As I heard my friends talk about their belief in Jesus, I could tell that what they were experiencing was more personal and joyful than what Christianity meant for me. I was too prideful to admit that they knew something I didn't and had something that I didn't have. So I didn't ask them why their experience was so different from mine. Big mistake! My pride caused me to wait much longer than I should have to understand the truth.

One night the message finally got through. In a meeting at church, I heard someone explain what I probably had heard a thousand times before, but this time the message sank in. The speaker said that Christianity is *not* just going to church or trying to be good or even believing that Jesus once walked this earth. He talked about a personal *relationship* with Jesus, a relationship that began with my decision to trust Jesus to forgive my sins and to direct my life. I prayed a prayer expressing that trust that night, and a new life and a new relationship with Jesus started. One of the things that immediately changed for me was the sense that I had a real purpose for my life, the purpose I had been searching for all of my life. I had finally begun a relationship with Jesus Christ that I would be building the rest of my life, and even into all eternity.

Teaching Tip

Take some time to tell *your* story of how you came to know Christ. A good way to tell it is to use the simple outline Paul used when he gave his testimony in the book of Acts.

My Life Before I Came to Christ

How I Came to Know Jesus Christ

My Life Since I've Come to Know Him

Make sure you take some time to focus on the relationship you began with Jesus when you became a believer; that part of your story will tie in to the idea of building a lifelong friendship with Jesus, which is at the center of this study.

Throughout the study, you'll want to talk about how you are continuing to get to know him. Make it as personal as possible. Remember that one of the keys for making doctrine come to life is to "make it personal."

The object of this study is simple: to get to know Jesus better. I want you to get to know your best friend, Jesus Christ. The teaching centers around getting to know Jesus as you would get to know anyone: by learning his names, by understanding his life history, and by appreciating and enjoying his personality.

Why Is This Important?

Why is this important? Why is it worth your time to get to know more about Jesus Christ? Two reasons:

1. **Knowing Jesus is life's continuing <u>PRIORITY</u>.**

Philippians 3:8 brings clarity to this truth when it says, "Everything else is worthless when compared with the priceless gain of knowing Christ Jesus my Lord" (Phil. 3:8 LB). Everything else! You could put everything you own on a ledger sheet and write across the page the word *worthless*. Worthless compared with the incalculable value of knowing Christ. That car you drive, that house you live in, even the relationships you have with family and friends can never compare in value to the grace, forgiveness, and eternal life we're given in our relationship with Christ.

Once a year, Christie's auction house in New York City offers a free appraisal weekend. People bring in items from the back of their closet or a corner of their attic hoping to learn they have had an undiscovered treasure right under their roof. Often the items are of little value, but one appraiser still remembers the woman who brought in an 11.4-carat ruby that a jeweler had told her was costume jewelry. According to Christie's president Kathleen Guzman, "We were able to confirm that it was made in 1904 by Tiffany and Co. They still had the original drawing for the piece, and, consequently, sold at auction to them for $385,000. But this was a lady who kept it in the back of her closet in her grandmother's costume jewelry box, along with everything else, and was convinced that this was fake."[1] She kept a piece of jewelry of great value in a costume jewelry box! As I heard this story I thought, "Lord, help me to always treat my relationship with you as something valuable rather than as something common. I want to put the fact that I can know you in the right box—the one marked 'priceless.'"

2. **Knowing Jesus is the believer's continuing <u>CHALLENGE</u>.**

Read this verse with me:

For as you know him better, he will give you, through his great power, everything you need for living a truly good life: he even shares his own glory and his own goodness with us!

—2 Peter 1:3 (LB)

Teaching Tip

As we've mentioned before, your goal as a teacher is to establish a connection with those to whom you are speaking. One way of doing that is by sharing a personal story, as you've already done with your testimony. A second way, discussed previously, is by asking questions that help people engage with what you're saying, questions that help them think about how what you are saying fits into their lives. As you teach the following points, notice that you'll be asking everyone to think of the name of one person they know at each of three relational levels. Who do they know only by name? Who do they know some life history about who is not yet a friend? Who do they count as friends?

Getting to know Christ is like any other relationship; it must be developed. The more we develop our relationship with Christ, the more we see how valuable that relationship is. Take a moment to think about how our relationships develop. Suppose you meet someone new at your office or in a class at school. You don't know it, but this person is going to become your best friend. Obviously, you're not best friends the day you meet. First you learn their name. How many people do you know on that level—you know them by name only? A few days or weeks later you may learn some details such as how many children they have or where they grew up. You probably know a lot of people on that level. What names come to mind? As a relationship develops you begin to enjoy and appreciate the other person—for their personality, their interests, and their heart. Who do you count as real friends?

What does the way relationships develop have to do with our study of the person of Jesus Christ? Everything! Is Jesus someone you know by name only? Do you just know him as a figure in history? Or do you count him as a friend?

As you study Jesus you are learning about someone who desires to be your best friend. I'd remind anyone who thinks of doctrine as just head knowledge that there is nothing more relational than a look at the truth about Jesus. The goal of this study is not just that you will become more informed about Jesus but that you will develop a deeper relationship with him. The more you know about Jesus, the more you realize how deeply he loves you and how he's given you the wonderful ability to love him in return.

You can learn a lot about Jesus just by looking at his names.

The Names of Jesus

One of the first ways we get to know another person is by learning his name. That's not such a simple task when it comes to Jesus. Elwell's *Topical Analysis of the Bible* lists 184 different names for Christ in the Bible.[2]

> The preacher Billy Sunday counted even more and said, "There are two hundred and fifty-six names given in the Bible for the Lord Jesus Christ, and I suppose this was because he was infinitely beyond all that any one name could express."[3]

> You could make a lifelong study of just the names of Jesus.

Remember, a name helps you to identify someone. The names of Jesus Christ help you to identify who he is.

A Fresh Word

A Person's Name

In the Bible, names had more significance than we sometimes give them today. A name was an indicator of three specifics about a person:

1. His purpose   2. His position   3. His promise

> If a little boy was given a name that meant "strong in battle," that name pointed to his reason for living, to his position in society, and to future promise.

> Now you see why Jesus has so many names! His life is filled with purpose, he has a position that is above all others, and the promise of his coming still impacts us every day.

> As we take a brief look at just a few of Jesus' names, listen for how they express his purpose and position, his promise in our lives.

- **The angel told Mary: Jesus (Luke 1:31).**

Jesus means "salvation of God."

> The angel told Mary in Luke 1:31 to name the baby "Jesus." The name Jesus (Joshua in the Aramaic language, which they spoke) means "salvation of God." Could any other name more clearly identify Jesus' purpose and the promise of his life?

I don't know of anyone who writes more vibrantly and passionately about Jesus than Max Lucado. Listen to his words about the name Jesus.

> Jesus.
>
> In the gospels it's his most common name—used almost six hundred times. And a common name it was.... If Jesus came today, his name might have been John or Bob or Jim. Were he here today, it is doubtful he would distance himself with a lofty name like Reverend Holiness Angelic Divinity III. No, when God chose the name his son would carry, he chose a human name. He chose a name so typical that it would appear two or three times on any given class roll. "The Word became flesh," John said, in other words. He was touchable, approachable, reachable.... "Just call me Jesus," you can almost hear him say.[4]

- **The angels told the shepherds (Luke 2:11):**

When the angels appeared to the shepherds, they announced that "a Savior," who "is Christ the Lord," was born in Bethlehem.

- **Savior: Showing Jesus' <u>PURPOSE</u>.**

  He came to save the world, to save each of us, from a life of separation from God both here and for eternity.

- **Christ: Showing Jesus' <u>PROMISE</u>.**

  Remember, Christ was not Jesus' last name! It wasn't "Jesus Christ, son of Mary Christ and Joseph Christ." Christ is his title. Christ is the Greek equivalent of the Hebrew word *Messiah,* which means "promised one from God." Many carried the name Jesus in that day, but there is only one Jesus Christ.

- **Lord: Showing Jesus' <u>POSITION</u>.**

  Even at his birth, Jesus was recognized as the Lord of the universe that he truly is.

  Think of it: for you and me as believers, Jesus is both our friend and our Lord! It's not often that people have a close relationship with someone we would consider our Lord. We tend to keep our distance from those who have such power over our lives. I know some believers who are very excited by the closeness they can have with Jesus but who don't take his lordship very seriously. They're more likely to seek Jesus' opinion in prayer than ask for his direction. Other believers have a great sense of Jesus' power over their lives as Lord but feel very distant in their relationship to him. I encourage and challenge you to walk this difficult line of Jesus being both friend and Lord for the rest of your life. Enjoy with all of your heart the fact that he desires to be your closest friend. Commit all of your life to the truth that he alone is your sovereign Lord.

We could go on and on with this look at the names of Jesus Christ. Even these few we have looked at are enough to let us know that Jesus is someone we'd like to get to know well. Yet there are many who would like to be close to Jesus who haven't taken the step of beginning a personal relationship with him. Some people, many people, know Jesus by reputation only. Let me encourage you, before we go any further, to start a relationship with him. That means recognizing his purpose as Savior of your life, and asking for his forgiveness. That means realizing his promise to each of us as the one sent from God. That means accepting his position as the Lord (the boss, the manager, the CEO) of your life.

You can begin a relationship with Jesus right now. For you to learn about Jesus without having a relationship with him would be life's greatest tragedy. I'm not talking about religion. I'm talking about the relationship with Jesus that you were made for, that he died on the cross to offer you. I would like to lead you in a prayer of commitment to Jesus right now. The words to this prayer are in front of you in your notes. The exact words are not important; what is important is a heart of commitment to Jesus.

> *Jesus Christ, today I want to begin a relationship with you. I don't want to just know about you; I want to know you personally. I ask you to forgive me for the wrong things I've done. I want to learn from you how to live. I choose today to begin to live by your direction and guidance. I don't even know all that that will mean, but I'm trusting you to show me the way. In Jesus' name, amen.*

If you just prayed that prayer for the first time, you have a new best friend, Jesus Christ, starting today. Let's continue to get to know him better.

Key Personal Perspective

The Bible does more than just list Jesus' names; it tells us of the power of his name!

Certain names *do* have power. List below some of the names in our world today that have certain power or authority or clout behind them.

List them on your outline and then call out some of the names.

Teaching Tip

If no one volunteers a name from their list after a few moments, resist the temptation to offer names yourself. Do not make the mistake of answering the question for them. If you do, you'll lose the opportunity to bring the group into the study and will find it even harder to get them to answer the next time. Instead, prompt some members of the group to get the ball rolling.

Look at all of those names we've written down. You could add all of the names of all of the people who seem to have "power" in this world, and they still wouldn't even merit a place on the page beside the name of Jesus. The TV documentary series *Biography* chose the hundred greatest figures of the last millennium. The list was topped by Gutenberg, followed by Isaac Newton, Martin Luther, Charles Darwin, William Shakespeare, Christopher Columbus, Karl Marx, and Albert Einstein. Add the significance of every name in that top hundred together and multiply them by every other person of import and impact that you could remember, and still you would not be able to approach the purpose and promise and power in the name of Jesus Christ.

1. Jesus' name is above all names (Phil. 2:9–11).

Just when it seems that words are not enough to express the greatness of Jesus' name, we're reminded of God's word to us in Philippians 2:9–11:

> Therefore God exalted him to the highest place and gave him the name that is above every name, that at the name of Jesus every knee should bow, in heaven and on earth and under the earth, and every tongue confess that Jesus Christ is Lord, to the glory of God the Father.
> —Philippians 2:9–11

2. As believers we live in his name!

We are anointed (James 5:14),
forgiven (1 John 2:12),
baptized (Acts 10:48),
and justified in his name (1 Cor. 6:11).

We assemble in his name (1 Cor. 5:4),
we bear his name (1 Peter 4:16),
believe in his name (John 1:12),
and call on his name (1 Cor. 1:2).

In his name we give thanks (Eph. 5:20),
have life (John 20:31),
preach (Acts 8:12),
speak (Acts 9:28),
and suffer (Acts 21:13; 1 Peter 4:16).

We do everything in his name (Col. 3:17).

Split Session Plan: If you're teaching this study over two sessions, end the first session here.

The Details of Jesus' Life

Suppose you're sitting down for a piece of pie at your favorite restaurant. Across the table from you is Jesus Christ. What would you talk about? How would you get to know him better? At some point (I hope) you would ask him to tell you more about the story of his life. Oh sure, you know where he was born. But how much do you really know about his family or his ministry? What do you know about his life before he was born? About his life after his resurrection?

Jesus' life did not begin with his birth and it did not end with his death. We're going to look at Jesus' life before, during, and after his time on this earth. If you did a time line of Jesus' life, his time on earth would be an exclamation point in the middle of an eternally long line. We see it as the larger part, and it is the most significant part for us, but in terms of real time, it is the shortest part.

What did Jesus do before he was born?
The pre-incarnate Christ

Pre-incarnate means before he came to this earth as a man. The term for Jesus' being born on the earth as a man is the *incarnation*. Incarnation comes from a Latin word that means "in the flesh." Jesus was God in the flesh. God became a man! What about Jesus before that day he was born in Bethlehem?

- **He has always existed: he is eternal (Mic. 5:2; John 8:57–58).**

What did he do before being born into this world? Certainly much more than just wait in heaven for that day.

- **He <u>CREATED</u> the universe (Col. 1:16).**

One of the "little" jobs that Jesus did before his earthly birth was create the universe that he would be born into (Col. 1:16).

- **He <u>MINISTERED</u> to people.**

Did he create the earth and then wait until Bethlehem to connect again with us in a direct way? No. A close look at the Bible reveals that before Jesus was born, he ministered directly to people on the earth.

The people Jesus ministered to included:

1. **Hagar (Gen. 16:7–14):**

   The angel of the Lord found Hagar near a spring in the desert.... Then the angel of the Lord told her, "Go back to your mistress and submit to her." The angel added, "I will so increase your descendants that they will be too numerous to count."
   —Genesis 16:7, 9–10

2. **Moses (Ex. 3:2–14):**

   The angel of the Lord appeared to him in flames of fire from within a bush.... God called to him from within the bush, "Moses! Moses!"
   —Exodus 3:2, 4

3. **Abraham (Gen. 18:1–2; 22:11–12):**

   The Lord appeared to Abraham near the great trees of Mamre.... Abraham looked up and saw three men standing nearby.
   —Genesis 18:1–2

As you read these passages you will come across a figure known as the "angel of the Lord." Why would we say that this angel was actually Jesus?

A Fresh Word

The Angel of the Lord

A number of times in the Old Testament a figure called "the angel of the Lord" appears to people. It is evident that this is more than an angel. He is spoken of in terms that relate more to God himself. There is no single biblical reference regarding the identity of the angel of the Lord, but the great majority of Bible teachers see these as appearances of Christ on earth before his human birth. No, he did not look like Jesus of Nazareth. He did not become a man as he would when he was born in Bethlehem. He simply took on the appearance of a man.

In Genesis 16 the angel whom Hagar saw said that he would increase her descendants; only God would say that. And Hagar recognizes this angel as "the God who sees me." The Bible itself refers to him as "the LORD who spoke to her."

In Exodus 3 we are told, "The angel of the LORD appeared to him in flames of fire from within a bush. . . . God called to him from within the bush, 'Moses! Moses!'" (Ex. 3:2, 4). And Genesis 18:1–2 tells us that the Lord appeared to Abraham, also in the form of a man.

Teaching Tip

For additional material on the angel of the Lord, see the appendix at the end of this study.

Jesus' life on earth

10

A short history

Although Jesus is eternal, we are most acquainted with the thirty-three short years that he walked this earth. One part of making friends with someone is getting to know the facts about him: where he was born, important relationships, memorable events, and so on. How do the stories you've heard about the life of Jesus fit into the overall history of his life? As we see the events of Jesus' earthly life, we have an opportunity to get to know him better.

Go back to that favorite restaurant we talked about a few minutes ago. As you're talking with Jesus, you say, "Tell me more about yourself," and his amazing story begins to unfold. Listen to these facts not as bits of history but as a personal story about someone you love.

A look at Jesus' life in six major periods

1. Jesus' <u>BOYHOOD</u>

Beginning: his birth (Matt. 1–2; Luke 1:1–2:38)

Ending: Jesus in the temple (Luke 2:41–50)

Significant Events:

   Jesus' dedication at the temple (Luke 2:22–39)

   Fleeing to Egypt (Matt. 2:13–23)

   Visit to the temple at age twelve (Luke 2:41–50)

As Jesus begins this story, you would hear first about his boyhood, beginning with the familiar story of his birth (Matt. 1–2; Luke 1:1–2:38) and ending with Jesus' visit to the temple at age twelve (Luke 2:41–50). Imagine Jesus' eyes lighting up as he tells you of the hope expressed the day he was dedicated in the temple (Luke 2:22–39), of the protection his Father provided when his family fled to Egypt because of the threats of King Herod (Matt. 2:13–23), and of that significant moment in his visit to the temple at age twelve (Luke 2:41–50).

Jesus' visit to the temple affords a great opportunity to see how very personal the story of Jesus' being both God and man truly is. You might remember that Jesus was "lost" on the return home from Jerusalem. Let me ask you, how would you have felt if you had been the parents who lost the Son of God! You can understand how this happened when you remember that at twelve, a Jewish boy became a man. Since caravans in that day often traveled with men and women separately— and the children traveled with the women—it is not so strange that Joseph and Mary did not miss Jesus for a few days. They both expected him to be with the other. Mary thought, "Now he's with the men," while Joseph may very well have been thinking, "He's still traveling with his mother."

They rushed back to Jerusalem to find Jesus. There he was, in the temple, teaching the teachers! You need to know that at twelve a Jewish boy would have been expected to begin to be involved in the work of his father. That is why, when they found Jesus in the temple, he made the amazing statement to his earthly parents, "Didn't you know I had to be in my Father's house?" He knew at that point that God was his Father.

"The Silent Years" of Jesus' Life

The Bible tells us nothing of Jesus' life between his infancy and this event when he was twelve. And after this event, we hear nothing until he is thirty years old. You might call these the silent years of Jesus' life. Although the Bible does not directly tell us about these years, it's surprising how much we can learn through a close look at Scripture.

- **Jesus grew as any child should grow.**

  And Jesus grew in wisdom and stature, and in favor with God and men.

  —Luke 2:52

- **His mother, Mary, was with him at his birth (of course! Luke 2:7), at his death (John 19:25), to witness his resurrection, and for the beginning of the church on the day of Pentecost (Acts 1:14; 2:1).**

  Can you imagine the life that Mary led! She gave birth to the Messiah, the Savior of the world. She watched Jesus grow up in her home, begin his public ministry, and saw the crowds flock to him. She saw him die, was a witness to an appearance of Jesus after his resurrection, and saw the beginning of the church on the day of Pentecost. What an incredible life!

- **His father, Joseph, probably died sometime after Jesus' visit to the temple in Jerusalem and before the beginning of his public ministry at age thirty. Joseph is never mentioned after the experience in the temple, although Mary is with Jesus numerous times. It would have been very unusual in that day for Mary to be traveling without her husband if he were still alive.**

  The fact that Joseph likely died at an earlier age would mean that Mary was a single parent, perhaps only when her children grew older, but a single parent nonetheless. Jesus likely spent part of his life growing up in a single-parent home.

  What did Jesus do in the years between twelve and thirty? As the oldest son, there would have been a time when he took care of his family. Jesus' example shows us that our ministry to our family is part of our ministry to the world. Jesus—God in human flesh—actually spent more of his life preparing for ministry and ministering to his family (thirty years) than he spent in public ministry (three years).

- **There were at least seven children in Jesus' family: Jesus, four half brothers, and at least two half sisters (half brothers and half sisters because God was the Father of Jesus, and Joseph was the father of the others). We know this from Matthew 13:55–56: "Isn't this the carpenter's son? Isn't his mother's name Mary, and aren't his brothers James, Joseph, Simon and Judas? Aren't all his sisters with us?"**

  Many people look at this and think, "I never knew that. I always thought that Jesus was an only child." But the Bible is clear, Jesus came from a large family.

What must it have felt like to be one of Jesus' brothers or sisters? What would it be like to have a sibling who never did anything wrong, and whose mother knew he would never do anything wrong?

The truth is, Jesus' own family struggled with having faith in him. In the New Testament you often see them accusing him of ignoring them, and there's a strong undercurrent of jealousy. But it did not stay that way.

- **His brother Judas wrote a book in the New Testament, the book of Jude.**

- **His brother James also wrote one of the books in the New Testament. Guess what it was named. Right . . . James! Judas and James were skeptics until they met with Jesus after his resurrection (John 7:5; Acts 1:14; 1 Cor. 15:7). James became a leader in the Jerusalem church (Acts 12:17; 15:13–21).**

It would be easy to spend weeks on any one of these periods of Jesus' life. We've spent a little more time focusing on the time of Jesus' boyhood; let's take just a few minutes on each of these next segments of his life. I primarily want you to see how the events you may be familiar with fit into the overall time line of his life.

2. **Beginning of Jesus' <u>MINISTRY</u>**

Four significant events mark the beginning of Jesus' public ministry at thirty years of age:
- **The ministry of John the Baptist (Mark 1:1–8; Luke 3:1–18)**
- **Jesus' baptism (Matt. 3:13–17; Mark 1:9–11)**
- **Jesus' temptation in the wilderness (Luke 4:1–13; Matt. 4:1–11)**
- **Jesus' turning the water to wine (John 2:1–11)**

Jesus' ministry begins with the preparation of John the Baptist, receiving the affirmation of his Father at his baptism, his being tempted by Satan with the three great tests in the wilderness, and the public declaration of his deity when he turns the water to wine at the wedding in Cana of Galilee.

3. **Jesus' ministry in <u>JUDEA</u>**

Beginning: Cleansing the temple (John 2:13ff)

Ending: Conversation with the woman at the well (John 4:1–42)

Significant Events: Conversation with Nicodemus (John 3)

Judea, you'll remember, was in the southern half of Israel. The city of Jerusalem would be the center of Jesus' activities in Judea. Those at the centers of power (Nicodemus was one of the top religious leaders of the day) quickly learned that they would have to deal with the light that Jesus was bringing into this world.

4. **Jesus' ministry in <u>GALILEE</u>**

Beginning: Healing the nobleman's son at Capernaum (John 4:46–53)

Ending:

> **Peter's statement of trust (Matt. 16:13ff)**
>
> **Jesus' Transfiguration (Matt. 17:1ff; Luke 9:28ff)**

Significant Events:

> **The Sermon on the Mount (Matt. 5–7)**
>
> **Calling the disciples (Luke 5:1–11; Mark 2:13–14; Luke 6:12–16)**
>
> **Feeding the 5,000 (Matt. 14:13–21; Mark 6:30–44)**

Jesus moves to the north of Israel for a fruitful period of ministry. This period begins with his healing a nobleman's son at Capernaum (John 4:46–53) and goes through Peter's confession of Jesus as "the Christ" (Matt. 16:13ff) and Jesus' transfiguration (Matt. 17:1ff; Luke 9:28ff). The familiar significant events during this segment of his ministry include the preaching of the Sermon on the Mount (Matt. 5–7), the calling of the disciples (Luke 5:1–11; Mark 2:13–14; Luke 6:12–16), and the feeding of the 5,000 (Matt. 14:13–21; Mark 6:30–44).

One quality of Jesus' life that jumps off the pages of the Bible is his love for people. Even before he gave his life for others on the cross, he gave his life to others in daily activities. In his book *The Jesus I Never Knew,* Philip Yancey writes about Jesus' love for people:

> Jesus was "the man for others," in Bonhoeffer's fine phrase. He kept himself free—free from the other person. He would accept almost anybody's invitation to dinner, and as a result no public figure had a more diverse list of friends, ranging from rich people, Roman centurions, and Pharisees to tax collectors, prostitutes and leprosy victims. People liked being with Jesus; where he was, joy was.[5]

5. **Jesus' journey to <u>JERUSALEM</u>**

Beginning: He "resolutely set out for" Jerusalem (Luke 9:51)

Ending: Mary anoints his body for burial (John 12:1ff; Matt. 26:6–13)

Significant Events:

> **Clashes with the Pharisees (Luke 14; Luke 16:14ff)**
>
> **The resurrection of Lazarus (John 11:1ff)**
>
> **Meeting Zacchaeus in Jericho (Luke 19:1ff)**

In Luke 9:51 we are told that Jesus "resolutely set out for Jerusalem," thus beginning a new chapter in his life. This is a time of increasing conflict and mounting tension, ending with Mary, the sister of Lazarus, anointing his body for burial (John 12:1ff). The significant events of these days are his clashes with the Pharisees (Luke 14; Luke 16:14ff), the raising of Lazarus from the dead (John 11:1ff), and Jesus' meeting with a short tax collector named Zacchaeus in Jericho (Luke 19:1ff).

6. Jesus' death, burial, and resurrection

Beginning: The triumphal entry into Jerusalem (Matt. 21:1–11)

Ending: The ascension into heaven (Luke 24:50–51)

Significant Events:

> **Cleansing the temple, the Garden of Gethsemane, trials (Luke 19:45–46; John 17–18)**
>
> **Jesus dies on the cross (Matt. 27:31–50; Luke 23:26–46)**
>
> **Jesus is buried in a tomb (Mark 15:42–47; John 19:38–42)**
>
> **Jesus is alive (Matt. 28:2–15; Mark 16:1–17; Luke 24:1–7; John 20:1–18)**

No week in Jesus' life is more familiar to us than his last week. It began with his triumphal entry into Jerusalem (Matt. 21:1–11) and ended with his resurrection from the dead. During that week are the unforgettable events that took place in the temple as he spoke with the religious leaders, in the Upper Room as he washed the disciples' feet and then offered them bread and wine as a symbol of his body and blood, and in the Garden of Gethsemane as he poured his heart out in prayer. A lifetime could be spent studying the few hours he spent on the cross, giving his life for us. Isn't it amazing that although you may have heard the story of his resurrection on the third day thousands of times, it is still a story that has the thrill of newness in it. Intuitively we know that this is the moment that everything changed! Death was defeated, and life was guaranteed for all who trust in him.

Key Personal Perspective

Jesus is a part of history. In the *Encyclopaedia Britannica*, following a discussion of the writings about Jesus outside of the New Testament, the following statement is made: "These independent accounts prove that in ancient times even the opponents of Christianity never doubted the historicity of Jesus, which was disputed for the first time and on inadequate grounds by several authors at the end of the 18th, during the 19th and at the beginning of the 20th centuries."[6]

H. G. Wells personalizes the historical foundations to Jesus' life.

"More than 1900 years later, a historian like myself, who doesn't even call himself a Christian, finds the picture centering irresistibly around the life and character of this most significant man. . . . The historian's test of an individual's greatness is 'What did he leave to grow?' Did he start men to thinking along fresh lines with a vigor that persisted after him? By this test Jesus stands first."[7]

Jesus really lived. Jesus really died. And . . . Jesus really rose from the dead on the third day! I can't think of a better expression of the personal impact that the events of Jesus' life have upon our lives than that found in John 3:16.

For God so loved the world that he gave his one and only Son, that whoever believes in him shall not perish but have eternal life.

—John 3:16

Because Jesus lived, you and I who trust him have life—abundant life and eternal life. What an indescribable gift!

Teaching Tip

As you come to John 3:16 in the study notes, tell your group that you are going to read something that is very familiar—but you want them to listen as if they are hearing this for the very first time. Then read the verse: slowly and joyfully!

The eternally existent Christ

Have you ever asked yourself what Jesus is doing right now? We know from Acts 1 that he ascended back to heaven, but what is he doing there? Let's answer together two questions about what Jesus is doing in heaven.

What does he look like?

All the evidence points to Jesus still existing in his <u>RESUR-RECTED</u> <u>BODY</u> in heaven:

- **He ascended to heaven in bodily form (Acts 1:9).**

- **He will return in bodily form (Acts 1:11).**

- **Stephen saw him in bodily form in heaven (Acts 7:55–56).**

- **Paul indicated Jesus now has a glorious body (Phil. 3:21).**

It is of course a part of the great mystery of God's greatness that Jesus still lives in this resurrected body in heaven. But beyond the mystery, take a moment to think about the reality of this truth. It means one day I'll be able to see his nail-scarred hands. I will be able to look into his joy-filled eyes. I will be able to walk beside him and talk about eternity. It means that one day I will be able to wrap my arms around him and give him an awe-filled hug; saying thank you for all that he's done for me!

> Discussion questions 2 and 3 can be used here.

What is he doing?

This world can be a very insecure place. When we look at what Jesus is doing right now in heaven, it gives us some rock-solid truths to stand on.

- **He is <u>RULING</u> at God's right hand (Eph. 1:20–22; 1 Peter 3:22).**

- **He is <u>PRAYING</u> for us (Rom. 8:34).**

- **He is holding the <u>UNIVERSE</u> together (Col. 1:16–17).**

- **He is anxiously <u>WAITING</u> for us to be with him (John 14:1–3; 17:24).**

Take a deep breath with me and let it out slowly, and think about how great Jesus' love is for you. Do it again. Consider the fact that he loves you more than you could ever imagine. Be amazed by the truth that we do not have the capacity to even grasp the greatness of his love for us. Let that love be your comfort and your motivation this week.

Acting on the Truth

Jesus Christ wants to be your best friend. Think of it—your best friend is ruling at God's right hand, is the one who holds the universe together. Let me encourage you to enjoy the fact that he is your friend this week by choosing to act as if he is your best friend. Here are three ways you can do that:

1. Say to yourself, "He accepts me even when I don't feel acceptable." Remind yourself throughout this week that you are Jesus' friend because of his grace, not because you somehow deserve that friendship.

2. Talk to him—like a friend. That's what prayer is. At least once this week take a few minutes to tell Jesus what is happening in your life much as you would talk to a best friend. Sure, he already knows what's happening to you. But it is life-changing for you to talk to him as a friend about what you're facing each day.

3. Listen to him—like a friend. When I'm reading the Bible I'm reading the book he gave me. This week, listen as you read. What is God saying to you about his love for you?

Discussion questions 4 and 5 can be used here.

Begin working on memory card 3, "The Truth about Jesus."

Appendix: Teacher's Resource

The Angel of the Lord

As a teacher, remember that the object in this study is to simply introduce the idea of the angel of the Lord. Whet the appetite of those in the group for learning more by introducing the idea, telling them that this could be a complete study in and of itself. The following material on the concept of the angel of the Lord is for your personal and background study.

There are two primary questions that you probably will hear from those you teach concerning the angel of the Lord:

First: How do we know that this is not just a powerful angel, but that this angel is to be identified with God? These are the two most convincing facts:

1. Divine names are given to him and claimed by him (Gen. 16:13; 18:1, 17, 20, 26, 33; Ex. 3:2–7; compare Ex. 13:21 with 14:19; and compare Joshua 5:13 with 6:2).

    He is called God by Hagar (Gen. 16:13), by Jacob (Gen. 32:30), to Moses (Ex. 3:4, 6), and by God himself (compare Gen. 31:13 with 31:11 and compare Ex. 3:6 with 3:2).

2. Divine attributes and authority are ascribed to the angel.

    Creative power. He promised Hagar: "I will so increase your descendants that they will be too numerous to count" (Gen. 16:10).

    He said to Abraham, "'I will surely return to you about this time next year, and Sarah your wife will have a son.' Now Sarah was listening at the entrance to the tent, which was behind him" (Gen. 18:10).

    Sovereignty. He claims both the right to answer prayer and to act out his will in his conversations with Abraham concerning Sodom and Gomorrah (Gen. 18:17–33).

    Judgment. In Genesis 18:25, Abraham gives to the angel of the Lord an amazing title, "Surely you will not destroy the good people along with the evil ones; then they would be treated the same. You are the judge of all the earth. Won't you do what is right?" (Gen. 18:25 NCV).

The second question is, how do we know that this "angel of the Lord" is to be identified with Jesus and not with the Father? This point is not as biblically clear as the first. By simple deduction we would expect that it would be Jesus who would be the person of the Godhead who would appear in some manner on earth. One of his primary purposes is to be the mediator between God and man. It's interesting to note the similarities in the ministries of the angel of the Lord and Jesus.

- The angel of the Lord did miraculous acts; so did Jesus (see John 2:9; Matt. 8:3; Luke 7:14; Matt. 15:32–38).

- The angel of the Lord taught and instructed people; Jesus was called "Teacher" or "Rabboni" (John 20:16).

- The angel of the Lord is a judge of mankind; in John 5:22 we see "The Father judges no one, but has entrusted all judgment to the Son."

- No one has ever seen the Father (John 1:18; 5:37) and the Holy Spirit is invisible. Hence, the angel of the Lord probably wasn't either of them.

The term theologians use for an appearance of Christ on earth before his birth in Bethlehem is *Christophany*. A theophany is a manifestation of God that is tangible to the human senses. A Christophany is such an appearance of Jesus.

Discussion Questions

1. **What does "having a relationship with Jesus" mean to you?**

2. **When you get to heaven and come face to face with the eternally existent Jesus:**
   - **What do you want to say to him?**
   - **What question do you want to ask him?**
   - **What emotions do you think you'll experience?**

Small Group Leaders: Let the group answer these three questions for a few minutes before giving them the follow-up question below.

This follow-up question is not a simple question—it is likely one that the group will need to wrestle with for a while. Remember that as a small group leader, silence sometimes is your best friend. It means people are thinking about how a truth fits into their lives. With challenging questions such as this, it's good to give the group some time before they answer—some leaders actually mentally count to thirty. The few moments of silence builds a kind of tension, and eventually somebody will speak. When they do, it often leads to an amazingly deep and fruitful discussion.

3. Here's the important follow-up: What is it that keeps us from telling him or asking him or feeling those emotions right now? What gets in the way of us sensing that Jesus is our best friend right now? (Talk about ways you may have broken through some of these barriers.)

4. What new thing did you learn about Jesus in this study?

5. At the end of the study we looked at three ways to begin to act on the truth that Jesus is your best friend this next week: remind yourself of his acceptance of you as a friend, talk to him as a friend, or listen to him as a friend. Which of these do you think would best help you to come to a new understanding and appreciation of your friendship with Jesus? Why?

Jesus

Part 2

 Life Change Objective

To develop an understanding of Jesus' nature as both God and man that will protect you against false teachings and give you confidence in trusting Jesus with a specific need.

Summary Teaching Outline

Jesus Is God

How do we know Jesus is God?

1. Jesus said he is God.

2. Others said he is God.

3. He is worshiped as God.

4. He does what only God can do.

What evidence supports Jesus' claim to be God?

Evidence 1: Fulfillment of prophecy

Evidence 2: His miracles

Evidence 3: His resurrection

Jesus Is Man

Jesus Is Fully God and Fully Man

Jesus limited himself.

Jesus did not lessen himself.

Teaching Tip

How do you build your confidence that God is going to use what you teach to make a difference in people's lives? This is one of the most important issues for any teacher. Anyone who has taught the Bible even a few times knows that confidence is much more than a matter of "thinking more positively" or "getting your confidence up." Those techniques may work for a business presentation, but they are not enough when facing the feelings of inadequacy that are inevitable when we attempt to communicate God's truth. As the apostle Paul said, "There is nothing in us that allows us to claim that we are capable of doing this work" (2 Cor. 3:5 GNT). He ends the verse by saying, "The capacity we have comes from God."

How do you focus with faith on what God has the capacity to do instead of focusing on the fact that you do not feel capable? Remember these two statements each week as you prepare and as you begin to teach.

Prayer is vital to keeping your faith focus. Tell God you trust that what you are going to say will make a lasting impact upon someone's life because of the power of his Word. Jesus told us to ask specifically— so ask him to work in specific ways in people's lives as you teach.

Turn your feelings of inadequacy into a decision to be vulnerable. Paul said in 2 Corinthians 4:7, "But we have this treasure in jars of clay to show that this all-surpassing power is from God and not from us." When you feel inadequate, the best thing to do is to admit that you *are* inadequate—you are a "jar of clay" that God uses in wonderful ways.

Discussion questions 1 and 2 can be used here.

What does it mean when we say that Jesus is both man and God?

Before we look in the Bible at what God has to say about his Son, take a moment to answer the question below. Don't be afraid of getting the wrong answer. Most of us have never thought about the nature of who Jesus is.

Is Jesus . . .

- **A man who became God?**
- **God indwelling a man?**
- **God appearing to be a man?**
- **A spiritual being ordered by God to become man?**
- **Fully God and fully man?**

Remember the scene in the third Indiana Jones movie where Indy is challenged to choose the cup of the Holy Grail (the mythical cup from which Christ drank at the Lord's Supper) from dozens of cups of various sizes, shapes, and appearance? A drink from the right cup would yield eternal life. A drink from the wrong cup would bring death. One of Jones's enemies grabs the cup that intuitively looks right to him—one made of gold and encrusted with jewels. He greedily drinks the water in the cup—and dies instantly. In one of the most memorable lines in the movie, the ancient crusader guarding the cups looks at Indiana Jones and says, in understated irony, "He chose . . . poorly."

Step into the movie with me. Suppose you have in front of you five cups, representing five different ways of believing who Jesus really is. Four cups represent beliefs that are destructive—they lead to spiritual death. The fifth cup represents the truth of who Jesus is, the living Water that leads to eternal life. How do you choose the right cup? Our intuition or reasoning is not enough—it can easily lead us astray. Others' opinions can also lead us astray—no matter how confidently they may speak. Our opinions on this issue aren't worth much. The *only* one who can tell us about the true nature of Jesus Christ is God himself.

At the very core of what God tells us about Jesus is this: Jesus is God and Jesus is man. He is fully God and he is fully man. Look at what these verses from John and First John tell us.

In the beginning was the Word, and the Word was with God, and the Word was God.

—John 1:1

Anyone who acknowledges that Jesus Christ came as a human being has the Spirit who comes from God.

—1 John 4:2 (GNT)

We're going to focus today on the truth that Jesus is God and Jesus is man. You and I need to know this so that we'll be protected against false teachings about Jesus. We need to know this so we'll see how freely we can turn to him as the one who not only understands our needs but can meet our needs.

Jesus Is God

How do we know Jesus is God?

1. Jesus said he is God.

Look at these verses:

He was even calling God his own Father, making himself equal with God.

—John 5:18

I and the Father are one.

—John 10:30

Anyone who has seen me has seen the Father.

—John 14:9

"I tell you the truth," Jesus answered, "before Abraham was born, I am!"
—John 8:58

Circle those two words "I am." "I am," you might remember, is the most holy name of God, the name God, in Exodus 3:13–14, told Moses to say to the Israelites if they asked who had sent him to them. That is the same name Jesus used in referring to himself in John 8:58. Some say he didn't mean those words in that way. But the Pharisees, in John 8:59, certainly understood what he was saying. They picked up stones to kill him because he referred to himself as "I am," the name of God. Jesus understood, and his enemies understood, that he was claiming to be God.

C. S. Lewis writes these classic lines concerning Jesus' claims about who he is.

> I am trying here to prevent anyone saying the really foolish thing that people often say about Him: "I am ready to accept Jesus as a great moral teacher, but I don't accept His claim to be God." That is one thing we must not say. A man who was merely a man and said the sort of things Jesus said would not be a great moral teacher. He would either be a lunatic—on a level with the man who says he is a poached egg—or else he would be the Devil of Hell. You must make your choice. Either this man was, and is, the Son of God; or else a madman or something worse. . . . You can try to shut Him up for a fool, you can spit at Him and call Him a demon; or you can fall at His feet and call Him Lord and God. But let us not come up with any patronizing nonsense about His being a great human teacher. He has not left that open to us. He did not intend to.[1]
>
> —C. S. Lewis
>
> **Josh McDowell says that Jesus is either "a liar, a lunatic, or the Lord."[2]**

2. **OTHERS** said he is God.

This started in the prophecies of Jesus' birth before he was born.

> And he will be called . . . Mighty God.
>
> —Isaiah 9:6

It continued with those who were closest to him, his own disciples.

> So that at the name of Jesus every knee will bow . . . and that every tongue will confess that Jesus Christ is Lord.
>
> —Philippians 2:10–11 (NASB)

Compare Philippians 2:10–11 with what is said of God in Isaiah.

> I am God, and there is no other. . . . Before me every knee will bow; by me every tongue will swear.
>
> —Isaiah 45:22–23

Remember that before the apostle Paul became a believer, he was a Pharisee—someone who knew the Old Testament backward and forward. When he explained the lordship of Jesus to the believers in Philippi, he deliberately chose to paraphrase the words of Isaiah concerning God's greatness. For Paul, it would have been blasphemy to use these words of anyone but God. Every knee will bow before Jesus because Jesus is God!

> For in Christ all the fullness of the Deity lives in bodily form.
>
> —Colossians 2:9

> In the beginning was the Word, and the Word was with God, and the Word was God. He was with God in the beginning.
>
> —John 1:1–2

3. He is **WORSHIPED** as God (Matt. 14:33; Phil. 2:10; Heb. 1:6).

- Many worshiped him: a healed leper (Matt. 8:2), women (Matt. 15:25), the mother of James and John (Matt. 20:20), a Gerasenes demoniac (Mark 5:6), a blind man (John 9:38).
- He accepted such worship (John 20:28–29; Matt. 14:33; 28:9–10).
- His disciples prayed to him (Acts 7:59).

And not once did Jesus say, "No, you're wrong. Don't worship me." When Thomas worshiped Jesus as "my Lord and my God" in John 20:28, Jesus affirmed Thomas for his belief. Paul and Barnabas told those in the town of Lystra who tried to worship them as Greek gods, "Men, why are you doing this? We too are only men, human like you" (Acts 14:15). If Jesus were not God, he would have rejected human worship in just the same way. But he instead accepted and blessed people as they worshiped him.

4. He does what <u>ONLY</u> <u>GOD</u> can do.

This drove the religious leaders who opposed Jesus absolutely crazy. They did not want to accept Jesus as God because it would radically change their world—and they didn't want any change. But Jesus kept doing things that, by the religious leaders' own beliefs, only God had the ability to do.

- **He has the power to forgive sin (Mark 2:1–12).**
- **All <u>JUDGMENT</u> is in his hands (John 5:27; Acts 17:31).**
- **He sends the Spirit (John 15:26).**
- **He will raise the dead (John 5:25).**
- **He is the <u>CREATOR</u> (John 1:3; Col. 1:16; Heb. 1:10).**
- **He is the Sustainer—upholding all (Col. 1:17; Heb. 1:3).**

Those are the facts, facts supported by the evidence.

What evidence supports Jesus' claim to be God?

Before Jesus came, the prophets said he would be God. While he walked the earth Jesus said, "I AM God." And after his death and resurrection, his followers continued to state that he is God.

But how do we know that what he was saying was true? Where is the evidence that backs up these bold claims of deity?

Obviously anyone could "claim" to be God. The difference with Jesus is that his life backs up those claims.

Suppose that you were in a courtroom hearing a case trying to prove that Jesus is God. Witness after witness says, "Jesus is God." The prophets, Jesus' own disciples, and Jesus himself have taken their place on the witness stand to say, "You have my word on it."

Added to the overwhelming weight of this personal testimony three powerful evidences of Jesus' claim to be God are now brought before us.

Evidence 1: <u>FULFILLMENT</u> <u>OF PROPHECY</u>

[Jesus] said to them, "This is what I told you while I was still with you: Everything must be fulfilled that is written about me in the Law of Moses, the Prophets and the Psalms."

—Luke 24:44

Look at the number of prophecies that Jesus fulfilled. Look at how detailed some of these prophecies were.

The Old Testament verses are the prophecy. The New Testament verses proclaim the fulfillment.

1. Born of a virgin (Isa. 7:14; Matt. 1:21–23).
2. A descendant of Abraham (Gen. 12:1–3; 22:18; Matt. 1:1; Gal. 3:16).
3. Of the tribe of Judah (Gen. 49:10; Luke 3:23, 33; Heb. 7:14).
4. Of the house of David (2 Sam. 7:12–16; Matt. 1:1).
5. Born in Bethlehem (Mic. 5:2; Matt. 2:1; Luke 2:4–7).
6. Taken to Egypt (Hos. 11:1; Matt. 2:14–15).
7. Herod's killing of the infants (Jer. 31:15; Matt. 2:16–18).
8. Anointed by the Holy Spirit (Isa. 11:2; Matt. 3:16–17).
9. Heralded by the messenger of the Lord (John the Baptist) (Isa. 40:3; Mal. 3:1; Matt. 3:1–3).
10. Would perform miracles (Isa. 35:5–6; Matt. 9:35).
11. Would preach good news (Isa. 61:1; Luke 4:14–21).
12. Would minister in Galilee (Isa. 9:1; Matt. 4:12–16).
13. Would cleanse the temple (Mal. 3:1; Matt. 21:12–13).
14. Would enter Jerusalem as a king on a donkey (Zech. 9:9; Matt. 21:4–9).
15. Would be rejected by Jews (Ps. 118:22; 1 Peter 2:7).
16. Die a humiliating death (Ps. 22; Isa. 53) involving:
    a. rejection (Isa. 53:3; John 1:10–11; 7:5, 48).
    b. betrayal by a friend (Ps. 41:9; Luke 22:3–4; John 13:18).
    c. being sold for thirty pieces of silver (Zech. 11:12; Matt. 26:14–15).
    d. silence before his accusers (Isa. 53:7; Matt. 27:12–14).
    e. being mocked (Ps. 22:7–8; Matt. 27:31).
    f. being beaten (Isa. 52:14; Matt. 27:26).
    g. being spit upon (Isa. 50:6; Matt. 27:30).
    h. piercing his hands and feet (Ps. 22:16; Matt. 27:31).
    i. being crucified with thieves (Isa. 53:12; Matt. 27:38).
    j. praying for his persecutors (Isa. 53:12; Luke 23:34).
    k. piercing his side (Zech. 12:10; John 19:34).
    l. being given gall and vinegar to drink (Ps. 69:21; Matt. 27:34; Luke 23:36).
    m. no broken bones (Ps. 34:20; John 19:32–36).
    n. being buried in a rich man's tomb (Isa. 53:9; Matt. 27:57–60).
    o. casting lots for his garments (Ps. 22:18; John 19:23–24).

17. Would rise from the dead (Ps. 16:10; Mark 16:6; Acts 2:31).

18. Ascend into heaven (Ps. 68:18; Acts 1:9).

19. Would sit down at the right hand of God (Ps. 110:1; Heb. 1:3).

A Closer Look

Some people call this fulfillment of prophecy a "statistical accident." He "just happened" to be born in Bethlehem, to be of David's line, etc. There are two answers to that argument. First, these predictions were more than just a matter of chance. He "just happened" to make a blind man see. He "just happened" to rise again from the dead. That's beyond statistical probability!

The second answer is the large number of prophecies that were fulfilled. Peter Stoner in his book *Science Speaks* has calculated the mathematical probability of even eight of these prophecies being fulfilled in one man.

> We find that the chance that any man might have lived down to the present time and fulfilled all eight prophecies is 1 in 10^{17}.

That would be one in 100,000,000,000,000,000. In order for us to be able to comprehend this staggering probability, Stoner illustrates it by supposing that:

> We take 10^{17} silver dollars and lay them on the face of Texas. They will cover all of the state two feet deep. Now mark one of these silver dollars and stir the whole mass thoroughly, all over the state. Blindfold a man and tell him that he can travel as far as he wishes, but he must pick up one silver dollar and say that this is the right one. What chance would he have of getting the right one? Just the same chance that the prophets would have had of writing these eight prophecies and having them all come true in any one man, from their day to the present time, providing they wrote in their own wisdom.[3]

And Jesus did not just fulfill eight prophecies, he fulfilled more than 300 specific prophecies of his life from the Old Testament!

What are the probabilities of one person fulfilling more than 300 prophecies? Instead of picking out a single silver dollar in Texas, it would be the chance of your randomly picking out a single atom from all of the atoms in the universe and having it be the one that had been marked with a microscopic X.

Evidence 2: His MIRACLES

When asked for proof, Jesus pointed to the miracles.

> When the men came to Jesus, they said, "John the Baptist sent us to you to ask, 'Are you the one who was to come, or should we expect someone else?'" . . . So he replied to the messengers, "Go back and report to John what you have seen and heard: The blind receive sight, the lame walk, those who have leprosy are cured, the deaf hear, the dead are raised, and the good news is preached to the poor."
>
> —Luke 7:20, 22

Here is a list of what Jesus was talking about—the places where he accomplished the very miracles he's speaking of here.

"the blind receive sight" (Matt. 9:27–31; Luke 18:35–43; Mark 8:22–26)

"the lame walk" (Matt. 9:2–7)

"those who have leprosy are cured" (Matt. 8:2–3; Luke 17:11–19)

"the deaf hear" (Mark 7:31–37)

"the dead are raised" (Matt. 9:18–19, 23–25; Luke 7:11–15; John 11:1–44)

"good news is preached" (Matt. 11:5)

Let's focus on just one of those miracles, when Jesus raised Lazarus from the dead, in John 11.

Jesus was a good friend of Lazarus and of his sisters, Mary and Martha. The three lived in Bethany, just a few miles outside of Jerusalem. When Jesus would go to Jerusalem he would often stop by for a meal or to stay the night. (And he always brought twelve disciples with him!)

The Bible tells us that when Jesus heard that Lazarus was near death, he did an amazing thing. Instead of rushing to Bethany, he stayed where he was for two more days. We'll see why in just a moment. When Jesus finally did arrive, Martha rushed to meet him and said, "Lord, if you had been here, my brother would not have died." She expressed faith and a rebuke at the same time! (Don't look at me like you've never talked to God like that.) The Bible tells us that when Jesus saw Mary and the Jews who had come with her to meet Jesus weeping, he broke down and wept. The pain of what death and grief do to our human hearts overwhelmed him.

He walked to the tomb and did three things. First, he ordered that the stone be rolled away. Martha protested that Lazarus had already been dead for four days, and that the smell of his body would be terrible. Jesus reminded her to trust God. Second, he prayed out loud for the benefit of those who were watching. In his prayer he said, "Father, I thank you that you have heard me. I knew that you always hear me, but I said this for the benefit of the people standing here, that they may believe that you sent me." Then Jesus does the third thing. He shouts the command, "Lazarus, come out!" And Lazarus, still wrapped in strips of cloth that even covered his face, walks out of that tomb alive.

He'd been in that tomb for four days! Remember that Jesus took his time getting to Lazarus. One of the reasons was so no one could say, "Lazarus wasn't really dead. He was just taking a long nap in there." When Jesus raised him from the dead, Lazarus had been dead and buried for four days.

And dozens, if not hundreds, of people were witnesses to this miracle. This was no rumor of some great miracle done in some remote place. Lazarus walked out of that tomb alive, just a few miles from Jerusalem.

Jesus is saying to you, "Are you one of those people who need proof? Then look at the miracles."

Teaching Tip

When you feel that the group's attention is beginning to wander, what do you do? Many teachers internalize these feelings and begin to feel discouraged about themselves and their skills even as they teach. That's exactly what Satan would love for you to do! Now you're focused on yourself and not on the truth you're teaching or the people being taught. When the group seems to be losing interest, the three words to remember are: do something different.

Move to a different spot, maybe closer to the group or a few feet to one side.

Speak differently. Speed up or slow down the cadence of your words.

Have the group do something different. Read a Bible verse together, turn to each other and discuss a question, or (in a long session) you can even get everyone to stand up for a moment.

Evidence 3: His **RESURRECTION**

14

The Resurrection is one of his miracles and a fulfillment of prophecy that deserves to be focused on separately.

It was one thing for Jesus to bring Lazarus out of the grave. It's infinitely greater for him to resurrect himself. When Lazarus was brought out of the grave, he was going to die (again) one day. But Jesus resurrected himself with a new body to live forever!

Jesus not only predicted it but told the number of days!

> Jesus answered them, "Destroy this temple, and I will raise it again in three days."
>
> —John 2:19

> For as Jonah was three days and three nights in the belly of a huge fish, so the Son of Man will be three days and three nights in the heart of the earth.
>
> —Matthew 12:40

> He then began to teach them that the Son of Man must suffer many things and be rejected by the elders, chief priests and teachers of the law, and that he must be killed and after three days rise again.
>
> —Mark 8:31

He called it! We live in a day where amazement comes when a coach predicts a win in a football game or a baseball player points with his bat to which field he'll hit a home run. That's nothing compared to Jesus' prediction that he would do something that no one had done before or has done since then!

He claimed the authority behind the Resurrection.

> The reason my Father loves me is that I lay down my life—only to take it up again. No one takes it from me, but I lay it down of my own accord. I have authority to lay it down and authority to take it up again. This command I received from my Father.
>
> —John 10:17–18

He didn't just say his resurrection would happen; Jesus said it would happen by his choice and his power.

> Discussion questions 3 and 4 can be used here.

Thomas Arnold (former professor of history at Oxford) writes of the Resurrection from a historical perspective: "I know of no one fact in the history of mankind which is proved by better, fuller evidence of every sort, to the understanding of the fair inquirer, than the great sign which God hath given us that Christ died and rose again from the dead."[4]

Simon Greenleaf, former professor at and one of the developers of the Harvard Law School, writes from a legal viewpoint concerning the evidence given by Jesus' disciples in the Bible: "It was therefore impossible that they could have persisted in affirming the truths they have narrated, had not Jesus actually risen from the dead, and had they not known this fact as certainly as they knew any other fact."[5]

The fulfillment of prophecy . . . the miracles . . . the Resurrection—all are clear evidence that Jesus is who he claimed to be. Jesus came into this world as God in human flesh.

Lee Strobel, a reporter for the *Chicago Tribune,* had clung to a belief in atheism all of his life. To him it seemed the most reasonable belief. Then events in his life began to stir a quiet suspicion that there could be some truth to what the Bible says about Jesus. Lee did something that took great courage. He decided to investigate, to search for the truth. Listen to his words describing where that search led.

> The date was November 8, 1981. It was a Sunday. I locked myself in my home office and spent the afternoon replaying the spiritual journey I had been traveling for twenty-one months....
>
> I'll admit it. I was ambushed by the amount and quality of the evidence that Jesus is the unique Son of God. As I sat at my desk that Sunday afternoon, I shook my head in amazement. I had seen defendants carted off to the death chamber on much less convincing proof! The cumulative facts and data pointed unmistakably toward a conclusion that I wasn't entirely comfortable in reaching....
>
> I realized that my biggest objection to Jesus also had been quieted by the evidence of history. I found myself chuckling at how the tables had been turned.
>
> In light of the convincing facts I had learned during my investigation, in the face of this overwhelming avalanche of evidence in the case for Christ, the great irony was this: it would require much more faith for me to maintain my atheism than to trust in Jesus of Nazareth! ...
>
> I talked with God in a heartfelt and unedited prayer, admitting and turning from my wrongdoing, and receiving the gift of forgiveness and eternal life through Jesus. I told him that with his help I wanted to follow him and his ways from here on out.
>
> There were no lightning bolts, no audible replies, no tingly sensations. I know that some people feel a rush of emotion at such a moment; as for me, however, there was something else that was equally exhilarating; there was the rush of reason.[6]

Split Session Plan: If you're teaching this study over two sessions, end the first session here.

Jesus is fully God, and Jesus is fully man!

Believe it or not, many of us have more problems with the second part of what I just said than the first. We find it easier to accept the fact that Jesus is God than to believe that he *really* became a man, a human being like you and me.

I've found that before we become believers, we all have a difficult time accepting the fact that Jesus is 100 percent God. I've also found that once you've become a believer and the longer you are a believer, the more difficult it is to see that Jesus Christ was also 100 percent man.

The truth is, we need to hold on to both to be able to fix our eyes on the real Jesus. And it's important throughout every day to have our eyes fixed on him!

What gets your attention gets you. Have you noticed how easily our lives get caught up in the routine, how our noses stay fixed to the daily grindstone? Anne Ortlund, writing about this all-too-human tendency, compares us to sheep:

> You know how a sheep is. He keeps his head down and goes nibble, nibble, nibble.
>
> Out of the corner of his eye he sees a new tuft of grass; he moves four inches right . . . nibble, nibble.
>
> When have you seen a sheep climb a tree, check the horizons, see where he's come from and where he wants to go, and climb down and strike out? Never.
>
> Are you identifying with a sheep? Do you pretty much live with your head down?
> Now it's time to go to work . . .
> Mustn't forget to pick up the pants at the cleaners . . .
> It's five o'clock; wonder what I should fix for dinner . . .
> It's Thursday and my book's due back to the library . . .
> It's five minutes till time for the school bus . . .
> Nibble, nibble, nibble . . . ?
> What consumes you? Where are you going? Have you pinpointed your aim? Does your life have a specific target?
> You know, deep inside, what you need.
> Fix your eyes on Jesus.[7]

Fix your eyes on Jesus! That is the goal of this study.

A lot of people try to fix their eyes on Jesus without taking the time to see who he really is. If you're going to focus your attention on the person of Jesus, you have to come to grips with Jesus' teaching that he is both man and God. This is important because it is at the center of who Jesus is!

Jesus Is Man

Just for a moment, imagine with me that you were in school with Jesus. What would that be like? He would really ruin the curve, wouldn't he? Suppose you were a competitive type, and you were trying to get a better grade than Jesus. Trying to beat him in geography (he made the world and everything in it). Hoping to do better than him in Bible study (he wrote it). How about history? (He watched history unfold.) How about PE? Did Jesus have a 200 mph fastball?

This brings up a question. Was Jesus some kind of a "superman" with man-of-steel kind of strength? No, he was a real human. When he hit his thumb with a hammer in his father's carpenter shop, it hurt him just as much as it would hurt you. (Although he probably said something entirely different than what you say!) Jesus was fully God, and he was also fully man.

How do we know that Jesus is man?

1. He had a human <u>BIRTH</u> (Isa. 7:14–16; Matt. 1:23; Gal. 4:4).

    (A virgin birth)

    Jesus came into this world the same way every one of us did: he was born as a baby. When you think about how vulnerable, how dependent, a baby is, you get a deeper look at the incredible humility that Jesus had to have to choose to be born as a human.

2. He showed human <u>GROWTH</u> (Luke 2:52).

    Notice the four human ways that Jesus grew:

    "In wisdom and stature, and in favor with God and man." Jesus grew:

    *   <u>INTELLECTUALLY</u>
    *   <u>PHYSICALLY</u>
    *   <u>SPIRITUALLY</u>
    *   <u>SOCIALLY</u>

    Jesus wasn't born with some superhuman baby brain, full of knowledge from the beginning. He had to learn just as we have to learn. He had to memorize the Old Testament that he wrote. He had to learn about the creation that he made. Jesus was perfect, but don't let that cause you to miss the fact that as he grew . . .

3. He experienced human <u>EMOTIONS</u>.

    This is why I hate most movies and television shows that show the life of Jesus. They take all of the emotion out of him. Jesus just wanders through life in some kind of mystical daze. *Not true!* Jesus was filled with emotion, filled with life!

    Jesus felt:

    *   **Grief (John 11:35)**

        Jesus grew up in a Jewish culture that knew how to show emotion. When the Jews wept, it wasn't a little tear trickling down the cheek. They wept openly. They wailed loudly. They even tore their outer clothes into shreds to express their grief.

    *   **Sorrow (Matt. 26:38)**
    *   **Amazement (Matt. 8:10)**
    *   **Love (for an unbeliever: Mark 10:21; for his friends: John 11:5; for his disciples: John 13:1; for his mother: John 19:26–27)**

- **Wonder (Mark 6:6)**
- **Distress (Mark 14:33)**
- **Compassion (Mark 1:41)**
- **Anger (Mark 3:5)**

  Anger is an emotion, not a sin. What we do with our anger is often sinful, but it doesn't have to be. Jesus was angry, but he never sinned.

4. **He had human <u>EXPERIENCES</u> and <u>NEEDS</u>.**

- **He was tired (John 4:6; Mark 4:38).**

  Imagine spending day after day with crowds, serving and teaching and healing and listening. He got tired.

- **He was hungry (Matt. 4:2).**
- **He was thirsty (John 19:28).**
- **He was in agony (Luke 22:44).**
- **He was tempted (Matt. 4:1–11).**

  He didn't fall to that temptation—but he was tempted.

- **He died (Luke 23:46).**

  Jesus went through the most human of all experiences—physical death.

Why did he do it? Why did Jesus leave the perfection of heaven to become a man? Because of his love for you!

A Fresh Word

Incarnation

The word *incarnation* is from the Latin for "in the flesh." When Jesus was born in Bethlehem, it was the incarnation of God into this world. God came to us in human flesh.

Discussion questions 5 and 6 can be used here.

Jesus Is Fully God and Fully Man

The council of Chalcedon was a group called together in 451 A.D. to deal with false teaching in that day as to the nature of Jesus. Look at their famous affirmation of the truth that Jesus is fully God and fully man.

Jesus exists "in two natures which exist without confusion, without change, without division, without separation, the difference of the natures having been in no wise taken away by reason of the union, but rather the properties of each being preserved, and both concurring into one person."

Wow! What does all that mean?

- Jesus became 100 percent God and 100 percent man 100 percent of the time (that's not good math, but it's excellent theology).

- Jesus was not God indwelling a man. He was not a man who became God. He was not God appearing to be a man. He combined in one personality the two natures: he was fully God and he was fully man.

- Jesus is perfect humanity wrapped around undiminished deity.

A Fresh Word

Hypostatic Union

The union of undiminished deity and perfect humanity forever in one person. That means that Jesus not only became God and man but that he will always be God and man.

1. Jesus always has been God (John 1:2).
2. Jesus became man while continuing to be God (John 1:14).
3. Jesus continues to exist as God and man (Acts 1:9–11).

The truth that Jesus is both God and man is so deep that it can easily become muddy.

It's easy to make the mistake of thinking that Jesus is somehow a "mixture" of man and God. Jesus being man does not diminish in any way the fact that he is God, and his being God does not take away in the least from the fact that he is fully man. Jesus is not separately God and man; he is fully both man and God.

Wait a minute. Didn't the fact that Jesus took on a human body make him somehow less than God? God is able to be everywhere at once, but Jesus, while he was on earth, was only able to be in one place at one time. While he was in this world, Jesus made a choice. Let me explain it this way:

Jesus limited himself—he became fully man.

But . . .

Jesus did not lessen himself—he remained fully God.

He limited himself but he did not lessen himself. Let's take a few minutes to look at that a little more closely.

Jesus limited himself.

After a Bible study about Jesus praying, a fourth-grade boy asked, "You talked about Jesus being God on this earth, but he prayed. Isn't that like Jesus was talking to himself, since he is God?" Wow, this young guy was a thinker! The truth of the incarnation is that Jesus, when he came to earth, *decided* to limit himself in certain ways.

- **By taking the form of a man (Phil. 2:6–8)**

- **By limiting his presence to one place and one time**

- **By taking a position in which the Father was "greater" (John 14:28)**

- **By limiting his understanding (Matt. 24:36)**

Jesus did not become any less God by deciding to limit himself. As he walked this earth, he still possessed the attributes of God's omniscience, omnipresence, and omnipotence. In fact, there are times when we see his omniscience, his ability as God to know everything, even as he lived as a man. For instance, Mark 2:8 says, "Immediately Jesus knew in his spirit that this was what they were thinking in their hearts, and he said to them, 'Why are you thinking these things?'" He could have exercised any of these attributes at any time, but he had decided to limit himself.

The idea of Jesus being limited and yet also being God is difficult to understand. This is one of those times when it's good to realize that God is so much greater than we are that some of the truths about him are difficult for us to grasp.

There is one word that best describes Jesus' decision to limit himself, and that is *love.* Have you ever limited yourself because of love? You probably have. Parents, have you ever limited yourself because of love? Sure you have. You'd love to be driving a convertible, but you're in a minivan. You limited yourself! You'd love to be at a nice restaurant for dinner, but you're at McDonald's. You limited yourself. So in some small way we can understand Jesus' decision to limit himself when he came to this earth to meet our needs.

Jesus did not lessen himself.

- He was still fully God even as he walked this earth.

- The decision to be born a man, to walk this earth, and to die on a cross was made by him as a part of the Trinity.

  Even while on earth, he limited himself by choice: He could have turned the stones to bread when Satan tempted him (Luke 4:3). He could have called 10,000 angels to save him from the cross (Matt. 26:53), but he chose not to.

I don't want us to leave this subject without seeing what God wants us to learn from the choice that Jesus made to limit himself and become a man.

Key Personal Perspective

Philippians 2:5–11 is one of the most exciting passages in the Bible about Jesus' willingness to become a man. As you read it, note that it says at the beginning, "Your attitude should be the same as that of Christ Jesus." What is Paul talking about? What attitude is revealed in Jesus' willingness to become a man?

Verses 3–4 share several specifics concerning this attitude:
- Do nothing out of selfish ambition.
- Don't act out of vain conceit.
- Consider others better than yourself.
- Don't just look out for yourself.
- Look out for the interests of others.

The attitude is <u>HUMILITY</u>.

The cross says something which may well astound us. It is this: God is humble. It cost God far more to redeem our world than to create it. God carries the whole universe on His shoulders with ease, but when He carried the cross to Calvary He staggered and fell! God can carry Orion and the Pleiades and the whole Milky Way in the fingers of one hand, but when He carried the burden of humanity's sin and guilt He sweat drops of blood; for (remember!) the heavenly Father suffered in all the sufferings of His incarnate son.[8]

Philip Yancey writes:

> In a memoir of the years before World War II, Pierre Van Paassen tells of an act of humiliation by Nazi storm troopers who had seized an elderly Jewish rabbi and dragged him to headquarters. In the far end of the same room, two colleagues were beating another Jew to death, but the captors of the rabbi decided to have some fun with him. They stripped him naked and commanded that he preach the sermon he had prepared for the coming Sabbath in the synagogue. The rabbi asked if he could wear his yarmulke, and the Nazis, grinning, agreed. It added to the joke. The trembling rabbi proceeded to deliver in a raspy voice his sermon on what it means to walk humbly before God, all the while being poked and prodded by the hooting Nazis, and all the while hearing the last cries of his neighbor at the end of the room.
>
> When I read the gospel accounts of the imprisonment, torture, and execution of Jesus, I think of that naked rabbi standing humiliated in a police station. Even after watching scores of movies on the subject, and reading the Gospels over and over, I still cannot fathom the indignity, the *shame* endured by God's Son on earth, stripped naked, flogged, spat on, struck in the face, garlanded with thorns.[9]

Jesus humbled himself and became a man, a man who was willing to suffer the public ridicule of a death on the cross. He did it to save us, but he also did it to give us an example of how we're to treat each other. He was willing to do this for me, and I can learn from his example and draw upon his power to humble myself for others: for my spouse, for my coworkers, for my kids, for my friends.

Where do you and I even begin to get the strength to act like Jesus acted, to live like Jesus lived? We draw it from who he is—from the fact that he is fully man and fully God.

As fully man, Jesus shows us that he <u>UNDERSTANDS</u> our needs.

25

As fully God, Jesus shows us that he can <u>MEET</u> our needs.

To receive strength from Jesus I need to know that he understands my needs! It helps to know that there is at least one other person who completely understands what I am going through. (By the way, Jesus obviously understood all of our needs even before he came to this earth. As God, he knew everything. But coming to this earth *showed us* how deeply he understands.)

But understanding is not enough. We also need someone who can do something about our needs. Jesus did not come to this earth just to give us a pat on the back and say, "I can sympathize with what you're going through." He came to show us that he has the power to make a difference in our everyday lives, with our everyday needs.

That's who he is, fully man and fully God. This is the foundation of everything we believe. If you leave out this foundation, that Jesus Christ is God and Jesus Christ is man, everything else crumbles.

The cross? It doesn't mean anything because there is no power there to make a difference.

The Day of Pentecost? It was just a show.

All of those books we have in the New Testament? Every one of them is a lie.

If this truth isn't true, then everything else comes crashing down—from Bethlehem to Calvary to Pentecost to today.

But it does not come crashing down. This truth is the truth upon which all of human history rests. Jesus Christ—God in human flesh—came into this world. Jesus lived for us. Jesus died for us. Jesus was resurrected for us. You can stake your life on it!

Discussion question 7 can be used here.

Finish memorizing memory card 3, "The Truth about Jesus."

Discussion Questions

1. **How have your friendships with other believers helped you to see God's love in new and fresh ways?**

2. **Share your experiences from this last week of acting on the truth that Jesus is our best friend. In what ways did you sense the closeness and friendship of Jesus as a part of your daily life? Where were you frustrated, left wishing you would have remembered how close Jesus is? (Don't be afraid to share your frustrations; it will be an encouragement to others who faced the same feelings this last week.)**

3. **Which of the three evidences for Jesus being God is the strongest for you? Why do you think this evidence is the most important for you?**

   Small Group Leaders: Remind your group that there is no one right answer here. This is an opportunity for them to say which of these evidences most clearly encourages their faith.

4. **Even with this evidence, many people still struggle to believe. What's the difference between physical proof and personal faith? Is faith something that we should have without any proof at all? Is proof a guarantee that we will have faith?**

   Small Group Leaders: Help your group to see that there is no amount of proof that can make faith happen in our lives. Faith is a matter of trust, not scientific proof. This evidence is the backbone of our faith, but not the heart of our faith! Evidence may encourage me in the faith that I have or challenge me to take a look at the need to have faith in God, but it can never *produce* faith. Faith comes about in our lives as a gift of God's grace. It is a decision of the *will,* not of the *intellect.* On the other hand, our faith is not empty of evidence. God does not ask us to lose our minds when we put faith in him. The difference between the Christian faith and the faith that some cult leader asks for is that Christianity has tangible proofs as a foundation for our commitment of faith.

5. **Which is harder for you to see as real: the fact that Jesus is completely God or the fact that Jesus is completely man?**

   Generally, unbelievers have a harder time seeing Jesus as being God, and believers have a difficult time seeing the human side of Jesus.

6. We know that Jesus can identify with our struggles and weaknesses because of the fact that he became a person. Right now, what are one or two areas where you are glad he is able to identify with you?

Tiredness Temptations Emotions Disappointment

Betrayal Relationships Stress Other: _____

7. The life of Jesus was all about serving others. Those who get close to him end up being more and more like him, wanting to serve others. Who needs your service in Jesus' name this next week? It doesn't have to be something big or noticeable.

In Matthew 10:42 Jesus says, "And if anyone gives even a cup of cold water to one of these little ones because he is my disciple, I tell you the truth, he will certainly not lose his reward."

This week, look for ways to do seemingly little acts of ministry in Jesus' name. You don't have to *tell* the people you're serving that you're doing it in Jesus' name. "I'm unselfishly bringing you this cup of coffee in the name of my Lord and Savior Jesus Christ!" Not that way! Just do it without calling attention to yourself.

For Further Study

Edersheim, Alfred. *The Life and Times of Jesus the Messiah.* McLean, Va.: MacDonald, n.d.

Elwell, Walter, ed. *Topical Analysis of the Bible.* Grand Rapids, Mich.: Baker, 1991.

Little, Paul. *Know What You Believe.* Wheaton, Ill.: Victor, 1987.

Lucado, Max. *God Came Near.* Portland, Ore.: Multnomah Press, 1987.

McDowell, Josh. *The New Evidence That Demands a Verdict.* Nashville: Nelson Reference, 1999.

Rhodes, Ron. *The Heart of Christianity.* Eugene, Ore.: Harvest House, 1996.

Strobel, Lee. *The Case for Christ.* Grand Rapids, Mich.: Zondervan, 1998.

Yancey, Philip. *The Jesus I Never Knew.* Grand Rapids, Mich.: Zondervan, 1995.

The Holy Spirit
Part 1

Life Change Objectives

- To experience a new sense of security in your relationship with God based on the presence of his Spirit in your life.

- To see with eyes of faith how the Holy Spirit is at work in your life.

Summary Teaching Outline

Historical Background

What Is the Role of the Holy Spirit Today?

The Holy Spirit regenerates me.

The Holy Spirit baptizes me.

1. The baptism of the Holy Spirit places the Christian into the body of Christ and into Christ himself.

2. The baptism of the Holy Spirit is a one-time event occurring at the moment of salvation.

3. The baptism of the Holy Spirit is a universal experience for believers.

The Holy Spirit indwells me.

The Holy Spirit seals me.

The Holy Spirit is the deposit of God's promise.

Close your eyes for a moment and picture some things for me. When I say "God the Father," what do you picture? Hopefully not a rocking chair. He's not the old man in heaven you sometimes see pictured. For many, God is seen as a picture of glorious light. How about Jesus the Son? That's easy. We've seen depictions of Jesus in paintings and in the movies. But what if I asked you to picture the Holy Spirit? What comes to mind? The Bible gives us some descriptions, but they are difficult to visualize. In John 3, Jesus says the Holy Spirit is like the wind. I can picture what the wind does, but it is difficult to picture "the wind." It is an unseen force. Jesus is saying to us that the Spirit is the unseen person of God at work in our lives. He's not visible, but he's real and he's powerful.

To most of us, the Holy Spirit seems mysterious. We can't fit him into a human form. The symbols used to represent him in Scripture (oil, fire, wind, dove) don't help much. The Bible teaches us that the Holy Spirit, like God the Father and God the Son, is to be worshiped, loved, and obeyed. We can get to know him personally.

The Holy Spirit tends to be a neglected member of the Trinity. Many people think of the Holy Spirit as an impersonal force. In this study, I want to introduce you to a *person*, the Holy Spirit.

When I say Father or Son, it's natural to picture them as persons—every father and son we've ever met are persons. But when you hear "spirit," you don't think *person;* you think of something more like Casper the Friendly Ghost. And yet you have a spirit, and you're a person. In fact, your spirit is the most important part of who you are!

Close your eyes once again for just a moment. This time picture yourself, but see a different you than you are now. You are growing in your faith like never before, even through some tough times. You have a deep and unshakable sense of God's love for you at the core of your being. If someone asked you to describe the experience of your everyday life, one of the words you would use would be "joy." You would say, "I know I'm far from perfect, but much of the time I'm living the life that God wants me to live."

Now you are picturing the Holy Spirit, seeing in your mind's eye the personal impact that he can make on your everyday life.

As we begin our look at the Holy Spirit, let's remind ourselves of the truth of God's Trinity that we studied a few weeks ago.

Review of truths about God:
1. **God relates to us as a Trinity, three persons in one being.**
2. **God is one, he is not three gods, but one God (Deut. 6:4).**
3. **The Father is God, the Son is God, and the Spirit is God.**
4. **The three are distinct from one another, separate but one.**

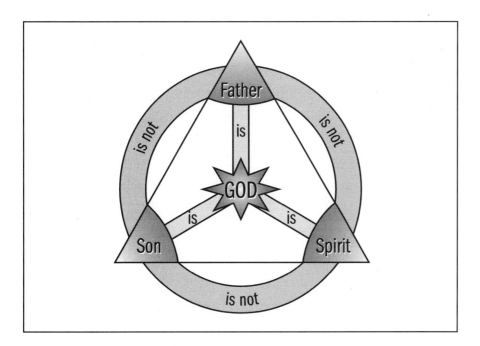

We're talking about God as we talk about the Spirit. We're not talking about a part of God or how God acts or feels. We're talking about God himself.

A bit of historical background will help you understand what the Bible teaches about the work of God's Spirit in your life.

Historical Background

In the Old Testament the Holy Spirit came upon people at <u>VARIOUS</u> times for <u>SPECIFIC</u> purposes. He never indwelt anyone <u>PERMANENTLY</u>.

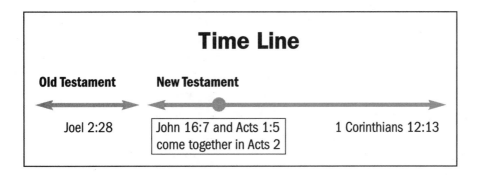

Look at this time line. It's a simple expression of the spiritual earthquake that changed everything when Jesus came.

Before Jesus came to earth, in the Old Testament the Holy Spirit was present in the world, but he did not permanently indwell the lives of believers. He came upon believers at certain times for certain tasks.

But God had something different in mind. In the Old Testament there is the promise of something new that God was preparing to do. Joel expressed it in the words of the Lord that came to him, saying God would "pour out" his Spirit on his people (Joel 2:28).

Jesus himself pointed back to this promise when he told his disciples, in John 16:7, "He [the Spirit] will come because I will send him to you" (NLT).

Take a close look at Acts 1:5 and 1 Corinthians 12:13. In Acts Jesus promises that we "will be" baptized with the Holy Spirit. In Corinthians, Paul tells the believers that they "were all baptized" by the Spirit. What happened between Acts 1 and 1 Corinthians 12? Acts chapter 2! In Acts 2 God's Spirit comes to indwell all believers, and at that moment everything changed! In one of the most important events in human history, God's Spirit came to permanently live in believers. The unique significance of this event is seen in the fact that God sent a rushing wind and tongues of fire to mark this moment. I guess you could say God makes his own fireworks! Seven weeks after the resurrection of Jesus, the sound of a mighty rushing wind burst into the Upper Room where the 120 believers were gathered. Flames of fire seemed to be coming out of the top of each of their heads. When they went out into the streets they found themselves able to communicate in the languages of the people who were in Jerusalem from all over the world to celebrate the Jewish holiday of Pentecost. God was making sure that no one would ever forget that day!

Teaching Tip

It's always a challenge to tell history with excitement. You likely remember the teacher who could make the most crucial moment in history sound like a monotone reading of the phone book. Tell the history above with excitement! The only way to do that is for you to be personally enthusiastic about what you are saying. Tell this as if you were telling the story of catching a record-breaking home-run ball. The truth is, the story of what happened on the day of Pentecost is much more exciting than that. It is a truth that will impact you for the rest of your life and into eternity.

Excitement is expressed by our body language as much as by the words we say. Studies show that about half of what we communicate is in our body language. Here are a few things you can do:

Step out from behind the lectern or pulpit.

Step toward the audience.

Stand on the balls of your feet, with a sense of anticipation.

Use larger arm motions. Don't flail your arms like a windmill, but don't be afraid to talk with your hands. That's what we do when we're excited about something.

Express the excitement you feel about what God has done for us with your *eyes* and with your tone of *voice*. (Tone of voice accounts for 30 to 40 percent of your communication. An excited tone of voice does not have to be loud. It simply needs to have passion.)

Question: Do we have to have an experience just like Acts 2 to be filled and empowered by the Holy Spirit? Of course not! These disciples had a unique experience as the Holy Spirit indwelt believers for the first time on the Day of Pentecost. But the fact that our experience will be different should not limit our expectation that the Holy Spirit will work in our lives.

There are two ways we limit the Spirit today:

First, we say the Spirit "can't do it that way." I have a deeply spiritual answer to that attitude. "Baloney!" He's God and he can do things any way he chooses. (The Spirit obviously is not going to work in a way that is inconsistent with God's character or with God's Word.)

Second, we say he has to do it "this way," matching the experiences of the disciples in the book of Acts. Yet nowhere does the Bible say that. You don't have to speak in tongues to prove you are filled by the Spirit. You don't have to have flames of fire on your head. Or have the power to heal or preach or see three thousand saved.

The important question is, what does the Bible say regarding how the Spirit works in the life of *every* believer? We're going to look at four specific ways God's Spirit works in each of our lives.

Discussion questions 1 and 2 can be used here.

What Is the Role of the Holy Spirit Today?

The Holy Spirit __REGENERATES__ me.

Definition: <u>TO</u> <u>GIVE</u> <u>REBIRTH</u>

The more common term for regenerate is "born again."

The phrase "born again" comes straight out of the Bible. Jesus used it in his talk with Nicodemus in John 3.

> **In reply Jesus declared, "I tell you the truth, no one can see the kingdom of God unless he is born again."**
>
> —John 3:3

Titus 3:5 talks about the new birth that the Spirit gives us.

> **He saved us. It was not because of any good deeds that we ourselves had done, but because of his own mercy that he saved us, through the Holy Spirit, who gives us new birth and new life by washing us.**
>
> —Titus 3:5 (GNT)

Here is the simple truth:

Before I came to Christ, I was <u>SPIRITUALLY</u> <u>DEAD</u>.

Now I am <u>SPIRITUALLY</u> <u>ALIVE</u> through the new birth.

> **What gives life is God's Spirit; human power is of no use at all. The words I have spoken to you bring God's life-giving Spirit.**
>
> —John 6:63 (GNT)

What does it mean to be spiritually dead? Or spiritually alive? Our spirit is the inner part of each of us that connects with and relates to the God who made us.

When Adam and Eve were first created, they were spiritually alive; they had a deep and intimate relationship with God. They walked with God and they talked with God. They were connected with the God who had made them. When they chose to sin, to eat the fruit of the tree that God had told them not to eat, they died spiritually. The results were immediately apparent: they became afraid of God, they hid from God, they knew they were separated from God.

If your car's battery is dead, the car won't start, and you have to put a new battery in before the car will run again. Something inside all of us is dead! (Don't give the person sitting next to you that "yeah, I knew it" look!) You see, as hard as we try, we cannot connect with God as we know we should. The desire is in many of us, but the ability to connect is missing. We're like a person in a car with no battery thinking, "If I turn this key as hard as I can one more time, maybe it will start."

Because of our sin, we are spiritually dead. No battery.

We need more than just a new "part." We need to become new people. So God sends the person of the Holy Spirit into our lives! Through our faith in Christ, God takes those who are spiritually dead, regenerating us through the work of the Holy Spirit, and makes us spiritually alive.

This is often a "hidden" transaction. God does not have to be showy to do something powerful. When the Holy Spirit came into your life and saved you, what happened? Did you tingle all over? Did you get goose bumps? Most don't. You don't all of a sudden get a halo. Jesus tells us that the Spirit is like the wind. Like the wind, you can't see the Spirit, but the Spirit has incredible impact!

We've looked in this section at a short history of the Spirit's work in our world and at the regenerating power of the Holy Spirit. Before we leave this, I want to invite you to take a few moments to cement in your heart how powerfully personal these truths are.

The end result of the historical work of the Holy Spirit is that by our faith in Jesus we have God's Spirit living in us.

The end result of the regenerating work of the Holy Spirit is that, based on your trust in Jesus, you are a new person.

I have friends who've told me, "I know now that the Holy Spirit came into my life when I became a believer, but it was years before anyone *told* me that, years before I discovered that he was there and available for me."

I don't want anyone to leave this study not knowing that the Holy Spirit is in your life. He is the one who made you spiritually alive. And he's available for you to call on.

Split Session Plan: If you're teaching this study over two sessions, end the first session here.

As we move from talking about the regenerating work of the Spirit to the baptizing of the Spirit, let me take just a moment to deal with some feelings that many face concerning this. When you come face to face with the truth that the Holy Spirit has come into your life and made you a brand-new person, one of the thoughts we all have is, "I still look and act like the same old person." We still have the same feelings, struggle with the same wrong thoughts, and feel the same weaknesses. If God is in my life through his Spirit, shouldn't it make a bigger difference?

Good question. Honest question. Those are the kinds of questions that you should be asking because now you're thinking about how the truth fits into your life.

Picture the power of what the Holy Spirit is doing in your life with these words: The Holy Spirit wants to make a Grand Canyon–sized difference in your life! When the powerful waters of the Colorado River first started flowing through the area that is now the Grand Canyon, it would not have been evident to you that anything was happening. There would have been no "wow," no "that's awesome." You would have thought, "It's just a river like all the other rivers." But slowly, imperceptibly, yet certainly and powerfully that river was carving out a Grand Canyon. God *loves* to work that way! It doesn't look like much is happening to the human eye, but he is transforming and changing everything.

The Christian life is a life of faith. By that faith we *know* that there is no more powerful force at work in this world than the work of God's Spirit in our lives. There is no greater power at work in the world today!

In light of that faith, let's talk about the truth of the Spirit's baptism.

The Holy Spirit <u>*BAPTIZES*</u> *me.*

What does it mean for the Holy Spirit to baptize us? How does this happen? When does this happen? And what does it mean?

One theologian writes:

> What is the baptism imparted to us by Christ? Sometimes we hear this spoken of as if He baptized us with something different from Himself, some sort of an influence or feeling or power. The truth is, the Spirit Himself is the baptism.[1]

The person of God comes into our lives through his Spirit.

As simple as that sounds, there is a great deal of talk and even disagreement among Christians on the baptism of the Spirit. The Spirit was sent to give us unity, but we create disunity by arguing about the very work of God's Spirit. If you think about it, that's pretty crazy, isn't it?

Let me take a moment to address this. It's important to understand that we often let our individual experiences become points of argument as to how the Holy Spirit must do things. Let me give you a picture of how this can get us into trouble.

Remember how Jesus healed blind people? With some, he simply touched their eyes and they were healed (Matt. 9:29). He spit on the eyes of others (Mark 8:23). For another Jesus put mud on his eyes and told the man to wash off the mud, and the man was able to see (John 9). I've often wondered what it would be like to get these blind people whom Jesus healed together, ten years later, to talk about how Jesus works in people's lives. One would say, "When Jesus heals of blindness he does it immediately, with just a touch." Another would argue, "My experience is that the way Jesus heals blindness is he spits; he is a spitting God." The man from John 9 would chime in and say, "No, when Jesus heals blindness he always takes mud and puts it on the eyes." I can imagine that last man starting a "Here's mud in your eye" denomination of churches.

God did not baptize us with his Spirit to create a point of contention. In fact, just the opposite. He intends the baptism of the Spirit to be a point of unity and assurance. We miss the point of the New Testament when we allow ourselves to get into arguments about the work of the Spirit and any one person's experience. In fact, when we do that we're playing right into Satan's hands. God sent his Spirit to give us unity and assurance. God does not want us to wonder if his Spirit is in our lives or not. He wrote to *assure* us of the presence of his Spirit in our lives, of the fact that we, as believers, are immersed in his Spirit. That assurance is a vital part of being able to live the Christian life.

Let's focus on that assurance.

1. **The baptism of the Holy Spirit is the placing of the Christian into the <u>BODY</u> <u>OF</u> <u>CHRIST</u> and into <u>CHRIST</u> <u>HIMSELF</u>.**

Let's all read this verse together:

Teaching Tip

Reading a verse together is one of the ways that you can focus the attention of a group. There are two things to remember as you read together:

1. Have people read out of one translation. We've all made the mistake as teachers of asking a group to open their Bibles and read a verse only to hear the muddled sounds of people trying to read in unison out of nine or ten different translations. When reading out of the study guide, everyone will be reading from the same translation.

2. Read slowly. To read in unison you must slow down and pause more often as you read the verse.

One other tip: It's amazing how a little change in your wording can capture people's attention as you invite them to read. Instead of simply saying, "Would you read this verse with me," try instead, "Would you read this verse with great enthusiasm," or "Would you read this verse as if your life depended on it."

For we were all baptized by one Spirit into one body—whether Jews or Greeks, slave or free—and we were all given the one Spirit to drink.
—1 Corinthians 12:13

One Spirit. One body. Being baptized by the Holy Spirit is a clear picture of our unity in the body of Christ—the church. If we could see with spiritual eyes, we would have seen that the moment we became believers we were instantly joined with every other believer around this world as a part of the body of Christ. This means that as a Christian you *never* need to be alone. Even in countries where you don't speak the language and come from an entirely different culture, there is an almost tangible connection when you meet another believer. You feel that instant connection because you are both a part of the body of Christ.

We are now together "in Christ."

There are 150 New Testament references to our being "in Christ" (Eph. 1:13).

God's Spirit puts us "in Christ." You don't have to do anything to put yourself into Christ. The moment you are saved, God himself puts you in Christ through his Spirit. What does it mean to be in Christ? It means that when God looks at you he sees you in light of your faith in his Son.

Let me picture it this way. This piece of paper in my hand represents your life. Obviously the paper is not a clean, white sheet of paper. (None of us is perfect.) It has been crumpled by your selfishness, muddied by your sinful habits, torn by great mistakes, and made ragged by your attempts to be good without God's strength. If I hold this piece of paper up for all to see, it's a pretty sad-looking sight.

I have a Bible in my other hand. This Bible represents Christ. I slip this piece of paper into the Bible and close it. Although the paper is in the Bible, all you see is the Bible. Putting this sheet of paper into the Bible is like God putting you in Christ. When he looks at you now, he sees the glory of his Son because he has put you in his Son. When God looks at you now, does he see this (the crumpled paper)? Or does he see this (the Bible that the paper is in)? He sees you "in Christ."

Teaching Tip

As you teach this, you'll want to use a piece of paper and a Bible as object lessons. Whenever you're going to do an object lesson for the first time, it's a good idea to show this to a few people individually (practice!) before you teach it to the entire group.

2. **The baptism of the Holy Spirit is a <u>ONE-TIME</u> <u>EVENT</u> occurring at the moment of salvation.**

In the next session we'll see that we need to have many fillings of the Spirit, but there is only one baptism of the Spirit in our lives. In 1 Corinthians 12:13 when Paul tells the believers that they "were all baptized," he puts it in the past tense. It is something that has already happened.

Think back to our look at the Trinity of God, the truth that God is one. This is an important truth when we're talking about God baptizing us in his Spirit. God is one. You don't get the Holy Spirit on the installment plan, part now and part later, depending on the life you're living. Being baptized by the Spirit is not the result of "deserving it" because of our actions or "wanting it" with our emotions. Being baptized by the Spirit is a gift of God's grace.

3. **The baptism of the Holy Spirit is a <u>UNIVERSAL</u> <u>EXPERIENCE</u> for believers.**

Circle the times the word "all" appears in these next two verses.

You are all sons of God through faith in Christ Jesus, for all of you who were baptized into Christ have clothed yourselves with Christ.
—Galatians 3:26–27

For we were all baptized . . . we were all given the one Spirit to drink.
—1 Corinthians 12:13

The baptism of the Holy Spirit is a universal gift to believers. Nowhere in the Bible are Christians instructed to desire or seek the baptism of the Holy Spirit. We should not pray for it, seek it, or try to achieve it. We already have it.

Billy Graham writes,

> All believers are baptized with the Holy Spirit. This does not mean, however, that they are filled or controlled by the Spirit. The important thing is the great central truth—when I came to Christ, God gave His Spirit to me.[2]

As believers in Christ, we all have an equal measure of God's Spirit in our lives, and that measure is *all*. There are no second-class citizens in God's kingdom, no haves and have-nots. We can never think, "I have more of God's Spirit in my life than he has," or say to someone, "Let me show you how to get more of God's Spirit in your life, as I have." Instead we are to encourage each other to live out the fullness of the Spirit already in our lives.

What about Christians who are struggling in living out the Christian life? The Corinthians Paul says were all baptized by the Spirit were frankly one of the worst bunch of believers you could find. They were jealous of each other, arguing with each other, accepting sexual immorality in their church. They even were having feasts as part of their Lord's Supper celebrations that led to drunkenness and arguments. And yet Paul writes to them and tells them they're all baptized in God's Spirit! They obviously weren't living by the power of God's Spirit in them. Paul writes to tell them, "Start living out who God has made you to be in Christ and through his Spirit."

The truth is that the Holy Spirit baptized you the moment you believed. Yet many believers don't immediately recognize the truth of the Spirit's presence.

Note: **Much of the confusion over the baptism of the Holy Spirit comes about because of the failure to make a distinction between the baptism of the Holy Spirit and the filling of the Holy Spirit. The baptism of the Holy Spirit is something God does for us in establishing our relationship with Jesus Christ. The filling of the Holy Spirit is the daily experience of our yielding to the Holy Spirit's control. We will discuss the filling of the Holy Spirit in detail in the next session.**

Have you ever felt a deep hunger to have a kind of experience with God through which you would never be the same again? An experience that would leave you in love with the Lord throughout every moment of the day? An experience that would bring you to a place where sin completely lost its attraction for you? Many believers feel this way. They have a deep sense that there must be something more to life as a Christian. They look for a single experience or commitment or step they can take that will get them to that place they long for.

Let me say two things about that desire: First, that experience will not fully be ours until we reach heaven. There are no perfect Christians in this world, just Christians growing toward perfection. That desire in your heart is one of the longings that is in the heart of every true believer. God does grow us while we're on this earth, but it is a slow process. Remember the Grand Canyon.

Second, while we don't become all that we want to be immediately, we do have all of God in us through his Spirit. While the process is slow, the promise is great!

Discussion question 3 can be used here.

The Holy Spirit INDWELLS me.

In the Old Testament, what place (or places) did God "indwell"?

Teaching Tip

Questions can become a barrier to communication rather than a connecting point with those you're teaching. This happens when the group knows you're going to answer the questions, and they "tune out" when the question comes. A simple way to change this is to have them answer a few questions. Just pause for a moment, or say, "What do you think?" You can't do this with every question you ask, but it's amazing how doing this even once during a session changes the way people respond when they hear a question.

Yes, the places where God allowed the Jewish people to experience his presence were the tabernacle and then the temple in Jerusalem. In fact, there was even a specific place in the temple where God's presence dwelt—the inner room of the temple, the Holy of Holies.

The reason that people traveled the dusty roads to Jerusalem so often was to be in this place of God's presence. Because of God's holiness, people could not actually enter this place, but being close to it was good enough for them. In fact, only one person, the High Priest, was allowed to enter this holy place of God's presence, and he was allowed to enter only once a year. After he had made purification for his own sins, he went in to offer a sacrifice for the sins of the people. Before he went in, they tied a rope to him. That way, if he died while in the Holy of Holies they could drag him out. They knew if anyone else went in, even to drag out the High Priest, they would die. That's how holy this place of God's dwelling was.

When Jesus died on the cross, something very significant happened to that Holy of Holies. Do you remember? There was a curtain that separated the rest of the temple from the Holy of Holies. As Jesus was dying on the cross, the sky became black. Then at the moment of his death, the earth shook, rocks split, and many holy people were raised from the dead and walked out of their tombs. But the most significant of these remarkable events was what happened to the curtain. At the moment when Jesus died, that curtain was ripped in two from top to bottom. God was sending the world his change of address. God was saying, "I don't live here anymore." The New Testament teaches us God no longer indwells a temple. He indwells his people (1 Cor. 6:19).

> Do you not know that your body is a temple of the Holy Spirit, who is in you, whom you have received from God?
>
> —1 Corinthians 6:19

The Holy Spirit came to live in our lives!

Now he indwells us! This experience of God's presence is now the everyday experience of every believer! That's something we should never get used to, that we should always be amazed by.

Sometimes I become too familiar with this truth. I go through an entire day or even days without thinking about the presence of God living in my life through his Spirit. In the next session we're going to talk about how to have a more constant sense of awareness of God's Spirit in our lives.

> Discussion question 4 can be used here.

The Holy Spirit SEALS me.

> And you also were included in Christ when you heard the word of truth, the gospel of your salvation. Having believed, you were marked in him with a seal, the promised Holy Spirit.
>
> —Ephesians 1:13

On some envelopes, even today, you'll see a decorative wax seal on the back. In the days that the Bible was written, the seal was not just a decoration, it was more like a padlock. If anyone opened the letter before it reached its destination, it would be obvious that the seal had been broken.

Just like the envelope of old, God's Spirit has sealed you until you reach the destination of eternity with him.

What exactly does that mean?

Sealing implies OWNERSHIP and PROTECTION.

Each person's seal had a design on it that was their mark; it was unique to them. It was a kind of notary stamp of that day. A seal on a document was a guarantee that it had not been forged. God decided to mark our lives with the seal of his own Spirit. Nothing can be more personal or more powerful.

The seal of the Spirit proclaims to us that we are not our own anymore. We have been bought with a price. God owns us now. You may be one of those who feel you don't have much of a heritage, that you don't really fit in anywhere. You are wrong! You're part of God's family.

Sealing also stands for God's protection. The envelope seal protected the document from being opened or tampered with during its journey.

God has put his spiritual protection over our lives; he has put his Spirit into our lives. He's there to say "I'm with you" in every circumstance that we face through the journey of life.

Discussion question 5 can be used here.

The Holy Spirit is THE DEPOSIT OF GOD'S PROMISE.

Read with me Ephesians 1:14 and 2 Corinthians 5:5:

. . . who is a deposit guaranteeing our inheritance until the redemption of those who are God's possession—to the praise of his glory.
—Ephesians 1:14

Now it is God who has made us for this very purpose and has given us the Spirit as a deposit, guaranteeing what is to come.
—2 Corinthians 5:5

In terms that we use, the Bible is saying that the Holy Spirit is God's "down payment" in our lives.

God is saying, "I have this great promise of heaven for you, and I want to let you know that I'm not going to let you down on that promise. And so, in order to let you know that the promise is real, I want to give you something now, a deposit guaranteeing what is to come." What did he give us? He gave us himself!

The depth of God's commitment to us in this promise is almost beyond belief. A deposit is something given as a pledge for a promise, earnest money guaranteeing that you will keep your promise. When the Bible was written, this deposit was taken very seriously. If the promise was not kept, the earnest money paid was lost. If you put down a deposit on land and then backed out of the deal, you would lose your deposit. If you gave an engagement ring as a pledge of your intention to marry someone and then broke the engagement, you would lose the ring.

God has guaranteed our eternal salvation with no less than his very self! Obviously that is a deposit that God cannot lose! That's how deeply he assures us that he will not take his Spirit from us. The Bible tells us in 2 Timothy 2:13:

If we are faithless, he will remain faithful, for he cannot disown himself.
—2 Timothy 2:13

God put up *himself* as the pledge—as the down payment—on our eternal life with him. He guarantees our salvation with his own existence. That's how deeply he's committed himself to us as believers. He has put his own Spirit into our lives!

How does this guarantee and promise make you feel? Do you think, "Wow, since my salvation is guaranteed in such a powerful way by such a loving God, I think I'll just live for myself until I get to heaven." Of course not. When you understand the truth of God's indwelling Spirit, there is an overwhelming sense of gratitude and joy. The more you understand the work of God's Spirit in your life, the less you live for yourself. You no longer have to serve God to earn credits. Instead you serve him to give praise.

Let's make this personal as we close.

Key Personal Perspective

1. You may have realized that you have never been born again; you have never experienced the regeneration of the Holy Spirit. Come to God, repent of living life to please yourself, and ask him to give you a new birth and eternal life with him.

2. You may have been confused about the baptism of the Holy Spirit. You've prayed and sought another experience with God that would change you forever. Now you see that the miraculous has already happened to you. Thank God for putting you in Christ where you belong with all in God's family. Thank him that his work is so powerful and complete that you never have to repeat it. Thank God that because you are in Christ, he now sees you covered by Jesus' righteousness. You are pure, spotless, and holy before him.

3. Thank God that his promises are faithful and that his pledge to keep you forever is true. Thank the Holy Spirit for sealing you so that you are safe from losing your salvation. Spend a few moments thinking of the time when you will receive all that has been promised to you; when God's engagement ring becomes a wedding ring, and you will sit with him at the Marriage Supper of the Lamb in heaven.

Discussion question 6 can be used here.

Begin working on memory card 4, "The Truth about the Holy Spirit."

Appendix

The Holy Spirit began a new work on the Day of Pentecost that has continued up to the present. Before Jesus' resurrection and ascension into heaven, the Holy Spirit came upon people from time to time, but he never actually indwelt or lived inside of a person.

The prophet Joel prophesied that one day God would "pour out [his] Spirit on all people" (Joel 2:28). Jesus promised his disciples that he would send his Spirit to them after he went back to be with the Father.

> But I tell you the truth: It is for your good that I am going away. Unless I go away, the Counselor will not come to you; but if I go, I will send him to you.
>
> —John 16:7

Ten days after Jesus ascended to heaven, 120 believers were gathered in an upper room to wait and pray. Suddenly there came the sound of a rushing wind that filled the place, and separate tongues of fire came to rest on each of the believers. All of them were filled with the Holy Spirit and began to speak in other languages as the Spirit enabled them (Acts 2:1–4).

A little later in the day, as Peter was explaining what had happened to a much larger crowd, he referred to the gift as the "gift of the Holy Spirit." He urged his audience to repent and be baptized and receive the Holy Spirit (Acts 2:38). Peter's understanding of the prophecy of Joel was twofold: not only was salvation promised to those the Lord calls but they also were to receive the gift of the baptism of the Spirit. Three thousand people responded that day and were baptized with water (Acts 2:41).

The three thousand do not seem to have experienced the same miraculous phenomena (rushing wind, tongues of flame, or speaking in other tongues) as the 120 in the Upper Room. What was the difference? The 120 were already believers and received the baptism of the Spirit months or years after they started following Jesus. The three thousand were unbelievers who received the forgiveness of their sins and the gift of the Spirit simultaneously. This distinction is of great importance because the norm for Christian experience today is that of the three thousand, not the 120. The fact that the experience of the 120 was in two distinct stages was simply due to historical circumstances—they could not have received the Pentecostal gift before Pentecost. But on and after the Day of Pentecost, forgiveness of sins and the gift (i.e., baptism) of the Spirit were received together.

Two other "exceptions" that confuse Christians are the accounts found in Acts 8 and Acts 19.

In Acts 8:5–17, Philip preached in Samaria and many believed and were baptized. But what is unusual is that when the apostles at Jerusalem heard about it, they sent Peter and John to verify the experience. One reason is because these believers were Samaritans and at that time Jews had "no dealings with Samaritans" (John 4:9). Their rivalry had lasted for centuries and might have continued, causing great division in the church. Possibly God withheld the gift of his Spirit from the Samaritan believers until two of the leading apostles investigated and, by the laying on of their hands, acknowledged and confirmed the genuineness of the Samaritans' conversion. Neither a two-stage experience nor the laying on of hands is the norm for receiving the Spirit today.

In Acts 19:1–7, the twelve men Paul met do not seem to be Christians. They were called "disciples," but the story reveals they were actually disciples of John the Baptist. Paul asks if they received the Holy Spirit when they believed, indicating that at first he thought they were believers. But they had never heard of the Holy Spirit and that the "One who is to come" was Jesus. Paul not only laid hands on them but first had to baptize them into the name of the Lord Jesus. Can anyone who has never heard of the Holy Spirit, nor been baptized into Christ, nor even apparently believed in him be called a Christian? No. These disciples of John certainly cannot be considered typical of the average Christian today.

We don't get God on an installment plan. God is not three Gods; he is one. You get Jesus when you get God, when you get the Holy Spirit. You don't receive them one at a time. They are three in one; they come together.

The point of the three "comings" of the Holy Spirit in the book of Acts is that God wanted to show that Jews, Samaritans (who had mixed Jewish and Gentile heritage), and Gentiles all had a place in his body. Christianity was not just a Jewish religion. It confirms the truth of Acts 1:8 that the Gospel would go to Jerusalem and Judea, to Samaria, and to the uttermost parts of the earth.

Discussion Questions

1. It's easy to focus in our Christian growth on how far we have to go rather than on how far we have come. Share with others in your group one or two examples of God's work in your life.

2. Why do you think we fall into thinking of the Holy Spirit as an impersonal (rather than a personal) and even sometimes as a "lesser" part of the Trinity?

3. Look again at John 3:1–16. Why do you think it was so difficult for a religious man like Nicodemus to understand spiritual rebirth? Do Jesus' words to him help you to better grasp what it means to be born of the Spirit?

   Small Group Leaders: Sometimes our religion keeps us from seeing what is truly spiritual. Someone has called religion "man's attempt to reach to God." When our relationship with God is shielded by man-made rules and traditions, it makes it difficult to see what the Spirit is doing. Jesus encouraged Nicodemus to return to the simple truths, beginning with birth.

4. The word *baptized* literally means "totally immersed." What does it mean for you to be totally immersed in the Spirit of God? Does it affect your perspective on other believers when you realize that we're all totally immersed in the Spirit of God?

5. The sealing of the Holy Spirit is a tremendous source of security in our lives as believers. What is one of the areas of your life where you regularly need to draw on that security account?

   Small Group Leaders: The people in your group may talk about needing security in parenting or in their job or in witnessing or in facing up to a fear. Help them to remember that we don't earn God's love by what we do. We do what we do as a response to the great love and security that God has already given to us.

6. Second Corinthians 3:3 reminds us:

   You show that you are a letter from Christ, . . . written not with ink but with the Spirit of the living God, not on tablets of stone but on tablets of human hearts.

   —2 Corinthians 3:3

   How do you see God "writing on the hearts" of those who are in your group? Take some time to make this a personal expression of encouragement.

Go around the circle in your group and share with each person, one at a time, "This is one way I see God's Spirit in your life." At least two or three should share with each person. This may feel a little uncomfortable at first, but if we cheer someone for hitting a home run or applaud their getting a promotion at work, how much more important is it to recognize God's work in the lives of others.

The Holy Spirit
Part 2

Life Change Objectives

- To gain a clear understanding of the difference between the baptism of the Holy Spirit and the filling of the Holy Spirit.

- To immediately begin to recognize and live out the truth that you are filled with God's Spirit.

Summary Teaching Outline

Our Need for the Filling of the Holy Spirit

The Bible says that everyone is in one of three spiritual positions:

 The natural man

 The spiritual man

 The carnal man

What Is the Filling of the Holy Spirit?

 Four truths from Ephesians 5:18–21

 Signs of the filling of the Holy Spirit

How Can I Be Filled with the Holy Spirit?

1. Recognize your thirst for filling and desire it.

2. Repent of your sins and receive God's cleansing.

3. Yield all of yourself to the Holy Spirit's control.

4. Trust God to fill you as he said he would.

It's what's on the "inside" that counts.

A car is meant to be filled with gasoline. You could fill it with water (a lot cheaper!), but then the car would not do what it's meant to do.

A swimming pool is meant to be filled with water. If you filled it with sand, it just wouldn't be as refreshing an experience.

If I filled this expensive glass vase with old weeds, we'd all see that as a waste.

One of the pictures in the Bible of you and me is that we're containers. We are meant to be filled with something.

With what do *you* fill your life? There are a lot of choices you can make. You can easily fill your life with work, with hobbies, with family, with church activities, with recreation, or with a thousand other things. As important as some of these are, you can have a full schedule but still have an empty life. The items on our calendar cannot truly fill our lives. We are made to be filled with God's presence.

Chuck Swindoll gives us this picture:

> What fuel is to a car, the Holy Spirit is to the believer. He energizes us to stay the course. He motivates us in spite of obstacles. He keeps us going when the road gets rough. It is the Spirit who comforts us in our distress, who calms us in times of calamity, who becomes our companion in loneliness and grief, who spurs our "intuition" into action, who fills our minds with discernment when we are uneasy about a certain decision. He is, in short, our spiritual fuel.[1]

Before we begin our look at the filling of the Spirit, a quick reminder of what we talked about in the last session.

Review

Before Jesus' resurrection and ascension into heaven, the Holy Spirit would come upon certain individuals at special times for a special reason. He never lived inside of a person permanently. But the Old Testament prophecy of Joel 2:28 was fulfilled on the Day of Pentecost when the Holy Spirit was poured out on believers in Jesus Christ. Since that time, all Christians have been baptized with the Holy Spirit at the moment of salvation.

We looked at four aspects of the Holy Spirit's work in us: regeneration, baptism, indwelling, and sealing.

1. Regeneration means "new birth." When I came to Christ I was given a new birth; I was born again.

2. The baptism of the Holy Spirit is:

   a. God placing me into the body of Christ (the church) and into Christ himself.

   b. A once-for-all-time event which happens at the moment of salvation.

   c. A universal experience for believers (1 Cor. 12:13).

   d. Receiving all of God at one time; I don't receive God one day, Jesus later, and the Holy Spirit at another time. God is a Trinity — three in one.

3. The indwelling of the Spirit means that God comes to personally live in me.

4. To be sealed by the Holy Spirit means that God places his mark of ownership and protection on my life.

5. As a deposit, God's Holy Spirit also guarantees that all that has been promised to me by God will be mine one day.

In this study we'll look together at the filling of the Holy Spirit.

Our Need for the Filling of the Holy Spirit

Let me ask you an important question as we begin. Was there ever a time when you were closer to God than you are right now?

If so, do you remember what that was like? What happened to change that closeness? If not, what is it that has brought the closeness to God that you are experiencing right now?

The sad truth is, many Christians have their past and their future taken care of—their sins are forgiven and they have a home in heaven—but right now their lives are characterized by:

- Up and down experiences (going from spiritual high to spiritual low)
- Weak prayer life (you never pray or never see answers to your prayers)
- Inconsistent Bible study
- A feeling that church is a duty
- A fear of telling others you are a believer
- No real joy or peace
- Going through the motions; faking it a lot. You act Christian and sing Christian and smile Christian, but the feeling in your heart is that it really makes no difference in your life that you are a Christian.
- Bad attitudes—critical, jealous, proud, bitter
- Constant doubt of God and his goodness
- Repeated defeat over the same sins

If I've just described you, it may be, quite frankly, because you are not yet a Christian. You may be trying to *work* your way to heaven by doing good or to *make* your way into heaven by attending church or to *fake* your way into heaven by doing what other Christians do. None of those work. You need the forgiveness and life that only Jesus can give you!

On the other hand, I know many people who are true believers who have these feelings. They have given their lives to Christ, trusting him for forgiveness and believing that he is the Lord they desire to follow.

These feelings are like a big red warning light on the dashboard. It's flashing faster and faster, brighter and brighter, telling you that something is terribly wrong with your Christian life. Don't ignore the warning light! If it had words on it, this warning light would read, "Warning: Trying to live life on your own power."

The Bible says that everyone is in one of three spiritual positions:[2]

The <u>NATURAL</u> man

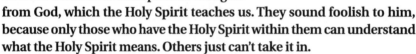

As for you, you were dead in your transgressions and sins, in which you used to live when you followed the ways of this world and of the ruler of the kingdom of the air, the spirit who is now at work in those who are disobedient.
—Ephesians 2:1–2

But the man who isn't a Christian can't understand and can't accept these thoughts from God, which the Holy Spirit teaches us. They sound foolish to him, because only those who have the Holy Spirit within them can understand what the Holy Spirit means. Others just can't take it in.
—1 Corinthians 2:14 (LB)

Have you ever tried to explain a truth from the Bible to an unbeliever only to have the feeling that you were on two totally different spiritual wavelengths? You were! Ephesians 2:1–2 reminds us that *all* of us were by "nature" separate from God at one time. First Corinthians 2:14 tells us that without God's Spirit, we just can't understand God.

Bill Bright, founder of Campus Crusade for Christ, has been used greatly to help believers understand the Spirit-filled life. These circle illustrations he developed have helped millions to understand the difference between these three spiritual conditions.[3] With the natural man, the "S" stands for "self" on the throne of your life. You're calling the shots. The cross is outside of your life because you haven't invited Jesus in. The dots represent the different activities and areas of your life, which are out of control. They couldn't be any other way because we aren't meant to live life on our own power or wisdom. It's amazing how, without God in their lives, even those with the greatest successes have this out-of-control and empty feeling.

The *SPIRITUAL* man

But the spiritual man has insight into everything, and that bothers and baffles the man of the world, who can't understand him at all.

—1 Corinthians 2:15 (LB)

The mind of sinful man is death, but the mind controlled by the Spirit is life and peace.

—Romans 8:6

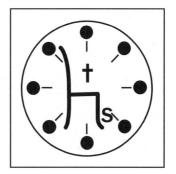

The spiritual man ("man" refers to mankind, both men and women) is the exact opposite of the natural man. You're not perfect, but God gives you insight as to his work in you and in the world (1 Cor. 2:15). Instead of self being on the throne, Christ is on the throne in your life. The priorities of your life become clear, and the activities of your life come into better alignment. You no longer have to do things to feel good about your life; you do things in response to God's awesome love for you. You begin to experience Romans 8:6, "The mind controlled by the Spirit is life and peace."

There is a third kind of person: the Christian who struggles with those experiences and feelings that we listed just a few moments ago.

The *CARNAL* man

Brothers, I could not address you as spiritual but as worldly—mere infants in Christ. I gave you milk, not solid food, for you were not yet ready for it. Indeed, you are still not ready. You are still worldly. For since there is jealousy and quarreling among you, are you not worldly? Are you not acting like mere men?

—1 Corinthians 3:1–3

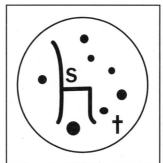

Read with me 1 Corinthians 3:1–3. The Bible tells us that we can make a choice as spiritual people to act like "mere men," like worldly people. What does that mean?

Look at the third circle. Although Christ is in our lives, self is back on the throne. This does not have to be with evil intent; it is a decision that slips into our lives for what we tell ourselves are good reasons. We need to "help God out." God needs us to "try harder." It makes us feel better to "be in control." We sometimes actually fool ourselves into thinking that we can get more done with ourselves on the throne than with Christ in charge.

Obviously, it doesn't work. The activities and priorities of our lives become jumbled, and we try harder. Yet the harder we try to live life on our power, the greater the mess inside us becomes.

Chuck Swindoll notes:

> It is one thing to become a Christian. It is another thing entirely to become a Spirit-filled Christian. The tragedy is that so many are converted and so few Spirit-filled. When this happens, a person misses the best God has to offer us on earth.[4]

There are a lot of Christians caught on the "trying harder for God" merry-go-round. How do you get off?

Let me read you a note from one Christian who felt the frustration of trying to live life apart from God's power.

> What I don't understand about myself is that I decide one way, but then I act another, doing things I absolutely despise....
>
> But I need something *more!* ... if the power of sin within me keeps sabotaging my best intentions, I obviously need help! I realize that I don't have what it takes. I can will it, but I can't *do* it. I decide to do good, but I don't *really* do it; I decide not to do bad, but then I do it anyway. My decisions, such as they are, don't result in actions. Something has gone wrong deep within me and gets the better of me every time.
>
> It happens so regularly that it's predictable. The moment I decide to do good, sin is there to trip me up. I truly delight in God's commands, but it's pretty obvious that not all of me joins in that delight. Parts of me covertly rebel, and just when I least expect it, they take charge.
>
> I've tried everything and nothing helps. I'm at the end of my rope.

Quite a description of the struggle we all face. But don't be discouraged because we truly do all face this battle. The letter that I just read you is the words of the apostle Paul, paraphrased by message author Eugene Peterson (Romans 7:15, 17–24 MESSAGE).

In Romans 7 Paul expresses this great frustration, yet Romans 8 is one of the most confident, spiritually assured chapters in the Bible. It's not too difficult to tell what makes the difference.

In Romans 7, the word *I* is used twenty-seven times. In Romans 8 the word *Spirit* is used nineteen times. What made the difference between the defeat that characterizes Paul in Romans 7 and the victory he describes in Romans 8? The filling of the Holy Spirit.

Discussion questions 1 and 2 can be used here.

What Is the Filling of the Holy Spirit?

The key doctrinal passage regarding the filling of the Holy Spirit is Ephesians 5:18–21.

Do not get drunk on wine, which leads to debauchery. Instead, be filled with the Spirit. Speak to one another with psalms, hymns and spiritual songs. Sing and make music in your heart to the Lord, always giving thanks to God the Father for everything, in the name of our Lord Jesus Christ. Submit to one another out of reverence for Christ.
—**Ephesians 5:18–21**

Remember, the Greek language that the New Testament was written in was a very precise language. It is much more exact than a language such as English. In these verses the grammar of the Greek words gives us some clarity on the meaning.

Four truths from Ephesians 5:18–21

The grammatical construction of these verses implies four truths:

1. **The verb used for "filled" is plural, implying <u>ALL</u> <u>ARE</u> <u>TO</u> <u>BE</u> <u>FILLED</u>.**

   This is a truth for all Christians. I am to be filled with the Holy Spirit. You are to be filled with the Holy Spirit. We *all* are to be filled with the Holy Spirit.

2. **The verb used for "filled" is present tense (be filled), implying <u>REPEATED</u> <u>ACTION</u>.**

   A repeated action. Something you do again and again throughout your days. It's like breathing.

   We all need air to live, but the only way to get it into our lungs is through the continual action of breathing. We breathe in, we breathe out. The average person takes in 21,600 breaths per day.

   Bill Bright likens the filling of the Spirit to spiritual breathing.[5] You breathe out (spiritually), recognizing the fact that God has forgiven you of your sins. You breathe in (spiritually), recognizing the truth that God's Spirit can now control and direct your life.

   Exhale (God, thank you for forgiving me of my sin).

   Inhale (God, fill me with your Spirit).

   Exhale . . . inhale . . . exhale . . . inhale . . . and so on throughout the day.

Do it with me now. Exhale: "Thank you, God, that you have forgiven the sins in my life, the sins that are coming to mind right now." Inhale: "Fill me with your Spirit. You take control."

There are two values to this picture. It reminds us that this is something we need to do wherever we are throughout the day—just as we breathe wherever we are. It also tells us that there should be no personal pride attached to the fact that God fills us with his Spirit. You wouldn't say, "Look at me, world, I'm breathing air! Notice what a great air breather I am." Everyone knows how to breathe, and we know that it's by the grace of God that we take our next breath. Likewise, God's Spirit fills any believer who trusts in him. Trusting him to fill us should be as natural to our Christian life as breathing air is for our physical life.

3. The verb used for "filled" is passive, implying the filling is SOMETHING DONE TO YOU.

Passive verbs in the Greek language usually indicate something being done to you rather than something you do yourself. It is God's work in you that causes the Spirit to fill your life.

How do you sort out your part and God's part in being Spirit filled? Think of it like this sponge and this basin filled with water. I put the sponge into the basin. That's a picture of immersion, of being baptized in the Spirit. The sponge represents you and the water represents the Spirit. When I put the sponge under the water, the water "fills" the sponge. You might say the sponge is now "baptized" in the water. Remember, baptized means "immersed." But what if I hold the sponge under this water and squeeze it? The sponge is still in the water, but my effort is keeping the water that the sponge is immersed in from filling the sponge at this moment. For the sponge to be filled again, what do I have to do? Right, all I have to do is release my hold on the sponge.

The experience of being Spirit filled is exactly like this: you decide to release control to God. The tighter you hold on to your life and plans and ideas, the more you squeeze out what God wants to do in and through your life. But the moment you release control, his Spirit's control comes flooding back into your life. Don't think of being Spirit filled as a strange mystical experience. Think of it as the way you, as a believer, are meant to live.

4. The verb for "filled" is imperative, implying A COMMAND.

God commands us to be Spirit filled. It is God's command for all believers to be Spirit filled all of the time, not just some of the time. Remember, the baptism of the Holy Spirit places us in a position to receive power; filling enables us day by day to walk in his power.

Baptism of the Holy Spirit	Filling of the Holy Spirit
A positional* truth	An experiential* truth
Not commanded	Commanded
A one-time event	A continuous event
Puts believer in the position to receive power	Power itself
*Positional truth is who we are because of our faith in Christ. Experiential truth is how we are to live based on that position. One is a root, the other is a fruit.	

Signs of the filling of the Holy Spirit

There is often confusion over "signs" that indicate the Holy Spirit has filled someone. We'll look at this in three sections: experiences that may or may not accompany filling, false ideas about filling, and true signs of the filling of the Spirit.

Although being Spirit filled is ultimately a matter of trusting that God will do what he says he will do, there are some indications that we are filled with the Spirit. The problem is, we often look to the wrong signs. Let's clear up some of the confusion.

Personal experiences that may or may not accompany filling

Emotionalism: emotion or feeling is not necessarily part of being filled.

Some say that to prove you're Spirit filled you have to jump for joy, cry crocodile tears, shout and yell. But people respond to great experiences in different ways. Just go to a few weddings to see that. Some families are very formal during the wedding, others weep their way through the ceremony, others laugh, and still others can't stop talking. To say "you must have this emotion" is to impose your personality on someone else's relationship with God.

Exceptional ability: God works within the framework of our limitations and natural abilities.

When you're Spirit filled you get a big "S" on your chest. You're "SuperSaint." You can win everyone in your office to Christ in a single day. That's not how it works.

If being Spirit filled is to be part of all of our lives, it must be a part of the routine of our life. I can be Spirit filled and wash dishes. (My wife tells me that's when I may be most Spirit filled.) The idea that being filled with the Spirit means you can't be playing with your kids at home or loving your wife or husband or doing a routine task is a lie that Satan would love to have us buy into.

Personal charisma: may be mistaken for filling.

Some people have more expressive or attractive personalities than others. That has nothing to do with being filled by the Spirit.

Tranquillity of mind and spirit: great Spirit-filled believers have experienced frustrations, discouragement, and disappointments.

Are Spirit-filled people ever frustrated or discouraged? Take a look at Paul in Second Corinthians or David in Psalms. Writing under the inspiration of the Spirit, they spoke of their fears and frustrations and discouragements. The Holy Spirit does help us to handle frustrations and discouragements in a different way, but they are still a part of our lives.

Tongues: throughout history, some Christians speak in tongues when filled, others do not.

Do some speak in tongues when Spirit filled? Of course. Just read Acts chapter 2. Does everyone have to speak in tongues when Spirit filled? Of course not. Just read Acts chapter 9 (where Paul is filled with the Spirit). Speaking in tongues is one of many different gifts the Spirit gives. Anytime we elevate one gift above the others in importance we head down a path that causes some to feel prideful because they have that gift and others to feel doubtful because they do not.

False teachings concerning what accompanies filling

Freedom from problems: filling doesn't make all problems disappear. It does give us the strength and wisdom to better face our problems. The apostle Paul is an example (2 Cor. 6:3–10).

Jesus was Spirit filled all of his life. Did he ever have any problems? Of course he did. He was criticized. He had nowhere to lay his head. He was persecuted. He was crucified.

Total freedom from temptation: Jesus faced one of the greatest times of temptation immediately after the Spirit came upon him following his baptism. Some who are filled experience more temptation than when not filled.

We think, "If I'm filled, I build this spiritual bubble around my life. Satan can't send any temptations in." Wrong! You'll still be tempted (as Jesus was), but you have a new power to say no to those temptations.

Sinless perfection: obviously this is not true. Every Christian sins and must trust in God's forgiveness and ask for renewed filling every day.

Biblical and universal signs of filling

The gifts of the Spirit:

A spiritual gift is given to each of us as a means of helping the entire church.

—1 Corinthians 12:7 (NLT)

These gifts are given so that we can better serve each other. One of the greatest signs of the filling of the Spirit is the willingness to serve others.

The fruit of the Spirit:

But the fruit of the Spirit is love, joy, peace, patience, kindness, goodness, faithfulness, gentleness and self-control.

—Galatians 5:22–23

As you see yourself growing in your ability to love, growing in the joy you experience, in the kindness that you express, you are seeing the results of the Spirit's work in your life. Fruit does not pop full grown onto the tree. It grows! When you see yourself growing in these character qualities, it's a sign of the Spirit's presence in your life. In Galatians 5 the Spirit-filled life is presented as the opposite of the selfish and sinful life. As you are filled with God's Spirit, your character will change!

The power of the Spirit:

The Holy Spirit gives power to witness (Acts 1:8; Eph. 3:20).

The apostles were not brash or egotistical, but they had confidence and boldness because of the filling (Acts 4:29).

You may not feel powerful yet see God working powerfully through your life. In fact, Paul reminds us in 2 Corinthians 12 that it is often when we feel the weakest and yet are obedient to God that the Lord does his greatest work. "My power works best in your weakness" (2 Cor. 12:9 NLT).

Before we move on, let's take a moment to make this personal. God's Spirit is personal. The person of God is living in us (I can't think of anything more personal than that). As you look at these signs of the Spirit's presence in our lives, it's very possible that you're not experiencing all of these in your life or I am certain that you are not experiencing them to the degree that you would like. Does that mean that his Spirit is not in your life? No. If you've trusted Jesus with your life, his Spirit is in your life, no doubt about that. But we are works in progress, masterpieces still on the easel.

Focus with me for just a moment on the work that God wants to do in your life. Think of the joy of letting God be at work in your life, making an impact on this world beyond what you can imagine. That is the result of the gifts of the Spirit.

Think of the deep fulfillment that comes as you see your character change. You're not as angry as you used to be, you feel a sense of peace that you've never had, you care for people as you've never cared before. That is the fruit of the Spirit.

See yourself setting aside a sin that has been marking your life for years. God's Spirit has given you the power to admit the sin, the courage to look for help, and the joy of seeing change. Oh, it's not that you're never tempted again, but you've found a new power to say no to that temptation by saying yes to God. He's working a genuine victory over sin in your life.

Think of the refreshing humility he wants to bring into your life. Instead of being constantly caught in the tangle of worrying about who notices you or whether you get your due, you are free to serve the people you love and people you've never met.

God is working to do all of this in our lives!

Discussion questions 3 and 4 can be used here.

Split Session Plan: If you're teaching this study over two sessions, end the first session here.

One of the most important questions in life is "How?" If I tell you that you can bake the greatest chocolate cake you've ever tasted, the next obvious question is "How?" If I tell you that you can take a free vacation to Europe with your family this summer your question is "How?" If I tell you that you can take off twenty pounds in five days, again you want to know "How?"

Teaching Tip

Let the group you are teaching get involved at this point. Instead of your saying "How?" at the end of each of the sentences above, pause and let them say it. As a teacher your goal throughout a study is to help people to be "active listeners." When people are listening actively they are engaged in what you are saying, and they are thinking about what it means for their lives. Even a simple thing like saying "How?" tends to break us out of the passive mode of listening that we all so easily fall into.

God commands us to be filled with his Spirit. The question is: how?

How Can I Be Filled with the Holy Spirit?

Some will be disappointed in what I'm about to say. It won't sound hard enough! God never commands us to do something that he does not give us the power to do. If you are commanded to be Spirit filled, you can count on the fact that God will give you the direction and resources that you need to be Spirit filled.

The filling of the Holy Spirit comes when we are cleansed from every known sin and every area of our life is surrendered to Jesus Christ.

Think of what it's like to have a guest in your home. You might go all out to please your guest: serving lavish meals and even sleeping on the floor so your guest can have your bed. (Actually, we usually make our kids sleep on the floor!) However, no matter how comfortable you try to make your guest, it's always known that it is your house and you are ultimately in control.

God's Spirit does not want to be a guest in your life. He wants you to hand over the ownership papers to him! He wants you to honestly admit every fault, scar, and sin to him—he knows it all anyway. He wants us to surrender every "room" of our lives to his control. Jesus tells us in John 14 that he sends his Spirit to live with us, to be *in* us.

> **And I will ask the Father, and he will give you another Counselor to be with you forever—the Spirit of truth. The world cannot accept him, because it neither sees him nor knows him. But you know him, for he lives with you and will be in you.**
>
> **—John 14:16–17**

How do we surrender our lives to God's Spirit?

1. **RECOGNIZE YOUR THIRST** for filling and desire it.

Open your Bibles with me to John chapter 7.

> **On the last and greatest day of the Feast, Jesus stood and said in a loud voice, "If anyone is thirsty, let him come to me and drink. Whoever believes in me, as the Scripture has said, streams of living water will flow from within him." By this he meant the Spirit, whom those who believed in him were later to receive. Up to that time the Spirit had not been given, since Jesus had not yet been glorified.**
>
> **—John 7:37–39**

Teaching Tip

This story of Jesus calling the thirsty to himself at the Feast of Tabernacles is central to the message of this study. Because you're teaching the deep need and desire that we all have to be filled with God's Spirit, it is crucial that you tell this story with passion. Slow down as you tell this to express the drama. As you talk about Jesus shouting to the crowd, it's important for you to speak in a "stage shout." Help people to feel that they were there that day. The way that you tell this story can change people's hearts.

This passage from John 7 takes place in Jerusalem during the Jewish Feast of Tabernacles.

Each morning of the feast, just after dawn, the high priest would lead a celebrating parade of worshipers from the temple down to the nearby Pool of Siloam. There he would fill a golden pitcher with water.

He carried this golden pitcher back through the south gate of the temple (which was called the Water Gate) and the people would recite Isaiah 12:3, "With joy you will draw water from the wells of salvation."

The priest then poured out the water at the altar as an offering to God. Besides being a prayer for rains for the harvest, this offering also served as a reminder of God's promise in Joel 2:28–29 to "pour out" his Spirit on all mankind.

Imagine this scene from John 7. Jerusalem is filled with worshipers who have packed the city for this celebration. With this ceremony on everyone's mind, perhaps even at the dramatic moment when the pitcher of water is about to be poured out, Jesus' voice rises above the crowd. Jesus *shouts*, "If anyone is thirsty, let him come to me and drink." Shocking! He was claiming to be the fulfillment of all of their hopes and dreams. It would be like someone standing up against the backdrop of a Fourth of July fireworks show and shouting, "If anyone wants true freedom, let him come to me!" Jesus is claiming to be able to fulfill us as nothing else can. Jesus shouted this because he knew that everyone in that crowd was thirsty that day for what he had to give. There was not a person who was not thirsty for God, thirsty for right relationships, thirsty for spiritual life.

Speaking of the moment when Jesus cried out, "If anyone is thirsty, let him come to me," Larry Crabb writes:

I can imagine a few brave souls running to Jesus, overwhelmed by the reality of their thirst. "Yes, Lord, I am thirsty. I admit it. I deeply desire what I do not have. If anyone is thirsty—" What did He say next? What He said was: "Come!" Neither deny your thirst nor focus on it. Christ's invitation to come to Him on the basis of perceived thirst grants legitimacy to the longings of our soul.[6]

You were created to thirst for God! You and I are thirsty. One of the most important questions we face every day of our lives is, "Where am I going to get my spiritual thirst quenched?" Satan comes and tempts us with the answers, "Financial gain, sexual sin, higher position—those will quench that inner thirst." That's a *lie!* You know it is, but Satan keeps telling us the lie.

Even the positive things in our lives cannot quench this thirst. As important as relationships are, as wonderful as a moment of relaxation can be, as significant as living out your purpose in ministry can feel, not even these can quench the thirst for connection with God. Only Jesus can do that.

So the next time you feel that deep sense of inner thirst, resist the temptation to think, "I'll call a friend . . . or go to a movie . . . or go shopping . . . or work harder in ministry . . . or rewrite my goals for this year." Those are all good things to do, but that is not the drink this thirst is inviting you to take. Instead, sit back and in a moment of quietness say to Jesus, "I need you more than I'll ever know, and I feel that need right now. Forgive me for looking to other things and other people to fill this place in my life. Would you fill me with your Spirit? I trust you to quench this thirst."

2. **<u>REPENT</u> <u>OF</u> <u>YOUR</u> sins and receive God's cleansing.** 11

Repent! In the battle for the meaning of words, Satan is winning with this word. The image that comes to many of our minds is of a crazy long-haired prophet with an angrily scrawled sign, "REPENT OR DIE!"

The truth is, "repent" is one of the most positive words in the dictionary. It means to turn around, to start again, to change your mind. Who wouldn't want that?

To repent is to agree with God about my sin; to stop making excuses and blaming others for my lack of obedience to God. Look at 1 John 1:9.

But if we confess our sins to him, he can be depended on to forgive us and to cleanse us from every wrong. (And it is perfectly proper for God to do this for us because Christ died to wash away our sins.)
—1 John 1:9 (LB)

The trouble most of us have with repenting is that we have to repent of our *sin.* It's much easier to admit that we had a "bad day" or a "bad attitude" or "hit a bump in the road" than it is to say, "God, I repent of the sin that is in my heart and in my actions."

I'll admit personally that the unwillingness to call sin sin is what often keeps me filled with myself rather than filled with God's Spirit.

Teaching Tip

The sentence above is a personal confession—one you should make only if it's true of you. (Of course, this happens to be an area that we universally struggle in.) When you share in a confessional way about your own struggles with sin, it entirely changes the tone of your teaching. Those listening hear you for who you really are—a fellow struggler just as in need of grace as every other person in the room.

My people have committed two sins: They have forsaken me, the spring of living water, and have dug their own cisterns, broken cisterns that cannot hold water.

—Jeremiah 2:13

Jeremiah 2:13 gives us a clear picture of the two reasons we need to repent. Would you circle "forsaken me" and "dug their own cisterns." We need to repent because we've stopped trusting in God's strength, and we need to repent because we've trusted instead in what we can do.

Imagine this picture. Every day we walk by a huge neon sign that points to Jesus with the flashing message, "Spring of living water . . . Spring of living water." We might even take a moment to marvel at the beauty of the sign, but then we grab a shovel and start digging our own well to get water. It's a sad, but honest, commentary on our hearts that we would rather dig cisterns that are "ours" even though they don't hold water.

Kay Warren tells this story about digging our own wells.

> I found myself feeling sad over a situation in my life. Instead of going to the spring of living water, where I knew that what I would have found was God's comfort, where I would have heard Him say such things as, "I will never leave you or forsake you," "I give my peace to those whose mind is stayed on me," I tried to dig my own well. Instead of coming to that font of living water, I walked right by God, said my hellos to Him, grabbed a shovel and began digging. Searching for a way to feel better I thought, "I'm hungry, maybe some food will help." I went into our kitchen and saw on the counter the three bags of my children's Halloween candy!

I thought, "This'll do it, this will make me feel lots better!" So I took a piece of candy from each of the three bags and I ate them. Even the chocolate didn't make me feel any better, so I dug a little deeper with that shovel. I went to the cupboard and got out the chips! I was soon full, but I was still sad, still depressed. So then I thought, "Aha, I'll call a friend. I'll get someone on the phone who will pat me on the back and tell me what a nice person I am. That's what I need to do." And as I walked over and picked up the phone I heard God saying to me, "Kay, you're digging your own well. I'm standing right here, I'm the spring of living water! I CAN QUENCH YOUR THIRST."

To be filled with God's Spirit you must confess that you have walked by him time after time, that you have tried to dig your own well to quench your thirst. To add insult to injury, what we usually do then is pray and ask God to help us to dig our own well! And then we get mad at him because he didn't help us dig our well. If you'll look at the unanswered prayers in your life, I'll bet you'll find that in many cases you were asking God to help you dig your own well. And when he would not, you got mad at him.

Say to the Lord who loves you, "I'm sorry that I so easily fall into trusting myself, and that I so often try to find satisfaction in trying to do it *my* way rather than trusting your way. God, forgive me for making excuses for my sin and for blaming others for my sin. I repent of my sin and ask you to fill me right now."

3. <u>YIELD</u> <u>ALL</u> <u>OF</u> <u>YOURSELF</u> to the Holy Spirit's control.

Being filled with the Spirit is not a matter of more or less, it's a matter of yes or no.

Sometimes you hear someone say something like, "Wow, he was *really* filled with the Spirit tonight." The Spirit's filling, however, is not a matter of amount or degree. You are not more filled or less filled—you simply are filled or you are not. Either you are allowing the Spirit to control your attitudes and direct your actions or you are not. Obviously, as we grow as Christians, we learn how to yield new areas of our lives in deeper ways to God's leadership. Being Spirit filled, however, is yielding all that I know and understand of myself to all that I know and understand of Jesus at this moment in my life.

This means that you make two choices:

• **Let Jesus be Lord daily.**

Say yes to Christ.

I have been crucified with Christ and I no longer live, but Christ lives in me. The life I live in the body, I live by faith in the Son of God, who loved me and gave himself for me.

—Galatians 2:20

• **Deny self daily.**

Say no to myself.

Then he called the crowd to him along with his disciples and said: "If anyone would come after me, he must deny himself and take up his cross and follow me. For whoever wants to save his life will lose it, but whoever loses his life for me and for the gospel will save it.

—Mark 8:34–35

Control is a word that is filled with concerns for most of us. We don't want anyone else to control our lives. For some of us, the greatest fear we have is the fear of being "out of control."

In every thrill ride, there is a moment of abandon. You get into the roller coaster, you start down the waterslide, you leap off of the bungee jump—you abandon yourself to the ride. Being filled with the Spirit is the decision to abandon yourself to the greatness of God's plan for your life. It is in essence the greatest true thrill of your life.

(By the way, I have a little secret for you. You aren't in control anyway! We fool ourselves into thinking we are by our familiar surroundings or daily habits or our limited perspective. But, in light of the vastness of eternity and the greatness of God, deep down we know we're kidding ourselves.)

Control is an even more serious issue than we are willing to admit. The truth is, we are in a battle with God over the issue of who controls our lives. Even as I say this it makes some of you feel very uncomfortable— deep down you don't want God intruding on certain parts of your life. He can have the time I am at church, but don't intrude on the way I run my business, or the hobbies that I might choose, or the way that I treat people to get things done. You're in a battle with God and, until you surrender control, that battle will continue. And it's not a one-time surrender, is it? It is a daily—even a moment by moment—surrender.

Discussion question 5 can be used here.

4. **TRUST GOD** to fill you as he said he would. 13

And then you trust. God will do what he says he will do. He always keeps his promise. You don't have to beg, you don't have to doubt—just trust. The God who commanded you to allow his Spirit to fill you will certainly do just that as you trust in him.

Bill Bright puts that trust in simple terms.

> The Christian does not need to beg God for that which is already his. Suppose that you went to cash a check for a hundred dollars. Would you go to the bank where you have several thousand dollars on deposit, place the check on the counter, get down on your knees, and say, "Oh, please Mr. Teller, cash my check?"
>
> No, that is not the way you cash a check. You simply go in faith, place the check on the counter and wait for the money which is already yours. Then you thank the teller and go on your way.
>
> Millions of Christians are begging God . . . for a life of victory and power which is already theirs—an abundant life just waiting to be appropriated by faith.[7]

How do you know if you're filled? *Do the things God said to do.*

At this moment you may very well be feeling:

"I could never do that! I'm just a normal guy." But then you remember what God has said about you.

"You're made new by my Spirit, baptized in my Spirit, indwelt by my Spirit, sealed and guaranteed through my Spirit. You're a temple of my Spirit." Let that Spirit fill you now.

Ray Stedman was pastor of the Peninsula Bible Church in Palo Alto, California, for forty years. He not only had a tremendously impactful ministry in the church he served, he also became a nationally known Bible teacher. He was powerfully used by God. I want you to hear what he said to the church that he served for so many years in his last message to them before his death. These are the words of a wise and experienced saint about how the power of God works in our lives.

> What I am trying to say is that the power of God, the resurrection power of God, is not a power that makes a great demonstration. It is quiet. We are so used to power that makes noises that we don't think we have power if we don't have noise. Things buzz, hum, pulsate, pound, explode, and bang, and these are seen as power. But this is power that you don't feel. You don't have any sense that it is happening, but it is happening.
>
> This power has a peculiar characteristic: It only happens when you begin to act! When you begin to exercise the gifts that God has given you, then the power begins to flow, not before. Then God will work through you to accomplish things that will leave you gasping, sometimes, at what he has done. You didn't feel this power. You don't suddenly feel strong, capable, and mighty. No, you felt weak; Paul says that God's power is made perfect in weakness, but we pay no attention, sometimes, to such a statement. If you feel weak, if you feel inadequate, if you feel ineffectual, this is no hindrance to being used of God and exercising the power of God—not in the least! That is what this is teaching us.
>
> Many people never discover what God could do in their lives because they keep waiting to feel powerful before they act. No, you won't feel powerful. Begin to reach out and act to meet the needs around, and suddenly you discover that there is unusual power at work.

I have a power toothbrush that runs by a battery. It has an unusual characteristic. When you get the toothpaste on the toothbrush and you are ready to brush your teeth, you look around for the button to turn it on. But you don't need a button to turn it on. The directions instruct you to put it up to your teeth and press, and suddenly the power will be there. I remember with what unbelief I tried this the first time, but, to my amazement, it worked. I put the toothbrush up and began to press against my teeth, and, suddenly, the brush began to move up and down—there was power available.

This is a trivial (and even silly) example of what the power of God is like, but resurrection power works much the same way. It works when you reach out to somebody. It works when you sit down to exercise a teaching gift, to comfort someone who is in trouble, or to confront someone who is taking a wrong course. It works when you expect it to be there. That is, it works by faith![8]

Will you act on the truths we've seen from God's Word in this study?

Acting on the Truth

1. Which circle represents your life at this moment? The natural, the spiritual, or the carnal? Probably, like most of us, you would like to "fudge" on this and say, "Well, I know that Christ is in my life, and although he's not Lord in everything, he's Lord in this or that area." The Bible doesn't give us a fourth option: we can't be partially carnal or partially spiritual. At this moment, Jesus is either Lord in all you know and understand of him or he is not. If he is not, will you give the throne in your life back to him?

2. Have you ignored or denied your thirst for God and right relationships? Can you admit your deep thirst today and come to him for the quenching of that thirst? Or have you been trying to dig your own well to satisfy your thirst?

3. What sins have separated you and God from fellowship together? What do you need to confess to him and repent of? Perhaps you need to spend some extended time with God, asking his Holy Spirit to reveal to you where you are wrong so you can trust again in God's forgiveness and ask to be filled again.

4. In what area of your life do you need to trust God for the power to do what he is leading you to do? Where do you need to act in faith? Who do you need to serve? How do you need to use the gifts that God has given you?

Discussion questions 6 and 7 can be used here.

Finish memorizing memory card 4, "The Truth about the Holy Spirit."
As you put these truths into your heart, expect the Lord to use them
to encourage you, and to encourage others through you.

 ## Discussion Questions

1. **Where do you cross the line between being an imperfect Christian living the Spirit-filled life to being a carnal Christian living a self-centered lifestyle?**

   Small Group Leaders: This is a thought question that has no one right answer. The purpose is not to see how much sin we can get away with. Instead, it is to have an honest talk about how easy it is to slip from a sinful action into a sinful lifestyle.

2. **Some Christian leaders say that up to 95 percent of believers are living worldly lives—lives characterized by some of those struggles we talked about in this session. The question that begs to be asked is why? Discuss in your group two or three reasons why you believe it is so easy and common to settle for less than God's best in our spiritual lives.**

   Small Group Leaders: Some ideas might include the influence of the world around us, lack of time to read God's Word, comparing ourselves with others, the material things we're surrounded by, our desire not to embarrass ourselves by standing out.

3. **If you could pick one place in your life where you would like to see God working in greater ways, where would it be?**

4. **If you could pick one of your character traits that you would like to see God develop in a greater way, what would it be?**

5. **What does it feel like to be filled with the Holy Spirit? What kinds of thoughts do you have when you're filled with the Spirit?**

   Small Group Leaders: This question gives you an opportunity to talk about the reality of the Spirit-filled life. At first it seems as if being Spirit filled would mean we would always feel giddy with joy, and that we would always be thinking about Jesus. The Spirit-filled life is deeper than that. We can be filled with the Spirit when we're facing depression or anger. We can be filled with the Spirit when we're thinking about work or kids or romance or relaxation.

6. **We learned that being filled is something that God does to you. What part, then, do you play in being filled with the Spirit?**

What is one small thing that you could do *tomorrow* to be more consistently filled with the Spirit?

7. As believers in Christ we cannot live the Christian life on our own power. We must have the daily power and filling of the Holy Spirit. There is likely nothing more important you could do for one another as a group than to be aware of and to pray for one another's needs in this all-important area. Take some time before you leave to make a list of each person's answer to what one thing they could do to more consistently be filled with the Spirit. Copy the list on a 3 x 5 card for each person in your group so you can all pray for each other. The list would look something like this:

> Specific prayer requests for my group—for each one's "one thing" to be more consistently filled with God's Spirit:
>
> John: A daily quiet time
>
> Mary: Trusting in God's forgiveness
>
> Bill: Thinking about God at the beginning of each hour
>
> Ellen: Taking the time to pray for my family
>
> Steve: Choosing to say yes to God
>
> Jan: Seeing the people at my work as people Jesus loves

Small Group Leaders: End the study by praying for each other that the work of God the Father, God the Son, and God the Spirit will be both personal and powerful in your everyday lives.

For Further Study

Bright, Bill. *The Holy Spirit: The Key to Supernatural Living.* San Bernardino, Calif.: Campus Crusade for Christ, 1980.

Elwell, Walter, ed. *Topical Analysis of the Bible.* Grand Rapids, Mich.: Baker, 1991.

Graham, Billy. *The Holy Spirit: Activating God's Power in Your Life.* Dallas: Word, 2000.

Ryrie, Charles Caldwell. *The Holy Spirit.* Chicago: Moody Bible Institute, 1965.

Sanders, J. Oswald. *The Holy Spirit and His Gifts.* Grand Rapids, Mich.: Zondervan, 1973.

Stott, John. *The Baptism and Fullness of the Holy Spirit.* Downers Grove, Ill.: InterVarsity Press, 1964.

Swindoll, Charles R. *Flying Closer to the Flame.* Dallas: Word, 1993.

Creation
Part 1

Life Change Objective

To deepen your conviction that the world and all that is in it are created by the personal action of a personal God.

Summary Teaching Outline

Why Did God Create?

1. God created for his own sake.
2. God created to express his sovereignty.
3. God created to reflect his character.
4. God created to show his wisdom.

How Did God Create?

Three major views that are important for all believers to understand:

Evolution

Theistic evolution

Supernatural creation

When Did God Create?

Listen to these words from the song "He Knows My Name."

I have a Maker,
He formed my heart.
Before even time began,
My life was in His hand.

He knows my name.
He knows my every thought.
He sees each tear that falls
And hears me when I call.[1]

That's the conviction I hope to build or to deepen in you as we study what God has to say about creation. I'm well aware of the fact that this subject is a matter of great scientific and theological argument. And we won't shy away from facing some of those issues. But I don't want you to miss the main point of any study of creation. You were personally created by a loving God.

As we begin our study of creation, I want you to see that it's not about something that happened a long time ago. It's about what's happening in your heart right now.

We study the origins of life because every one of us needs a sense of identity and purpose; what you believe about your origin affects:

<u>YOUR SELF-WORTH</u>

<u>YOUR RELATIONSHIPS</u>

<u>HOW YOU VIEW GOD</u>

Your self-worth. Which of these statements gives you a stronger foundation for self-worth?

> I am a personal creation of a loving God.
>
> I am the result of random chemical reactions in a primordial soup.

One reason why we are so fascinated with the question of where life began and where we came from is because the answers to these questions form the foundation of who we are.

Your relationships. Think the questions of creation don't impact our thoughts about everyday life and relationships? Let me give you an example. In an episode of the TV situation comedy *Home Improvement,* the husband, Tim, is caught by his wife, Jill, looking at another woman as she walks by their table in a restaurant. Jill, angry and confused, goes to ask the wise neighbor Wilson, who speaks from behind the fence, why Tim would do this. Wilson explained to Jill that cavemen needed to mate with many women in order to propagate the species—so it's "just natural" that men would have these feelings.

That's *very* different from the picture the Bible gives us of the first man and woman. Adam and Eve were given to one another by God to become one with each other for a lifetime. Wives, which would you rather have your husband think? "I have an inborn natural desire to mate with many women that I'm going to have to suppress for the rest of my life," or "I was created by God to be fulfilled through my faithfulness to unity with one woman for the rest of my life."

How you view God. The way we understand the truth about creation deeply impacts our beliefs about God. The farther you feel God is from the act of creation, the farther you tend to feel from God. It's much easier to develop a personal relationship with God when you realize he had a personal hand in creating you.

> Discussion question 1 can be used here.

This study is somewhat different from any other in *Foundations.* In our other studies most of the quotes are from the Bible. In this study you'll also see a lot of quotes from and about scientists who study the subject of creation. Since this very biblical subject is much discussed in our science classrooms, universities, and labs, I wanted you to be able to hear from some of these experts. I also admit to you from the beginning that we'll only be able to touch on this subject. If this study can get you thinking so that you'll study more for yourself, it will have been a huge success.

In this study we're going to answer three simple questions. Simple to ask, that is. The answers involve who God is, who we are, and why we are here. The three questions are:

1. **Why did God create?**
2. **How did God create?**
3. **When did God create?**

Why Did God Create?

1. **God created for <u>HIS</u> <u>OWN</u> <u>SAKE</u>.**

   God created because he enjoyed creating. Read with me Psalm 104:31.

   May the glory of the LORD last forever! The LORD rejoices in all he has made!
   —**Psalm 104:31** (NLT)

   He didn't have to create, he simply wanted to create. It brought him joy. Look at Colossians 1:16 and circle the words "for him."

   All things were created by him and for him.
   —**Colossians 1:16**

   Ultimately, creation is for God and not for you. He wants us to enjoy his creation and to enjoy him, but creation is "for him."

   I'm very aware that from our human perspective that sounds selfish. But God is not selfish. God created for the pure joy of creating. Have you ever done that? Have you ever made something not thinking about who would see it or how much you could sell it for but just for the joy of making that thing? It may have been a woodworking project you built or a poem you wrote or a garden you planted or a garment you sewed or a song you wrote. If you've ever felt the joy of just making something, you have a clue of what it means for God to create for his own sake.

2. God created to express his <u>SOVEREIGNTY</u>.

Sovereignty, you may remember from our study of God, means that God is ultimately in charge. God is in control. God's creation expresses his control. Listen to these verses:

> **The heavens are yours, and yours also the earth; you founded the world and all that is in it.**
>
> —Psalm 89:11

> **The earth is the LORD's, and everything in it, the world, and all who live in it.**
>
> —Psalm 24:1

The earth is the Lord's. He owns everything you see, including you. We have these things on loan for just a brief time while we are on this earth. It is true that some in his creation recognize his ownership, while others do not. But it is just as true that those who are acting as if the landlord will never return will one day see clearly the truth that you cannot ignore God's sovereignty. God is a gracious owner, but he is the owner. God is a patient owner, but he is the owner. God is a loving owner, but he is the owner.

Teaching Tip

Repetition is a communicator's best friend. The sentences that end the paragraph above are obviously repetitive, but that is often what helps those listening to really hear what you are saying.

Don't be afraid to repeat yourself. No one hears all that you say the first time. Even if they did, we usually have to hear a truth more than once to begin to incorporate that truth into our lives. Sometimes as teachers we think, "I said that last week. I'd better not say it again." It needs to be said more than once. Say it with a different emphasis, but say it again.

Some of the ways to use repetition as you speak are:

- Repeating a phrase for emphasis (as above with the phrase "he is the owner").
- Reviewing material from the previous session before you begin a new study.

- Saying the same thing in different ways in the teaching outline. In the outline points you're teaching here, we could have just noted that God created to show his nature. But by looking at his character and his wisdom and his sovereignty, the truth has an opportunity to sink in. It's like looking at a diamond. As you turn it in your hand to see the different facets, the beauty shines more and more clearly.

- Repeating from session to session the core truths you want to be sure those in a study learn and live by. (For instance, one of the core truths of *Foundations* is that what you believe about God deeply impacts the way you live in his world.)

3. **God created to reflect his <u>CHARACTER</u>.**

The heavens declare the glory of God; the skies proclaim the work of his hands. Day after day they pour forth speech; night after night they display knowledge.

—**Psalm 19:1–2**

From the time the world was created, people have seen the earth and sky and all that God made. They can clearly see his invisible qualities—his eternal power and divine nature. So they have no excuse whatsoever for not knowing God.

—**Romans 1:20** (NLT)

Psalm 19:1–2 tells us that the heavens declare God's glory. Day after day, night after night, year after year that incredible display of sun and stars in the sky shouts, "God is a great and wonderful God!"

Look at Romans 1:20—we can see God's character in what he has made.

If we were to turn this class into a pottery-making class, you would clearly see people's character in the way each of us made our pottery. Some of you are very detailed, and you would be able to see that in the time and energy you put into your pot. You would fashion the clay with great care, making sure that it was perfectly smooth. If you had a stick you might cut an intricate design onto the sides of your pot. Others of you are . . . shall we say . . . less detailed. Your basic goal would be to see how quickly you could make your pot. Or maybe you'd try to make more pots than anyone else in the room. You would see your character in what you have made. Some of you would be throwing little balls of clay at everyone near you. I don't even want to talk about *your* character.

A Closer Look

The Bible is filled with verses that tell us God's creation is an expression of God's character. To look more deeply into this, take some time before the next session to read through these verses.

Neh. 9:5–6; Ps. 19:1–4; Ps. 104:30–32; Isa. 43:7; Rom. 1:20; 2 Cor. 4:6; Ps. 8:1, 3; Ps. 104:24; Isa. 51:12–13, 16; Amos 4:13

4. God created to show his <u>WISDOM</u>.

> LORD, you have made many things; with your wisdom you made them all. The earth is full of your riches.
>
> —Psalm 104:24 (NCV)

> By wisdom the LORD laid the earth's foundations, by understanding he set the heavens in place.
>
> —Proverbs 3:19

Let's do something together. Make a list with me of just a few of the ways that creation shows the wisdom of God. For instance, I see God's wisdom in the way the earth rotates perfectly around the sun, in the way that he made a bird to fly, even in the persistence with which he gifted the ant! (Isn't "What a wise and wonderful God you are" *your* first thought when you find your kitchen counters crawling with ants?) Where do you see God's wisdom as you look at how God made the universe and at how God made you?

Teaching Tip

Take a few moments here to let the group talk back to you—as you make a list together of the ways we see God's wisdom in his creation. It's not always easy to get people started. If no one says anything immediately, you can often break the ice with as simple a statement as, "This is the interactive part of our study," or "Help me out with this one."

The answer to why God created is the foundation for understanding creation. With those truths under our belt, now we're ready to tackle questions of how God created and when he created.

Discussion question 2 can be used here.

How Did God Create?

And God said, "Let there be light," and there was light.

—Genesis 1:3

Read Genesis 1:3 with me. That settles it. God said light and there was light. That's how God created. Next question.

Somehow that's not enough for us, is it? We have an intense desire to figure out the "how." Sifting through all that is said and written on this subject:

There are three major views that are important for all believers to understand:

Evolution

This is not a view of "creation" because evolution does not involve a creator. In simplest terms, the view of evolution is that life originated from natural processes, beginning with the first living substance (a single cell) and continuing with the evolving of species.

There is a widespread belief that evolution has been proven by science, thereby making the biblical account of creation untrue.

But let me remind you.

It is impossible to prove <u>SCIENTIFICALLY</u> any theory of origins. This is because the scientific method is based on <u>OBSERVATION</u> and <u>EXPERIMENTATION</u>, and it is impossible to make observations or conduct experiments on the origins of the universe.

It's important to remember that there is no such thing as an unbiased approach to the study of creation and evolution. We all have a set of beliefs and ideas based on our experiences. The only question is, which is the better bias? We'll admit the bias in this study: the belief that God is the Creator of the world and all that is in it, that he made man in his image (man did not evolve from apes), and that the Bible can be trusted as a book of information about creation.

Evolution and creation are not just matters of science on the one hand and religion on the other. There can be no doubt that evolution and creation are positioned in our society as competing beliefs. Just look at the back of our cars! Little fish symbols on the back of Christians' cars responded to by little "Darwin symbols" on the back of others' cars. And then came the inevitable big fish eating the little Darwin, and vice versa. These are the actions of competing beliefs.

Often, as believers, we feel defensive about even discussing creation. Science seems to have the high ground, with the assumption that the theory of evolution is a proven fact. Any scientist would tell you, however, that there is no value to a science in which we cannot challenge assumptions and test theories. We should not be afraid to clearly state, as those who believe in a personal creator, that we have real problems with the theory of evolution.

The problems with the theory of evolution:

1. God is left out of creation.

One of the greatest problems when buying into an evolutionist position is that it paints God as either nonexistent or as cold and distant in the act of creation. The idea that God started it all with a big bang and then let things work themselves out is totally foreign to the God we read about in the Bible. He is a personal God who is intimately involved not only in creating but also in sustaining the creation he made.

How about the idea that God somehow created *through* evolution. We'll look at that more closely in a moment. Darwin rejected this idea from the beginning.

Darwin himself rejected the idea of adding intervention by God into the concept of evolution:

> **I will give absolutely nothing for the theory of natural selection if it requires miraculous additions at any one stage of descent.[2]**

2. The probability of evolution by <u>CHANCE</u>

What are the chances that life could begin by chance chemical reactions in a prehistoric sea? What are the probabilities of evolution successfully occurring?

Discussing the possibility of even one chain of amino acids combining by chance,

Francis Crick, codiscoverer of the molecular structure of DNA, wrote:

> **This is an easy exercise in combinatorials. Suppose the chain is about two hundred amino acids long; this is, if anything, rather less than the average length of proteins of all types. Since we have just twenty possibilities at each place, the number of possibilities is twenty multiplied by itself some two hundred times. This is conveniently written 20^{200}, that is a one followed by 260 zeros!**
>
> **This number is quite beyond our everyday comprehension. For comparison, consider the number of fundamental particles (atoms,**

speaking loosely) in the entire visible universe, not just in our own galaxy with its 10^{11} stars, but in all the billions of galaxies, out to the limits of observable space. This number, which is estimated to be 10^{80}, is quite paltry by comparison to 10^{260}. Moreover, we have only considered a polypeptide chain of a rather modest length. Had we considered longer ones as well, the figure would have been even more immense.[3]

The possibility of even this first step of evolution occurring by chance is a statistical impossibility.

Some of you *love* numbers such as 10 to the 260th power. Others are thinking right now, "Could you say that a little more simply?"

Charles Ryrie did.

It requires an incredible amount of faith to believe that evolution could have caused by chance all life that ever did or does now exist.[4]

To make it even more simple and clear than that, one writer pictured it this way:

The current scenario of the origin of life is about as likely as the assemblage of a 747 by a tornado whirling through a junkyard.[5]

3. **The lack of evidence for species-to-species evolution**

Charles Darwin conceded that point, the lack of evidence, in his writings:

Not one change of species into another is on record. . . . we cannot prove that a single species has been changed.[6]

The Bible tells us that God made each animal "after its kind." This is easily verified not only by the fossil record but also by modern scientific observation and experimentation. Animal breeders have successfully created new breeds of animals but have never changed one species into another.

There is no proof. In fact, some of what was thought might prove the theory of evolution has had to be thrown out.

We are now about 120 years after Darwin, and knowledge of the fossil record has been greatly expanded. Ironically, we have even fewer examples of evolutionary transition than we had in Darwin's time. By this I mean that some of the classic cases of Darwinian change in the fossil record, such as the evolution of the horse in North America, have had to be discarded or modified as a result of more detailed information.[7]

4. The irreducible <u>COMPLEXITY</u> of living things

By irreducibly complex I mean a single system composed of several well-matched, interacting parts that contribute to the basic function, wherein the removal of any one of the parts causes the system to effectively cease functioning. . . . An irreducibly complex biological system, if there is such a thing, would be a powerful challenge to Darwinian evolution.[8]

"Irreducible complexity" refers to something which is so intricate in its creation that it couldn't have evolved step by step. It had to have been made all at once.

One example among hundreds is the woodpecker.

The forces involved in the woodpecker's hammering away at trees are incredible, for the suddenness with which the head is brought to a halt during each peck results in a stress equivalent to a thousand times the force of gravity. This is more than 250 times the force to which an astronaut is subjected in a rocket during liftoff.

How is the woodpecker able to withstand such forces? What prevents woodpeckers from beating out their brains?

The woodpecker survives this head-bashing and these exceptional forces because God in His wisdom has designed the head, beak, and neck in a special way. For starters, the Creator has greatly reinforced the woodpecker's skull with bone. This is necessary if the head is not going to break into pieces. He has given the woodpecker a stronger bill than most birds. It must be strong enough to dig into a tree without folding up like an accordion. The bill is chisel-tipped, and when the woodpecker is chiselling away there is a lot of sawdust. Normally in birds, the sawdust would enter the nostrils, but the woodpecker has been designed with slit-like nostrils covered by fine wiry feathers to prevent the sawdust from entering.

Also, the beak and brain itself have been cushioned against impact. In most birds, the bones of the beak are joined to the bones of the cranium—the part of the skull that surrounds the brain. But in the woodpecker the cranium and beak are separated by a sponge-like tissue that takes the shock each time the bird strikes its beak against a tree. The woodpecker's shock-absorber is so good that scientists say it is far better than any that humans have invented.

For added protection to its brain, the woodpecker has special muscles which pull its brain-case away from its beak every time it strikes a blow. But this is only part of the story. If the woodpecker's head were to twist even slightly while hammering the tree, the rotation of its head, combined with the force of pecking, would tear away the bird's brain. But God, the ultimate Designer, has created the woodpecker with superbly coordinated neck muscles to keep its head perfectly straight. Thus the bird can withstand the enormous shock it inflicts on itself year in, year out, many thousands of times a day.[9]

Teaching Tip

You may have noticed that there are a good number of quotes in this study. In a study such as creation, it is important to bring in the statements of scientists and others who have made a lifelong study of creation. As you may remember from an earlier Teaching Tip, it's a good idea to print these quotes out on 3 x 5 cards and to read from there. When you pick up the card and read, it's then clear to those you're teaching that this is a quote. Also, this allows you to walk away from the pulpit or lectern as you're reading. With a long quote such as the one above, you may want to highlight certain sections of the quote and read only those. (You've seen this tip once before. If you didn't remember it or haven't been using it, consider this an example of the value of repetition.)

One of the greatest disagreements that Christians have with the theory of evolution is at this point. Evolution would say that the woodpecker developed these attributes at incredible odds because of the threats that nature posed to its existence. The truth of creation says instead that the woodpecker was intricately designed to these exact specifications as an expression of the magnificence of God. Do not allow any theory, any science, any belief to steal from you the truth that all that you are and all that you see were wonderfully created by God.

Split Session Plan: If you're teaching this study over two sessions, end the first session here.

Throughout this study of creation, I want us to keep before us that sense of joy that we have in everything that God has made.

Listen to this simple request from an English book of prayers:

> O heavenly Father, who has filled the world with beauty: Open our eyes to behold your gracious hand in all your works; that, rejoicing in your whole creation, we may learn to serve you with gladness; for the sake of him through whom all things were made, your Son Jesus Christ our Lord. Amen.

"God, open our eyes to see—*you!*" There is no better prayer as we look at some of the intricacies and complexities of creation.

When you look at the problems with evolution that we just studied, a natural question emerges. If the probability of evolution occurring on its own is so low, is it possible that God somehow helped the process along? In other words, could God have used the process of evolution as the means through which he created? This leads to a second major theory of origins:

Theistic evolution

Theistic evolution is the idea that God somehow used the process of evolution as the means by which he created everything.

This theory is attractive to some because it seems that we can have both. The easiest way to solve an argument is to say that everyone is right. Can we do that with evolution and creation? Will the two ideas somehow fit together? Let's take a closer look.

Although this view is very attractive to all who want to integrate the discoveries of science with the Bible, there are some significant problems with the idea of theistic evolution.

1. **The Bible pictures God as being intimately and actively <u>INVOLVED</u> in each aspect and moment of Creation.**

Look again at Psalm 19:1 and at Nehemiah 9:6.

The heavens tell the glory of God, and the skies announce what his hands have made.

—**Psalm 19:1** (NCV)

You alone are the LORD. You made the heavens, even the highest heavens, and all their starry host, the earth and all that is on it, the seas and all that is in them. You give life to everything, and the multitudes of heaven worship you.

—**Nehemiah 9:6**

And read with me these verses from Psalm 33:

By the word of the LORD were the heavens made, their starry host by the breath of his mouth. . . . For he spoke, and it came to be; he commanded, and it stood firm.

—**Psalm 33:6, 9**

As you read these verses, they tell us of a God who was very present in all that he made. They don't give you the picture of a God who started the process, walked away, and just let it play out.

There's a logical gap in the thinking that God personally designed everything through the process of random natural selection. Greg Koukl writes,

The problem with any form of theistic evolution . . . is that it means design by chance. That's like a square circle. There is no such thing. Blending evolution with creation is like putting a square peg in a round hole. It just doesn't fit.[10]

Evolution as a theory supposes that God is nonexistent or is absent as life is being created on our planet. It is a theory of natural selection, not supernatural creation. To take a theory that has its foundation on the idea that God was not a part of the creation process and then try to add God back into that theory has some obvious and fatal problems. It's like taking the foundation out from under a house and then trying to put it back on top of that house.

Teaching Tip

The following is a personal experience. As we've noted before, you are welcome to use this as a part of your teaching. However, if you or someone in your study had a similar experience, it will be much more meaningful to use that. The most personal way to say something is the most powerful way to say it.

Theistic evolution was the theory of creation that I (Tom Holladay) tried to make work in my mind as a new believer in Christ. As someone with a real love for science, it made logical sense to me to try to fit creation and evolution together. Let me tell you how some older Christians helped me to work through this. When I told them what I believed, these friends didn't pressure me to change my position. Instead they encouraged me to take my time and to study this issue more deeply. I'll always be grateful to them for that. Instead of forcing me into an argument, my friends gave me the opportunity to allow God to work in my heart.

Our views on how we were created are very important to us—they go to the core of who we are. If what we're talking about is bringing up questions, it's well worth taking the time to study this more fully.

2. **A <u>POETIC</u> rather than <u>HISTORICAL</u> view of Genesis 1–11**

The way you read the first pages of a book determines the way you read the rest of that book. If you discover in the first few pages that you're reading a murder mystery, you read the entire book as fiction. If the first pages contain lists of recipes, you'll read the book as a cookbook. If you see in the first pages that you're reading through an encyclopedia, you'll likely get another book.

If you're told that the first pages of the Bible are poetically interesting but don't describe what really happened, it impacts how you read the entire Bible. This is why there is such a great battle over the meaning of the first page of the Bible. It impacts the way we read the entire Bible.

Concerning this battle over the meaning of the first verses of Genesis, Ray Bohlin says:

We must realize that the book of Genesis is the foundation of the entire Bible. The word Genesis means "beginnings." Genesis tells the story of the beginning of the universe, solar system, earth, life, man, sin, Israel, nations, and salvation. An understanding of Genesis is crucial to our understanding of the rest of Scripture.

For example, Genesis chapters 1–11 are quoted or referred to more than 100 times in the New Testament alone. And it is over these chapters that the primary battle for the historicity of Genesis rages. All of the first eleven chapters are referred to in the New Testament. Every New Testament author refers somewhere to Genesis 1–11. . . .

How can the first 11 chapters be separated from even the rest of Genesis? The time of Abraham has been verified by archeology. The places, customs, and religions spoken of in Genesis related to Abraham are accurate. The story of Abraham begins in Genesis 12. If Genesis 1 is mythology and Genesis 12 history, where does the allegory stop and the history begin in the first 11 chapters? It is all written in the same historical narrative style.[11]

3. Placing God's <u>CREATION</u> and God's <u>WORD</u> on equal footing as revelations of God

While the heavens do "tell the glory of God," they cannot do so as faithfully and clearly as the Bible.

The grass withers and the flowers fall, but the word of our God stands forever.
—Isaiah 40:8

Heaven and earth will pass away, but my words will never pass away.
—Matthew 24:35

The words of Isaiah in chapter 40 verse 8 and the words of Jesus in Matthew 24:35 tell us the same thing. God's Word is more authoritative than creation because it will outlast creation.

Make no mistake, nature and our study of nature are a great source of human knowledge. But we cannot hold what the stars seem to be telling us through the Hubbell telescope on equal footing with what the God who made those stars clearly tells us in his Word.

Remember: God's Word and nature are not two separate sources of revelation. Nature is designed to teach us certain facts about God, but the Bible is designed to lead us to the God about whom nature speaks. So the two are complementary. The same God who reveals himself through the Bible is the God who created nature. In fact, he built into nature things that would reveal his character.

Think about that for a moment. God didn't just find examples in what was made to teach us. He made them! As he was creating, he knew that one day he would use certain aspects of his creation to teach us.

He would need to teach us how hard work pays off—so he created the ant. (Not the only reason he made the ant, but one of the reasons.) God needed to show us how dependent we are—so he created a sheep. Sheep are, shall we say, not the brightest of animals. When they're not following the shepherd, they have a tendency to wander off and do things like walk off the side of cliffs. As God built a sheep he knew he would one day compare us to sheep. You can almost hear the laughter from heaven.

Discussion questions 3 and 4 can be used here.

We've looked at evolution and at theistic evolution. Now let's turn to the third major view of how things came to be.

Supernatural Creation

God personally and supernaturally created the heavens and the earth.

At this point, I'd like us to take a hard look together at the difference between scientific evidence for a supernatural creation and personal faith in a God who supernaturally created. It's important to understand that science can't prove God. It never will. Science can provide us reasonable evidence, but ultimately this is a matter of faith. It's the only way it can be. You can't scientifically prove an invisible God. It's also the way that God wants it. He desires a personal relationship with each of us, a relationship based on faith.

Science may provide reasonable evidence, but ultimately it is a matter of faith.

Let me give you two examples of this.

1. **Science shows us the big bang, but it takes faith to believe God said, "Let there be light."**

Science can point to a creator.

- **On May 4, 1992, *Time* magazine reported that NASA's Cosmic Background Explorer satellite—COBE—had discovered landmark evidence that the universe did in fact begin with the primeval explosion that has become known as the Big Bang. "If you're religious, it's like looking at God," proclaimed the leader of the research team, George Smoot.[12]**

But only by faith can we believe in our Creator.

- **In Genesis 1:3 the Bible says, "And God said, 'Let there be light,' and there was light."**

It comes down to this: either the universe had a beginning or it didn't. If it had a beginning what caused it to begin? That's where God comes into the picture.

God said . . . and it happened! We'll talk about that more in the next session.

2. **Science shows us the intelligent design of the universe, but it takes faith to believe God personally created that universe.**

Science can point to a creator.

- **A July 20, 1998, *Newsweek* article entitled "Science Finds God" reported:**

  Physicists have stumbled on signs that the cosmos is custom-made for life and consciousness. It turns out that if the constants of nature—unchanging numbers like the strength of gravity, the charge of an electron and the mass of a proton—were the tiniest bit different, then atoms would not hold together, stars would not burn and life would never have made an appearance. "When you realize that the laws of nature must be incredibly finely tuned to produce the universe we see," says John Polkinghorne, who had a distinguished career as a physicist at Cambridge University before becoming an Anglican priest in 1982, "that conspires to plant the idea that the universe did not just happen, but that there must be a purpose behind it." Charles Townes, who shared the 1964 Nobel Prize in Physics for discovering the principles of the laser, goes further: "Many have a feeling that somehow intelligence must have been involved in the laws of the universe."[13]

  An intricate design proves the existence of a designer. Would someone loan me their watch? Thank you. Suppose I took this hammer and smashed this watch but promised that you could put it back together. Here's how. I would take the pieces and put them in this paper bag, shake the bag, and eventually the laws of probability would put the watch back together. Would you let me smash the watch? I hope not!

  William Paley, who first popularized the creation illustration that a watch must have a maker in the early 1800s, said it this way:

  "The marks of design are too strong to be got over. Design must have had a designer. That designer must have been a person. That person is GOD."[14]

But only by faith can we believe in our Creator.

- **In Genesis 1:1 the Bible says, "In the beginning God created the heavens and the earth."**

  In an honest search for truth, we will inevitably see God. We can see God in the creation that he has made: whether we're enjoying the stars on a cold, cloudless night or we are studying the stars through a space telescope.

Listen to this statement by Robert Jastrow, founder of NASA's Goddard Institute for Space Studies:

A sound explanation may exist for the explosive birth of our Universe; but if it does, science cannot find out what the explanation is. The scientist's pursuit of the past ends in the moment of creation. This is an exceedingly strange development, unexpected by all but the theologians. They have always accepted the word of the Bible: In the beginning God created heaven and earth. . . . For the scientist who has lived by his faith in the power of reason, the story ends like a bad dream. He has scaled the mountains of ignorance; he is about to conquer the highest peak; as he pulls himself over the final rock, he is greeted by a band of theologians who have been sitting there for centuries.[15]
—Robert Jastrow, founder of NASA's Goddard Institute for Space Studies

Our human reason can only take us so far. Ultimately there is a moment of faith in which I must decide: "I and all I see are the personal creation of a loving God."

Discussion question 5 can be used here.

There is a third question for us to answer before we end this study.

When Did God Create?

28

1. **All evolutionists believe that Earth is <u>BILLIONS</u> <u>OF</u> <u>YEARS</u> <u>OLD</u>.**

2. **Creationists are divided; most believe in a <u>YOUNG</u> <u>EARTH</u>, but there are some who believe it is an <u>OLD</u> <u>PLANET</u>.**

Could God create everything in six days? Of course he could, he's God. He could have created everything in six seconds if he had so chosen. If you don't believe that, your perspective on God is way too small. In the arena of faith, the question of God creating just as outlined in Genesis is a no-brainer. Of course he could do that.

It's in the arena of science that things get confusing. There is a huge mass of evidence for the universe and our world seemingly being a very old place. Evidence from geological records to radioactive dating to the time it would take light to reach our planet from the stars would seem to indicate that our universe is billions of years old.

The debate between these views centers around the translation of the word *day* (*yom* in Hebrew) in the Genesis 1 text. *Yom* can mean any of the following:

1. **A 24-hour day, which is the most common usage in the Old Testament**
2. **An unspecified period of time**
3. **An era**

The vast majority of the time the word *yom* is used in the Old Testament, it means a twenty-four-hour day. But there are enough times that it has a different meaning that opinions differ on what *yom* means in Genesis 1.

It might interest you to hear Americans' views on creation. They are a surprise to many. A recent Gallup Poll found:

- 44 percent held a strict creationist view (that God created the world in six actual days)
- 39 percent with a combination creation and evolution view
- 10 percent held a strict evolutionist view[16]

We could discuss this for hours and days. My goal here is to briefly help you to understand both sides and then to look at the single most important theological question that needs to be answered in this discussion.

 A Closer Look

Two Questions

1. **How could "old earth" creationists believe that the earth is billions of years old when the Bible says that God created it in just six days?**

   They believe that the days detailed in Genesis 1 represent millions of years or that there was a significant gap between the days of Creation.

   Old earth creationists do not believe in theistic evolution. They believe in a God-ordained creation which took a long time. They don't believe that mankind evolved, but that we were created in a single moment of creation after the universe had been in existence for at least millions of years.

2. **How could "young earth" creationists believe that the earth is thousands of years old in light of the scientific evidence?**

   They believe that God created the universe in full working order—with the starlight already reaching the earth and the ecosystem fully mature. They believe that this fact (along with the cataclysm caused by a worldwide flood) calls into question the apparent time lines deduced from radioactive dating, the earth's magnetic field, petroleum gas deposits, planet rotations, etc.

In this discussion of when God created, there is a burning theological question that I know many of you have on your minds, "But what about the dinosaurs?"

In the Bible's account of creation, mankind and land animals were created on the same day. No matter how you interpret the word *day,* we were created in the same time period. There was a time of perfection on this earth after the creation of animals and man and before the sin of Adam and Eve. This means that man and dinosaur would have walked the earth together—not as caveman and terrible beast on a volcanic earth, but as creations of God in God's perfect world. When did the dinosaurs become extinct? It was obviously due to dramatic climate changes on earth. Some scientists theorize that this was because of an ice age or a meteor impact upon the earth. Many scientists who are believers think it may have been the climactic changes that came after the worldwide flood in Genesis. No one knows for sure.

There is a question even more important than that about the dinosaurs.

The major theological question concerning when God created is, When did sin and death enter the world?

Since . . .

The Bible tells us that it was Adam's personal choice to sin that brought death and the fall of creation.

> **When Adam sinned, sin entered the entire human race. Adam's sin brought death, so death spread to everyone, for everyone sinned.**
> **—Romans 5:12 (NLT)**

Romans 8:20 tells us that the whole of creation suffers because of Adam's sin. Our sin infected all of creation.

And since . . .

The salvation that Jesus brings to us is tied in the New Testament to the historical fact of Adam's sin.

> **For since death came through a man, the resurrection of the dead comes also through a man. For as in Adam all die, so in Christ all will be made alive.**
> **—1 Corinthians 15:21–22**

Therefore . . .

Any idea of creation that theorizes the death of human beings and the fall of God's creation before the sin of Adam and Eve is contrary to the clear teaching of God's Word.

G. Richard Bozarth, in *American Atheist* magazine, shows that even skeptics have a grasp on this truth when he writes, "Christianity has fought, still fights, and will fight science to the desperate end over evolution, because evolution destroys utterly and finally the very reason Jesus' earthly life was supposedly made necessary. Destroy Adam and Eve and the original sin, and in the rubble you will find the sorry remains of the Son of God. If Jesus was not the redeemer that died for our sins, and this is what evolution means, then Christianity is nothing."[17]

He's saying, and he's right, that the reason that the subject of creation is so emotional for us is because it is so personal for us. The truths that we've looked at in this study are not just facts about geological records and historical time lines. Creation truths are truths about why we are here, who we are to be, and where we are headed.

This is a study that calls us to settle some issues in our hearts. The point of any study of creation is not just information about what has been made, but is a new commitment to our maker.

Acting on the Truth

1. **Today will you settle the matter of who made you and the world? Will you believe what God says about himself? And then will you determine to let his Word set the agenda for your life?**

2. **Today will you refresh your belief (or believe for the first time) that God's creation of you means that you have significance and importance to him?**

3. **Today will you make a fresh commitment to stand for the truth that God is the personal Creator of all that we see?**

4. **Every day this week, praise and worship God for all his mighty works. As you drive or walk, enjoy the beauty you see. As you work, enjoy the abilities that God has given you. As you spend time with others, enjoy the unique and marvelous ways that God has made each of us.**

As we close, let me tell you about Liz. At the end of this study, after walking through the four action steps above, she raised her hand and said, "I have something to say. That fourth one, where it says 'praise and worship God for all his mighty works,' that's exactly what I did. I wasn't a person who believed in Christ, but a friend encouraged me to just begin to look at what God had made. This was my first step, the first step in seeing and now knowing the God who loves me."

She got it! As we look at God's creation, we should be led to a deeper trust in him. Even in our imperfect world, it's spread out before us every day—the awesome and personal love of God, evidenced in all that he has made.

Begin working on memory card 5, "The Truth about Creation."

Discussion Questions

1. One of the statements at the beginning of our study of Creation was, "What you believe about your origin affects your self-worth, your relationships, and how you view God." In what ways do you feel that your view of God as our creator is impacting your daily thoughts about yourself and this world?

2. What is it that amazes you—simply amazes you—about the creation of God?

3. How can we discuss Creation in such a way that we don't appear scientifically illiterate? What are some ways that we can express to others that we are not ignoring the seeming evidence but just seeing it differently?

4. Does a discussion of topics such as irreducible complexity and fossil records excite you or bore you to tears? Why do you think people are different on this point: why do some love to study these details while others could happily do without them?

5. What one thing could you do to advance the idea of God as Creator and God's Word as reliable above the idea of evolution? In your community? With other believers? In your own family?

Creation
Part 2

Life Change Objective

To build a strong foundation for worshiping and obeying God as your Creator.

Summary Teaching Outline

Seven Truths about Creation That Are Foundations for Our Lives

God Created Everything out of Nothing

Creation Was Done in Proper Order

God Saw That It Was Good

Man Is the Crown of Creation

    How exactly did God create man?

    How are we created in God's image?

       1. Our personality: mind, will, emotions

       2. Our sexuality: created as male and female

       3. Our morality: created as moral beings, with a moral consciousness

       4. Our spirituality: created with the ability to relate to God

God Finished the Job

God Rested on the Seventh Day

God Now Sustains All That He Made

There is a bird that lives in the outback of Australia named the Megapode. The bird weighs about 3-1/2 pounds, but lays eggs that are ostrich size, about a half pound each. It lays up to thirty-five of these in one season! Question: how does this tiny bird sit on all of these eggs to get them to hatch?

It builds an incubator. (In fact, it's also called an "incubator bird" or a "mound bird.") The male builds an incubator mound and uses wet grasses to create compost heat and makes air holes to give proper ventilation. The bird also uses sand to insulate the mound in the summer so that the inside temperature stays at 92°. Male incubator birds have temperature-sensitive areas in their mouths that allow them to sample a mouthful of soil and determine its temperature so they can maintain the eggs at 92°F ± one or two degrees. If the temperature varies any more than that, the eggs won't hatch.[1]

How do they know how to do all of this? The wisdom of God.

In the last session we looked at the important issues in the great evolution vs Creation debate. We talked about some truths that we all need to wrestle with. That's good—the truth needs to be wrestled with!

In this study I want to give you some truths that we all can embrace. I want you to enjoy, to the depth of your being, the truth that God is your creator.

Seven Truths about Creation That Are Foundations for Our Lives

You might think of these as seven truths for the seven days of your week. In the last session we looked at how the doctrine of Creation impacts the broad issues of our lives such as who we are and why we are here. We're now going to look at how the truth about creation works its way into the everyday and the week to week.

Sometimes we're so intent on looking at creation through a microscope or a telescope that we fail to see the real scope of what God is telling us.

God Created Everything out of <u>NOTHING</u>

By faith we understand that the universe was formed at God's command, so that what is seen was not made out of what was visible.
—**Hebrews 11:3**

And God said, "Let there be light," and there was light.
—**Genesis 1:3**

Would you circle the word "said."

God simply spoke, and Creation happened.

God said, and it happened!

Imagine this with me. God said, "Land . . . water . . . sun . . . bird . . . whale . . . flower . . ."

Is this a poetic way of stating the natural processes that God used? No. He said, and it happened. To miss that is to miss the most essential truth about Creation.

Everything was created out of nothing.

What materials did he use to create? Nothing—just his word. That is hard for us to grasp. We think, "What did the nothing look like before God created everything out of it?" It didn't look like anything. It was just nothing. For us, creativity is rearranging the things God has made; putting them together in different ways. For God, creation is making it all out of nothing.

Scientifically impossible? Of course it is! Science studies how creation works. But a study of how things work will not necessarily tell you how they began.

To try to figure out Creation from the natural processes that God built into his creation is like trying to figure out what an orange tree looks like by looking at an orange, or an okra plant by looking at an okra. If you've never seen an okra plant, you might think okra grows on trees, in bunches like bananas.

Teaching Tip

Bring an orange and an okra—or any other fruits or vegetables you like—to hold up.

God said, and it was made.

Everything that you see is an example of the creative mind of God.

Don't let our human need to figure everything out steal away from you the wonder of what God has done. Don't let anyone or anything steal that sense of awe. It is one of the responses in you that God most enjoys.

This week, let the truth about Creation fill you with the wonder you need to face the realities of life.

C. S. Lewis portrays that sense of awe and wonder as he writes a picture of creation in *The Magician's Nephew* from the Chronicles of Narnia. This is not a doctrinal explanation of exactly how Creation happened, but it does capture the wonder that we need in our hearts as we think about creation. Aslan the Lion (who represents Jesus in these books) is about to make a world. Among others, two children named Digory and Polly and an English cab driver are witnessing this scene.

Hush!" said the Cabby. They all listened.

In the darkness something was happening at last. A voice had begun to sing. It was very far away and Digory found it hard to decide from what direction it was coming. Sometimes it seemed to come from all directions at once. Sometimes he almost thought it was coming out of the earth beneath them. . . .

Then two wonders happened at the same moment. One was that the voice was suddenly joined by other voices; more voices than you could possibly count. They were in harmony with it, but far higher up the scale: cold, tingling, silvery voices. The second wonder was that the blackness overhead, all at once, was blazing with stars. They didn't come out gently one by one, as they do on a summer evening. One moment there had been nothing but darkness; next moment a thousand, thousand points of light leaped out—single stars, constellations, and planets, brighter and bigger than any in our world. There were no clouds. The new stars and the new voices began at exactly the same time. If you had seen and heard it, as Digory did, you would have felt quite certain that it was the stars themselves who were singing, and that it was the First Voice, the deep one, which had made them appear and made them sing.

"Glory be!" said the Cabby. "I'd ha' been a better man all my life if I'd known there were things like this."[2]

God created everything out of nothing! Recapture the wonder of that this week! Whatever you face this week, this is a "wonder full" world.

> Discussion question 1 can be used here.

Creation Was Done in <u>PROPER</u> <u>ORDER</u>

God said, "Let there be light" . . . God called the expanse "sky'" . . . "Let the water under the sky be gathered to one place, and let dry ground appear. . . . Let the land produce vegetation." . . . The land produced vegetation: plants bearing seed according to their kinds and trees bearing fruit with seed in it according to their kinds. . . . "Let there be lights in the expanse of the sky to separate the day from the night, and let them serve as signs to mark seasons and days and years. . . . Let the water teem with living creatures, and let birds fly above the earth. . . . Let the land produce living creatures according to their kinds. . . . Let us make man in our image."

—Genesis 1:3–26

Notice the order that is a part of God's creation from the very beginning. First light, then sky, then water, then land, and then plants and animals. He created in proper order, and God also built order into his creation. Circle "seasons and days and years"—he built order into astronomy. Circle "according to their kinds." He built order into biology.

- **Both evolutionists and creationists believe in a well-ordered creation.**

- **Evolution is the idea that order evolved out of chaos.**

- **The Bible teaches instead that order was created by design.**

  The order in God's creation literally shouts, There is a plan here! Watch the planets. Look at a salmon. Study a beehive. Look at how cells divide. Delve into the properties of light. There is a plan here.

  God made bees with a fascinating order in the hive: Queen bees and workers bees and scout bees. The scout bees had to have a way to tell the worker bees where to find the pollen—and God even designed wonderful order into that! The bee scouts do a dance that tells the other bees where to go. In this dance they show the distance to the food source by the number of times the dancer circles and by wiggling her abdomen. The greater the distance, the more slowly she wiggles. The direction is revealed by the direction and angle the dancing bee cuts across the circle. It took the Nobel Prize–winning entomologist Karl Von Frisch twenty years to decipher this dance! God put it into the bee's brain in a moment of creation.[3]

  What does that mean for you and me as we live day to day?

This week: Let God's creation be a constant reminder that God has a plan!

  The sun still comes up each morning, plants continue to grow, the stars keep shining at night, and the bees keep dancing. He has a plan for this world, and he has a plan for you!

Discussion question 2 can be used here.

God Saw That It Was <u>GOOD</u>

God saw that the light was good, and he separated the light from the darkness.

—Genesis 1:4

God called the dry ground "land," and the gathered waters he called "seas." And God saw that it was good.

—Genesis 1:10

The land produced vegetation: plants bearing seed according to their kinds and trees bearing fruit with seed in it according to their kinds. And God saw that it was good.

—Genesis 1:12

. . . to govern the day and the night, and to separate light from darkness. And God saw that it was good.

—Genesis 1:18

So God created the great creatures of the sea and every living and moving thing with which the water teems, according to their kinds, and every winged bird according to its kind. And God saw that it was good.
—Genesis 1:21

God made the wild animals according to their kinds, the livestock according to their kinds, and all the creatures that move along the ground according to their kinds. And God saw that it was good.
—Genesis 1:25

God saw all that he had made, and it was very good. And there was evening, and there was morning—the sixth day.
—Genesis 1:31

It may sound simple to say that creation is "good," but some of the most destructive false teaching in the history of the church has revolved around this idea of the creation being evil. Look at these two bullet points in your outline:

- **God's creation is not evil. The world did not make people evil; people brought evil into the world.**

- **Don't make the mistake of thinking that because something is of the physical world it must therefore be evil.**

God richly gives us everything to enjoy.
—1 Timothy 6:17 (NCV)

A false teaching to watch out for is the idea that material things are inherently evil. The belief that "things" are where evil resides will take you in one of two directions. You can see this happening again and again down through Christian history. One direction this false teaching takes is, "Hey, this body and this world are evil, so it really doesn't matter what I do with them. When I get to heaven I'll be perfect, but I may as well sin in this body, because it's evil and I can't help myself and because it's going to be tossed aside anyway." The other direction this false teaching takes is, "If everything is evil in this world, I can't touch anything in this world, can't be a part of anything in this world, can't enjoy anything in this world." Don't make the mistake of thinking that just because something is of the physical world it has to be evil. That's not what the Bible teaches.

Many believers act as if we can't enjoy anything until we get to heaven. God created this world too. Even though it's scarred by sin, that does not take away the truth of creation. Don't wait until you get to heaven to enjoy what God has made. Start now.

I picture the joys that God gives us on earth and the joys that God gives us in heaven like this. This chocolate candy bar is one of the joys on earth. (Hold up one of those little bite-sized candy bars.) And *this* candy bar (hold up the largest chocolate bar you can find!) represents the joy we will have in heaven. What we have now is only a taste of what we will experience then, but it is a wonderful taste!

This week: enjoy God's creation!

Discussion question 3 can be used here.

Man Is the <u>CROWN</u> <u>OF</u> <u>CREATION</u>

Let's get some perspective on this by looking at how God created man.

How exactly did God create man?

Then the Lord God took dust from the ground and formed a man from it. He breathed the breath of life into the man's nose, and the man became a living person.
—Genesis 2:7 (NCV)

So the Lord God caused the man to sleep very deeply, and while he was asleep, God removed one of the man's ribs. Then God closed up the man's skin at the place where he took the rib. The Lord God used the rib from the man to make a woman, and then he brought the woman to the man.
—Genesis 2:21–22 (NCV)

When God made Adam, he took some dirt from the ground and formed it into a man. (Which means a woman is being biblically accurate if she says to a guy who has treated her badly on a date, "You're dirt.")

When God made Eve, he took a rib from Adam's side and out of that rib created a woman.

While God made the rest of creation with a word, he made us from the dust of the ground and from a rib. Why? Adam being made from the dust of the ground is a reminder of our connection to the rest of creation. It's a reminder that although we are the crown of creation, we must humbly remember that we are created by God. Eve's creation from Adam's rib is a reminder of our connection to one another.

At the tip of your fingers you have something that no one else in the world has or ever will have. Your fingerprints! If someone finds your fingerprint in a room, they know that you've been there. Being created in God's image means that God's fingerprints are all over our lives! His heart, his character, his values—his person—are all to be seen in who we are.

Listen to these words from Steven Curtis Chapman's song "Fingerprints of God."

The person in the mirror doesn't look like the magazine
Oh, but when I look at you, it's clear to me that . . .
I can see the fingerprints of God
When I look at you
I can see the fingerprints of God
And I know it's true
You're a masterpiece that all creation quietly applauds
And you're covered with the fingerprints of God[4]

Split Session Plan: If you're teaching this study over two sessions, end the first session here.

The fact that we are created in God's image is one of the most humbling truths that I know. Just to make sure you don't allow this to become instead a source of pride, let me remind you of a few facts.

More cubic yards of dirt are moved by earthworms every day than all our machines could move in a lifetime.

Snowflakes are tiny things, but put enough of them together and they can bring a city to its knees.

You could work out in a gym every day of your life and still not gain the relative strength of an ant (who can lift fifty times its own weight).

A single flare on our sun releases an energy roughly that of "one billion"[5] hydrogen bombs.

Just a few little facts to keep things in perspective! Now let's talk about the fact that we're made in the image of God and what it means for us to be created in God's image.

How are we created in God's image?

1. Our <u>PERSONALITY</u>: mind, will, emotions

God thinks, we think. God decides, we decide. God feels, we feel.

Animals don't think like we do, they don't reason. Insects don't decide, they respond to a built-in control we call instinct. Plants don't have feelings. They don't feel rejected because you didn't water them last week. In all of creation only mankind has these aspects of God's person.

The next one might surprise you. We are also like God in our sexuality. That got your attention!

2. Our <u>SEXUALITY</u>: created as male and female

> **So God created man in his own image, in the image of God he created him; male and female he created them.**
>
> —Genesis 1:27

Notice in Genesis, each time after saying "in his own image," God reminds us that means "male and female he created them." What is God saying?

For one thing, he wants to make it clear that it's not *just* men or *just* women created in God's image—it is both.

But there is something deeper here than even that. Genesis doesn't say "both male and female," it says "male and female he created them." In some way our sexuality is tied up with what it means to be created in God's image. Many theologians go so far as to believe that sexuality is actually part of what it means to be created in the image of God.

This is very important for us to understand in our world. We live in a world that has made sexuality into just sex. We've reduced its meaning dramatically. For many, sexuality is merely physical.

There's a better answer. God made men and women to be very different. How many of you would say amen to that? As I recognize what it means to be created in God's image, I begin to rejoice in those differences. My distinctives as a man [or woman] reflect God's image. Your distinctives as a woman [or man] reflect God's image just as much.

Let's be very clear about this because it is easily misunderstood. God reveals himself in a male image: Father, Son, and Spirit. Jesus came to this earth as a man. But that does not mean that we all, men and women alike, do not reflect the image of God as we live out who he created us to be. God chose to create both male and female to reflect the person and character of God on earth.

It's amazing how quickly we get into trouble when we forget this truth— as individuals and as societies. The root cause of gender confusion and sexual immorality is in not trusting that our greatest joy is in living out who God made us to be as men and women.

A Closer Look

Because *all* mankind was made in the image of God:

Both <u>MALE</u> and <u>FEMALE</u> have equal value and worth.

Each <u>RACE</u> has equal value and worth.

From one man he made every nation of men, that they should inhabit the whole earth; and he determined the times set for them and the exact places where they should live. God did this so that men would seek him and perhaps reach out for him and find him, though he is not far from each one of us. "For in him we live and move and have our being."

—Acts 17:26–28

3. Our <u>MORALITY</u>: created as moral beings, with a moral consciousness

We know right from wrong. A dog doesn't know right from wrong. You can train a dog to do what you tell it, but it has no moral conscience that causes it to think, "I shouldn't be eating out of garbage cans, I need to get into a recovery program." "Hi, my name is Spot and I eat garbage."

A mouse that invades your house doesn't have a conscience. It doesn't lay awake at night wondering if it was right to steal that piece of cheese, agonizing over its place in the world.

When Adam and Eve sinned, they immediately felt shame. God created us to be moral beings. Acts 24:16 reminds us that we all have a conscience.

Then the eyes of both of them were opened, and they realized they were naked; so they sewed fig leaves together and made coverings for themselves.

—Genesis 3:7

So I strive always to keep my conscience clear before God and man.

—Acts 24:16

Our moral nature includes both freedom of choice and responsibility for our choices.

With freedom comes responsibility. Any of you have teenagers? When you get the car keys out and you're going to let your car out of your sight for the evening, what do you tell your son or daughter? "With freedom comes responsibility." That's what God tells us in giving us freedom of choice.

4. Our <u>SPIRITUALITY</u>: created with the ability to relate to God

> Now we rejoice in our wonderful new relationship with God—all because of what our Lord Jesus Christ has done in dying for our sins—making us friends of God.
>
> —Romans 5:11 (LB)

The relationship that Adam and Eve had with God was broken, shattered, when they disobeyed him in the Garden of Eden. Romans 5:11 reminds us that through Jesus Christ that relationship is restored. Our spirit is brought back to life through God's Spirit.

We've just touched the surface of what it means for us to be created in God's image. When you and I begin to allow our view of the world and the choices we make to be more and more determined by the image that we've been created in rather than the images we see around us, we will begin to live out what it means to be God's children. Which is going to make a deeper impact on your life and decisions this week: the image you see on a billboard or the image you have been created in? The image on a TV screen or the fact that you've been made in the image of God? As we focus on being made in the image of God, we become more and more healthy—more and more whole people for the rest of our lives.

This week: intentionally focus throughout each day on the fact that you are made in God's image.

Discussion question 4 can be used here.

God <u>FINISHED</u> the Job

> **Thus the heavens and the earth were completed in all their vast array.**
> —Genesis 2:1

Circle the word "completed" in Genesis 2:1. Read with me Hebrews 4:3, and circle the word "finished."

> **God's work was finished from the time he made the world.**
> —Hebrews 4:3 (NCV)

- **The universe is not some vast unfinished symphony.**

- **This world and universe are not works in progress.**

- **The universe is a finished work of creation that has been marred by the presence of sin.**

Do you see the incredible difference this makes in the way we think about this world? An unfinished work in progress is like a house with only the frame completed. A finished work that has been marred is like a Victorian mansion that has been neglected for years. One needs to be finished. The other needs to be restored. We don't need finishing; we need restoring!

This world does not need to be made better, it needs to be brought back to what it was originally. We don't need to construct a new and better model of mankind, we need to be restored to our relationship with God. We cannot improve on God's original creation.

This week: look forward to God's restoration of his creation.

Discussion question 5 can be used here.

God <u>RESTED</u> on the Seventh Day

By the seventh day God had finished the work he had been doing; so on the seventh day he rested from all his work. And God blessed the seventh day and made it holy, because on it he rested from all the work of creating that he had done.

—Genesis 2:2–3

Why did God rest?

Two reasons:

Teaching Tip

It's amazing how much a simple statement such as "two reasons" can help those who are listening to you. When you say this, those listening immediately begin to look for what these two things will be. Whenever you give people a number to listen for, it builds a kind of anticipation into what you are saying.

It's important, of course, to very clearly let people know these two reasons as you are stating them. Every communicator has had the experience of not making clear the fact that you are now stating the second reason, only to have people get that confused look as they wait for the point that never comes.

The first reason:

• **To give us an <u>EXAMPLE</u> to follow**

Work and get everything done during six days each week, but the seventh day is a day of rest to honor the LORD your God. . . . The reason is that in six days the LORD made everything—the sky, the earth, the sea, and everything in them. On the seventh day he rested.
—Exodus 20:9–11 (NCV)

God did not need to rest because he was tired. God never gets tired or weary. He decided to cease working on the seventh day to give us an example of how we are to live. Do you rest one day a week? You were built to. If you don't rest, you'll break down.

Those of you who are musicians know that every musical score is literally filled with rests. During the rests, you don't play—and that is what makes the music beautiful. If you tried to play music without any rests, you would just hear a cacophony of jumbled noise. God, the great composer of every one of our lives, has intentionally built rests into our lives. If you keep playing through the rests, you aren't creating better music, you're just making more noise.

A brief caution here. Resting on the seventh day is a favorite subject of legalists. They not only want to tell you to rest on the seventh day, they want to tell you *how* to rest on that day! The Bible says how you rest is up to you. In fact, the New Testament indicates that we shouldn't get hung up on the exact day, as long as we rest one day out of seven. God is talking about a kind of rest that focuses on him, not just a day off. For most of you this day of rest will be Sunday, because that is the day that you worship with others.

The second reason God rested on the seventh day is:

- **To teach us his plan for the ages**

   There remains, then, a Sabbath-rest for the people of God; for anyone who enters God's rest also rests from his own work, just as God did from his. Let us, therefore, make every effort to enter that rest.
—Hebrews 4:9–11

Circle in this verse the phrase "enters God's rest."

God rested from his work to teach us that, spiritually, we must enter his rest. In the way that God created, he built a reminder that our relationship with him is not found in our works, it's found in trusting and resting in his work in our lives. We'll be taking a closer look at what that means when we study salvation. This verse reminds us that in order to find salvation we must rest from our works and enter into his rest. We must stop depending on what *we* can do and start resting in what only *he* can do.

Rest doesn't mean that we don't do anything. Look at the last phrase in Hebrews, "make every effort to enter that rest." It takes great effort of heart and faith to stop trusting in your work and to start trusting in God's work in you.

This week: take a day of worshipful rest.

Discussion question 6 can be used here.

God Now Sustains All That He Made

> He existed before everything else began, and he holds all creation together.
>
> —Colossians 1:17 (NLT)

The word used for God's continuing and active work in holding creation together is the "providence" of God. Never make the mistake of thinking that God made it all and then somehow left it to run on its own. There are literally hundreds of verses throughout the Bible concerning God's intimate and intricate sustaining of his creation.

From the smallest dewdrop to the greatest nations, God sustains it all!

Look at Job 38 and Psalm 47.

> Who fathers the drops of dew?
>
> —Job 38:28

> God reigns over the nations; God is seated on his holy throne.
>
> —Psalm 47:8

Imagine yourself trying to put together a simple plastic world globe. You take the four pieces that came in the box and fit them carefully together with your hands. As long as you keep your hands around the globe it stays together. The moment you let go, it falls apart in pieces. The glue holding that globe together is you.

God is the glue that holds all of the universe together. And in this case, there is no other glue strong enough to suffice. Without his "hands" around everything every moment, it would all fall apart, come apart, fly apart.

God is your sustainer! You may think that it's your paycheck that sustains you. It's not. The paycheck is one of the supply lines that God is giving you to sustain you right now, but he is the supplier. Never confuse the supply line with the supplier. Never confuse the means that God uses to sustain you with the fact that he and he alone is your sustainer.

This week, look to the God who sustains the universe to give you sustaining strength throughout each day.

We end this look at creation with an opportunity for you to personally respond to God as your creator. Try to filter out all of the distractions in and around you, and let's spend a few moments thanking God as our creator. Would you agree with me that we don't spend nearly enough time doing that? Let's do it now.

 Acting on the Truth

How to Praise God as Your Creator

"Seeing creation as an expression of your love . . ."

He made the sun and the moon. His love continues forever. He made the sun to rule the day. His love continues forever. He made the moon and stars to rule the night. His love continues forever. . . . He gives food to every living creature. His love continues forever.

—Psalm 136:7–9, 25 (NCV)

"I kneel before you in humility . . ."

Come, kneel before the LORD our Maker, for he is our God. We are his sheep, and he is our Shepherd. Oh, that you would hear him calling you today and come to him!

—Psalm 95:6–7 (LB)

"praising you for this day . . ."

This is the day the LORD has made; let us rejoice and be glad in it.

—Psalm 118:24

"and thanking you for creating me."

I praise you because you made me in an amazing and wonderful way. What you have done is wonderful. I know this very well.

—Psalm 139:14 (NCV)

Lord, thank you for making me to be the person that I am. Forgive me for comparing myself to others and for sometimes wanting to be a copy. Help me to live out the uniqueness of who you've made me to be.

In Jesus' name, amen.

Finish memorizing memory card 5, "The Truth about Creation"—you'll be amazed at how often you'll share this particular truth!

Discussion Questions

1. What stands out in your mind as one of the most powerful pictures of the creative mind of God? Be specific.

2. In what ways does God's creation speak to you specifically about the person and character of God? Example: when I look at the stars . . . at the ocean . . . at the Grand Canyon, etc.

3. How does the truth that God is the Creator help you to look at this world with a greater sense of security?

4. Do you tend to look at material things as "good" or as "evil"? Discuss the difference between recognizing that evil is present in this world and thinking that *everything* that is material must be evil.

5. What feelings do you have when you focus your thoughts on the truth that mankind is created in God's image?

6. How well are you doing at following God's example to rest? What are one or two practical things that you could do to better follow his example? (We know, this question *assumes* we aren't doing so well!)

For Further Study

Geisler, Norman L. *Origin Science.* Grand Rapids, Mich.: Baker, 1987.

Ham, Ken. *The Genesis Solution.* Grand Rapids, Mich.: Baker, 1988.

Ham, Ken. *The Lie: Evolution.* El Cajon, Calif.: Creation Life, 1987.

Huse, Scott M. *The Collapse of Evolution.* Grand Rapids, Mich.: Baker, 1983.

McGowan, C. H. *In Six Days.* Van Nuys, Calif.: Bible Voice, 1976.

Morris, Henry. *The Beginning of the World.* El Cajon, Calif.: Creation Life, 1991.

Ross, Hugh. *Creation and Time.* Colorado Springs: NavPress, 1994.

Ross, Hugh. *The Fingerprint of God.* Orange, Calif.: Promise, 1989.

Stoner, Don. *A New Look at an Old Earth.* Eugene, Ore.: Harvest House, 1997.

Notes

Introductory Study

1. Charles Colson and Nancy Pearcey, *How Now Shall We Live?* (Wheaton, Ill.: Tyndale, 1999), 14.

2. Charles Swindoll, *Growing Deep in the Christian Life* (Sisters, Ore.: Multnomah Press, 1986), 12–13.

3. Glenn Tinder, *Political Thinking: The Perennial Questions*, 4th ed. (Glenview, Ill.: Scott, Foresman, 1986), 1.

4. J. I. Packer, *Truth and Power* (Wheaton, Ill.: Shaw, 1996), 16.

5. Robert Bellah, *Habits of the Heart* (Berkeley: University of California Press, 1985), 228.

Session 1. The Bible: Part 1

1. Charles Swindoll, *Growing Deep in the Christian Life* (Sisters, Ore.: Multnomah Press, 1986), 56.

2. Norman L. Geisler and Ronald M. Brooks, *When Skeptics Ask* (Wheaton, Ill.: Victor, 1990), 159–60.

3. Erwin Lutzer, *Seven Reasons Why You Can Trust the Bible* (Chicago: Moody Press, 1998), 73.

4. Norman Geisler, *Baker Encyclopedia of Apologetics* (Grand Rapids, Mich.: Baker, 1999), 47.

5. William F. Albright, *The Archaeology of Palestine* (Harmondsworth, Middlesex: Pelican, 1960), 127.

6. Josh McDowell, *Evidence That Demands a Verdict* (San Bernardino, Calif.: Here's Life Publishers, 1972), 19–20.

7. John MacArthur Jr., *Is the Bible Reliable?* (Panorama City, Calif.: Word of Grace Communications, 1988), 5.

8. R. W. Funk et al., *The Five Gospels* (New York: Macmillan, 1993).

9. Geisler and Brooks, *When Skeptics Ask*, 145.

10. J. I. Packer, *Truth and Power* (Wheaton, Ill.: Shaw, 1996), 16.

11. C. H. Spurgeon, "Is God in the Camp?" (sermon delivered at the Metropolitan Tabernacle, Newington, on Thursday evening, 9 April 1891), www.spurgeon.org/sermons/2239.htm.

Session 2. The Bible: Part 2

1. Anne Ortlund, *Fix Your Eyes on Jesus* (Dallas: Word, 1991), 130–31.

2. John Pollack, *Billy Graham: The Authorized Biography* (London: Hodder and Stoughton, 1966), 80–81.

3. Howard Hendricks, *Living by the Book* (Chicago: Moody Press, 1991), 19.

4. John Ortberg, *The Life You've Always Wanted* (Grand Rapids, Mich.: Zondervan, 1997), 188.

Session 3. God: Part 1

1. A. W. Tozer, *Knowledge of the Holy* (New York: Harper and Row, 1961), 9.

2. Robert Hughes, "Visionaries: Seeking the Spirit," *Time* (21 May 1997): 32ff.

3. Avery Willis, *The Biblical Basis of Missions* (Nashville: Convention Press, 1984), 16.

4. Carla Power et al., "Lost in Silent Prayer," *Newsweek International* (12 July 1999): 48.

5. Adapted from Philip Yancey, *What's So Amazing about Grace?* (Grand Rapids, Mich.: Zondervan, 1997), 49–51.

6. J. P. Moreland, Saddleback Church men's retreat, 7 February 2000.

Session 4. God: Part 2

1. Billy Graham, *The Holy Spirit: Activating God's Power in Your Life* (New York: Warner, 1980), 27–28.

2. Walter A. Elwell, ed., *The Shaw Pocket Bible Handbook* (Wheaton, Ill.: Shaw, 1984), 359.

Session 5. Jesus: Part 1

1. Christie's Auction House Offers Free Appraisal, *Weekend Edition*, National Public Radio, 6 April 1996.

2. Walter Elwell, ed., *Topical Analysis of the Bible* (Grand Rapids, Mich.: Baker, 1991).

3. Billy Sunday, in a sermon, "Wonderful," quoted in Elijah P. Brown, *The Real Billy Sunday: The Life and Work of Rev. William Ashley Sunday, D.D., The Baseball Evangelist* (Dayton, Ohio: Otterbein Press, 1914).

4. Max Lucado, *God Came Near* (Portland, Ore.: Multnomah Press, 1987), 54.

5. Philip Yancey, *The Jesus I Never Knew* (Grand Rapids, Mich.: Zondervan, 1995), 89.

6. *Encyclopaedia Britannica*, 15th ed., s.v. "Jesus Christ."

7. H. G. Wells, quoted in Philip Yancey, *The Jesus I Never Knew* (Grand Rapids, Mich.: Zondervan, 1995), 17.

Session 6. Jesus: Part 2

1. C. S. Lewis, *Mere Christianity* (New York: Macmillan, 1952), 55–56.

2. Josh McDowell, *Evidence That Demands a Verdict* (San Bernardino, Calif.: Here's Life Publishers, 1979), 103–7.

3. Peter W. Stoner, *Science Speaks: Scientific Proof of the Accuracy of Prophecy and the Bible*, 3rd rev. ed. (Chicago: Moody Press, 1969), 100–107.

4. Thomas Arnold, *Sermons on the Christian Life: Its hopes, its fears, its close*, 6th ed. (London: T. Fellowes, 1859), 234.

5. Simon Greenleaf, *The Testimony of the Evangelists* (New York: Baker, 1874), 28.

6. Lee Strobel, *The Case for Christ* (Grand Rapids, Mich.: Zondervan, 1998), 259–69.

7. Anne Ortlund, *Fix Your Eyes on Jesus* (Dallas: Word, 1991), 22.

8. J. Sidlow Baxter, *Majesty: The God You Should Know* (San Bernardino, Calif.: Here's Life Publishers, 1984), 25.

9. Philip Yancey, *The Jesus I Never Knew* (Grand Rapids, Mich.: Zondervan, 1995), 199.

Session 7. The Holy Spirit: Part 1

1. A. B. Simpson, *The Holy Spirit* (Camp Hill, Penn.: Christian Publications, 1994), 317.

2. Billy Graham, *The Holy Spirit: Activating God's Power in Your Life* (New York: Warner, 1980), 91.

Session 8. The Holy Spirit: Part 2

1. Charles R. Swindoll, *Flying Closer to the Flame* (Dallas: Word, 1993), 75.

2. The following three illustrations are taken from *The Spirit-Filled Life,* used by permission from Campus Crusade for Christ.

3. Bill Bright, *Have You Made the Wonderful Discovery of the Spirit-Filled Life?* (Orlando, Fla.: New Life Publications, © Campus Crusade for Christ 1966, 2000), 2–3. All rights reserved. Used by permission.

4. Swindoll, *Flying Closer to the Flame,* 75.

5. Bill Bright, *The Holy Spirit: The Key to Supernatural Living* (San Bernardino, Calif.: Campus Crusade for Christ, 1980), 89.

6. Larry Crabb, *Inside Out* (Colorado Springs, Colo.: NavPress, 1988), 71.

7. Bright, *The Holy Spirit,* 76–77.

8. Ray Stedman, "The Power You Already Have," 29 September 1991, sermon preached at Peninsula Bible Church, Palo Alto, Calif., available at www.pbc.org/dp/stedman/misc/4308.html.

Session 9. Creation: Part 1

1. Tommy Walker, "He Knows My Name," on *Never Gonna Stop,* Doulos, 1996.

2. R. E. D. Clark, *Darwin: Before and After* (London: Paternoster, 1948), 86.

3. Francis Crick, *Life Itself, Its Origin and Nature* (New York: Simon and Schuster, 1981), 51–52.

4. Charles C. Ryrie, *Basic Theology* (Wheaton, Ill.: SP Publications, 1986), 177.

5. Fred Hoyle, *The Intelligent Universe* (New York: Holt, Rinehart and Winston, 1983), 19.

6. Francis Darwin, *Life and Letters of Charles Darwin* (New York: Basic Books, 1959), 1:210.

7. David Raup, "Conflicts Between Darwin and Paleontology," *Field Museum of Natural History Bulletin* 30 no. 1 (1979): 25.

8. Michael J. Behe, *Darwin's Black Box: The Biochemical Challenge to Evolution* (New York: Free Press, 1995), 39.

9. David Juhasz, "The Incredible Woodpecker," *Creation* 18 (December 1995–February 1996): 10–13.

10. Gregory Koukl, *Michael Behe's Theistic Evolution,* transcript of Stand to Reason Radio, 24 December 1997, accessed 1 February 2003 at www.str.org.

11. Dr. Ray Bohlin, *Why We Believe in Creation.* Accessed 1 February 2003 at www.probe.org.

12. Michael D. Lemonick, "Echoes of the Big Bang," *Time* (4 May 1992), 62.

13. Sharon Begley, "Science Finds God," *Newsweek* (20 July 1998), 46–51.

14. William Paley, *Natural Theology* (London, England: R. Faulder, 1802).

15. Robert Jastrow, *God and the Astronomers,* 2d ed. (New York: W. W. Norton, 1992), 106–7.

16. Kenneth Chang, *Evolutionary Beliefs* (New York: ABC Internet Ventures, 1999), accessed at http://abcnews.go.com/sections/science/DailyNews/evolution-views990816.html.

17. G. Richard Bozarth, "The Meaning of Evolution," *American Atheist* (20 September 1979): 30.

Session 10. Creation: Part 2

1. *New Encyclopaedia Britannica,* 15th ed., s.v. "Megapode."

2. C. S. Lewis, *The Magician's Nephew* (New York: Macmillan, 1955), 98–100.

3. *Collier's Encyclopedia,* s.v. "bee."

4. Steven Curtis Chapman, "Fingerprints of God," *Speechless,* Sparrow Records, 1999.

5. NASA website, http://helios.gsfc.nasa.gov/cme.html.

Resources Available

Audiotapes of Foundations. Audiotapes of each of the *Foundations* studies, taught by Tom Holladay and Kay Warren, are available at www.pastors.com.

Purpose-Driven Church. (see following pages)

Purpose-Driven Life. (see following pages)

Celebrate Recovery. (see following pages)

40 Days of Purpose. A forty-day campaign for churches that builds on *The Purpose-Driven Life* as a foundation, adding sermons, small group resources and video tapes, and training for leadership teams. This is a forty-day emphasis that promises to permanently change your church. (contact PurposeDriven.com)

Purpose-Driven Youth Ministry. The essentials of a healthy, Purpose-Driven youth ministry from Saddleback's youth pastor, Doug Fields. (Zondervan)

Pastors.com and PurposeDriven.com have additional resources for those in full-time ministry. Pastors.com specializes in messages and helps for the pastor as a communicator, including sermons and books. PurposeDriven.com specializes in tools and program materials to help churches focus on our God-given purposes.

MEMORY CARDS

---

1 — The Truth about the Bible

The Bible is God's perfect guidebook for living.

---

2 — The Truth about God

God is bigger and better and closer than I can imagine.

---

3 — The Truth about Jesus

Jesus is God showing himself to us.

---

4 — The Truth about the Holy Spirit

God lives in me and through me now.

---

5 — The Truth about Creation

Nothing "just happened." God created it all.

---

6 — The Truth about Salvation

Grace is the only way to have a relationship with God.

---

7 — The Truth about Sanctification

Faith is the only way to grow as a believer.

---

8 — The Truth about Good and Evil

God has allowed evil to provide us with a choice.
God can bring good even out of evil events.
God promises victory over evil to those who choose him.

---

9 — The Truth about the Afterlife

Heaven and hell are real places.
Death is a beginning, not the end.

---

10 — The Truth about the Church

The only true "world superpower" is the church.

---

11 — The Truth about the Second Coming

Jesus is coming again to judge this world and to gather God's children.

How great is the love the Father has lavished on us, that we should be called children of God!

—1 John 3:1

All Scripture is inspired by God and is useful to teach us what is true and to make us realize what is wrong in our lives. It straightens us out and teaches us to do what is right.

—2 Timothy 3:16 (NLT)

You alone are the LORD. You made the heavens, even the highest heavens, and all their starry host, the earth and all that is on it, the seas and all that is in them. You give life to everything, and the multitudes of heaven worship you.

—Nehemiah 9:6

Don't be drunk with wine, because that will ruin your life. Instead, let the Holy Spirit fill and control you.

—Ephesians 5:18 (NLT)

For in Christ all the fullness of the Deity lives in bodily form, and you have been given fullness in Christ, who is the head over every power and authority.

—Colossians 2:9–10

And we know that in all things God works for the good of those who love him, who have been called according to his purpose.

—Romans 8:28

I have been crucified with Christ and I no longer live, but Christ lives in me. The life I live in the body, I live by faith in the Son of God, who loved me and gave himself for me.

—Galatians 2:20

You have been saved by grace through believing. You did not save yourselves; it was a gift from God.

—Ephesians 2:8 (NCV)

Therefore, prepare your minds for action; be self-controlled; set your hope fully on the grace to be given you when Jesus Christ is revealed.

—1 Peter 1:13

You should not stay away from the church meetings, as some are doing, but you should meet together and encourage each other. Do this even more as you see the day coming.

—Hebrews 10:25 (NCV)

Set your minds on things above, not on earthly things.

—Colossians 3:2

Foundations

Tom Holladay and Kay Warren

> *"Foundations is the biblical basis of the Purpose-Driven Life. You must understand these life-changing truths to enjoy God's purposes for you."*
> —RICK WARREN

The complete communicator's resource for teaching Saddleback Church's Foundations course in your church or group

From Saddleback Church

This is a proven, tested curriculum that has helped change thousands of lives!

For the past ten years, *Foundations* has been used as the doctrinal course at Saddleback Church, one of America's largest and best-known churches. Thousands of Saddleback members have benefited from this life-transforming experience. This course is explained in detail in Rick Warren's groundbreaking book, *The Purpose-Driven Church*. Currently, Purpose-Driven churches all around the world are using *Foundations* to *raise up an army of mature believers* equipped for ministry in the church and prepared for mission in the world.

> *"At last! A curriculum that will root hearts and heads in the solid ground of God's Word in a way that makes sense in this complex and challenging world. I am thrilled to recommend it!"*
> —DR. JOSEPH M. STOWELL, PRESIDENT, MOODY BIBLE INSTITUTE

The complete *Foundations* kit includes:
- **2 Teacher's Guides (volumes 1 & 2)**
- **1 Participant's Guide**
- **1 CD-ROM** with PowerPoint® presentations, programming resources, and additional handouts

Curriculum Kit: 0-310-24072-7

Ideal for Sunday-night or midweek series, weekday Bible studies, Sunday school classes, and study groups of any size

---

> *"... excellent ... Never has our crazy world so needed such help."*
> —JILL BRISCOE, AUTHOR, EXECUTIVE EDITOR, *JUST BETWEEN US* MAGAZINE

Pick up a copy today at your favorite bookstore!

ZONDERVAN™

GRAND RAPIDS, MICHIGAN 49530 USA

WWW.ZONDERVAN.COM

A groundbreaking manifesto on the meaning of life

The Purpose-Driven® Life
What on Earth Am I Here For?

Rick Warren

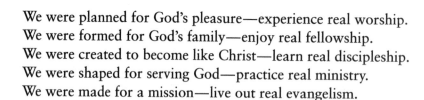

THE #1 NEW YORK TIMES BESTSELLER

RICK WARREN

THE PURPOSE DRIVEN *Life*

WHAT ON EARTH AM I HERE FOR?

The most basic question everyone faces in life is *Why am I here? What is my purpose?* Self-help books suggest that people should look within, at their own desires and dreams, but Rick Warren says the starting place must be with God—and his eternal purposes for each life. Real meaning and significance come from understanding and fulfilling God's purposes for putting us on earth.

The Purpose-Driven Life takes the groundbreaking message of the award-winning *Purpose-Driven Church* and goes deeper, applying it to the lifestyle of individual Christians. This book helps readers understand God's incredible plan for their lives. Warren enables them to see "the big picture" of what life is all about and begin to live the life God created them to live.

The Purpose-Driven Life is a manifesto for Christian living in the twenty-first century—a lifestyle based on eternal purposes, not cultural values. Using biblical stories and letting the Bible speak for itself, Warren clearly explains God's five purposes for each of us:

We were planned for God's pleasure—experience real worship.
We were formed for God's family—enjoy real fellowship.
We were created to become like Christ—learn real discipleship.
We were shaped for serving God—practice real ministry.
We were made for a mission—live out real evangelism.

This long-anticipated book is the life-message of Rick Warren, founding pastor of Saddleback Church. Written in a captivating devotional style, the book is divided into forty short chapters that can be read as a daily devotional, studied by small groups, and used by churches participating in a "40 Days of Purpose" campaign.

Hardcover: 0-310-20571-9
Unabridged Audio Pages® CD: 0-310-24788-8
Unabridged Audio Pages® cassette: 0-310-20907-2
ebooks:
  Adobe® eReader™: 0-310-25482-5
  Microsoft® Reader: 0-310-25481-7
  Palm™ Reader: 0-310-25484-1
  Gemstar eBook: 0-310-25483-3

Also available from Inspirio, the gift division of Zondervan:

  Purpose-Driven Life Journal: 0-310-80306-3
  Purpose-Driven Life Deluxe Journal: 0-310-80555-4

Pick up a copy today at your favorite bookstore!

ZONDERVAN™
GRAND RAPIDS, MICHIGAN 49530 USA
WWW.ZONDERVAN.COM

www.pastors.com

A Purpose-Driven® Discipleship Resource

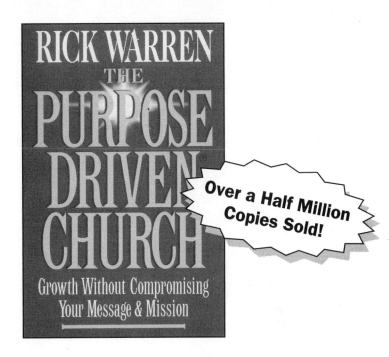

Over a Half Million Copies Sold!

The Purpose-Driven® Church
Growth without Compromising
Your Message and Mission

Rick Warren

Every church is driven by something. Tradition, finances, programs, even buildings can be the controlling force in a church. But for a church to be healthy, it must become purpose-driven.

Rick Warren, the founding pastor of Saddleback Church, shares a proven, five-part strategy that will enable your church to grow …

- Warmer through fellowship
- Deeper through discipleship
- Stronger through worship
- Broader through ministry
- Larger through evangelism

Discover the same practical insights and principles for growing a healthy church that Rick has taught to over one hundred thousand pastors and church leaders from over one hundred countries. *The Purpose-Driven Church* shifts the focus away from church building programs to emphasizing a people-building process. Warren says, "If you will concentrate on building people, God will build the church."

Hardcover: 0-310-20106-3
Unabridged Audio Pages® cassette: 0-310-222901-4
Abridged Audio Pages® cassette: 0-310-20518-2

ebooks:
Adobe® eReader™: 0-310-24465-X
Microsoft® Reader: 0-310-24466-8
Palm™ Reader: 0-310-24918-X
Gemstar eBook: 0-310-24467-6

Pick up a copy today at your favorite bookstore!

GRAND RAPIDS, MICHIGAN 49530 USA
WWW.ZONDERVAN.COM

www.pastors.com

Celebrate Recovery

A Program for Implementing a Christ-Centered Recovery Ministry in Your Church

Rick Warren and John Baker

Alcoholism • Divorce • Sexual Abuse
• Codependency • Domestic Violence •
Drug Addition • Sexual Addiction

These words are about more than "issues." They're about people who sit as close to us as the next pew—or in our own. People struggling with problems that sermons or Bible studies alone won't solve. But there is a way the church can help the hurting move beyond their wounds to experience the healing and liberty of Christ. *Celebrate Recovery* fills a long-standing need in the church in its role as Christ's healing agent. Developed by John Baker and Rick Warren of the renowned Saddleback Church, this program's life-changing effectiveness has gained it an explosive, grass-roots popularity. Drawn from the Beatitudes, *Celebrate Recovery* helps people resolve painful problems in the context of the church as a whole. Rather than setting up an isolated recovery community, it helps participants and their churches come together and discover new levels of care, acceptance, trust, and grace. Whether your congregation is large or small, this fellowship-based curriculum truly will be a celebration of Christ in the life of your church and its members. Everything you need is here!

- 20-minute videotaped introductory guide for leaders
- 1 Leader's Guide
- Participant's Guides 1–4
- 3.5" diskette with 25 lessons

- Road to Recovery series
- 8-tape audio cassette series
- sermon transcripts
- 3.5" diskette
- Reproducible promotional materials

All in a proven, groundbreaking program, painstakingly and prayerfully developed to help people discover new dignity, strength, joy, and growth in the image of Christ.

Curriculum Kit: 0-310-22107-2

Pick up a copy today at your favorite bookstore!

ZONDERVAN™

GRAND RAPIDS, MICHIGAN 49530 USA

WWW.ZONDERVAN.COM